Challenges of Contemporary India

Challenges of Contemporary India

• Polity • Justice • Education • Empowerment and • Judiciary

Dr Hemlata Singh
Dr Rajkumar Singh

KALPAZ

ISBN: 978-93-5128-209-9

Price: ₹ 950

First Published, 2016

Published by

Kalpaz Publications
C-30, Satyawati Nagar,
Delhi – 110052
E-mail: kalpaz@hotmail.com
Ph.: 9212142040

Printed at: G. Print Process, Delhi

Cataloging in Publication Data—DK
Courtesy: D.K. Agencies (P) Ltd. <docinfo@dkagencies.com>

Singh, Hemlata, 1965- **author.**
Challenges of contemporary India : polity, justice, education, empowerment & judiciary / Dr Hemlata Singh, Dr Rajkumar Singh.
pages cm
Includes bibliographical references.
ISBN 9789351282099 (hardback)

1. India—Politics and government. 2. Social justice—India. 3. Women in development—India. 4. Education—India. 5. Judicial power—India. I. Singh, Raj Kumar, 1958- author. II. Title.

JQ231.C43 2016 DDC 320.954 23

Contents

Dedicated to:

Smt Lalmani Devi
Mother of Dr Hemlata Singh
Mother-in-law of Dr Rajkumar Singh

Preface

The present political system of India ensures all citizens-justice liberty, equality and fraternity in the entire social, economic and political spheres of human activity. The framework of politics in a democratic society is characterised by the general and special features of the interaction between politics and the social structure. The general feature of politics in all democratic societies is that it intervenes to influence society and that it also reflects the social reality. In post-Independence era, all basic changes in Indian society are initiated by the state. The Indian state is the agency of change in society, and for performing such a role the state seeks its legitimacy through the democratic verdict of the people. Politics in India is a pre-eminent factor in societal changes and this alone is responsible for the complexity of the interactions between politics and society.

The presented book, ***Challenges of Contemporary India- Polity, Justice, Education, Empowerment and Judiciary*** is an exclusive piece of creation on complexities of Indian social structure and its actual operation in the democratic process, in the politics of today and tomorrow with a thin silver line to overcome the facts of social life and bare truths of politics. In contemporary India, the large masses of the people suffer from social and economic discriminations and they look to the State functionaries for protection and survival while those who belong to the vulnerable strata of society seek protection from the state, the privileged and powerful seek to control state institutions and resources for protection and promotion of their material interests. Although while keeping in mind the complexity of the relationship between politics and society it may be stated that the politics of transnational societies reveal more complexities than the politics of polarised ones. In all transitional societies the social structure, institutions, relationships, roles and identities are in a state of flux and the new and emerging social categories and linkage are involved in a continuous struggle with established social norms and relations. The relationship between politics and society can be neatly observed if the society has reached a stage of polarisation rather than in a society where numerous levels of relationship are involved in a struggle between the old and the new. In this context, India is attempting a reconciliation between modern democratic political systems with a social system which has its firm foundation in ancient culture.

In independent India the constitution makers were highly influenced by the feeling of social equality and social justice. The term "justice" in the Preamble embraces three distinct forms – social, economic and political, secured through various provisions of Fundamental Rights and Directive Principles. In fact, the entire social issues were understood in proper perspective and the demand for reservation was made to get rid of social injustice done earlier in India. Under the system of Varna-Jaathi, the Brahminical upper castes have undue, unearned and unjust privileges, whereas the Sudra and Panchama castes suffer from suppression, neglect and discrimination. Because of the graded inequality practised based on the mere incident of birth of a person in a caste group, the lower castes were denied educational opportunities and a share in the administration by the priestly and the ruling classes.

In the circumstances, reservation policy is one of the constitutional means adopted by India to address the problems of centuries of discrimination inflicted on certain groups resulting in all types of inequalities. It is an arrangement to make for the handicap or disability from which the lower castes suffer due to the caste system. Reservation in education and a job opportunity is not of the various means that could act as a corrective to the historical disadvantages. No one treats reservation as a substitute for social justice. Reservation is an arrangement, an aspect of policy, whereas social justice is a basic principle that lays emphasis on equality of opportunity and welfare of all by dispensing with equality. The policy has been in existence for more than half a century and it has been many difficulties as well as twists and turns. In this context, education too is most important as it transforms a person to live a better life. It is only the education which promotes good habits, values and awareness towards anything like terrorism, corruption and much more. It is the only fundamental way by which a desired change and upliftment in the society can be taken into effect.

Education plays a very significant role in the development of women position in India. From early twenty century their statuses have been changed slowly and gradually. Although today we have seen the women occupied the respectable positions in all walks of the fields, yet they are not absolutely free from some discrimination and harassment of the society. But lastly the governments of the time decided to empower women which means equipping women to be economically independent, self-reliant and enable them to face any difficult situation along with their participation in development activities. It was felt for long that the socio-economic development of women is deeply intertwined and if one dimension remains absent, the outcome would suffer. To overcome these challenges the National Mission for Empowerment of Women (NMEW) was launched by the Government of India on International Women's Day in 2010 with the aim to strengthen overall processes that promote all round development of women.

The present mission aims at strengthening the processes that promote holistic development of women, gender equality and gender justice through inter-sectoral convergence of programmes impacting women, forging synergy amongst various stakeholders and creating an enabling environment conducive to social change. In line, the National Resource Centre for Women (NRCW) has been set up to carry out studies and research project in various domain and sub-domain areas and is responsible for carrying out the impact assessment studies of policies, schemes and programmes of the government. The NRCW will also be responsible for devising a suitable media strategy to highlight the programmes and schemes of the mission and their achievements as well as public service campaign strategies to focus on retrograde social practices which afflict the society. Thus, the mission, with its objective of ensuring that the benefits of schemes and programmes of the Central, as well as of State Governments, reach their intended beneficiaries through convergence and coordination and it will also bridge the gap between 'what is' and 'what ought to be'. But in order to make this a reality, the Central Government, States, and civil society would need to work together. Every citizen of this country has a role to play in making it successful.

To a large extent, the success of all constitutional structures and aspirations as well were seen to be subjected to the rule of law in modern sense. In line the British legal system was basically maintained and a new constitution put in place that combine the principles of liberal democracy with socialist aspirations of general equality and welfare. But over the decades the role of Indian judiciary has gradually got a face-lifting and today a strong ambivalence clouds the public image of the

Indian judicial system. On the one hand, judicial activism is seen as a sign of hope to set shortcomings right. Social awareness, insistence on human rights and the attempt to check governmental lawlessness are said to have 'transformed the Supreme Court of India into a Supreme Court for Indians'. On the other hand, symptoms of inefficiency haunt the courts as they do other state institutions. The courts are not free of corruption. The legal process is even said to have become more and more intractable, dilatory, whimsical and protective of the criminal and law-breaker having influence or financial clout. There are serious complaints of widely reported allegations of judicial misconduct and a disconcerting compromise of integrity and impartiality. Especially, backlog and delay in the resolution of civil disputes in India erode public trust and confidence in legal institutions, and act as significant barriers to India's chosen path to social justice and economic development.

In the past decade India has emerged as a global economic powerhouse, and has been resilient during the global financial crisis and economic downturn, it however, still faces huge challenges in grappling with poverty, population growth and illiteracy. It continues to remain a puzzle to many in the West- a country of vast contradictions but also one that presents tremendous opportunity. The challenge of establishing inclusive growth dominates the policy debate within India, with government and other sectors of society focusing on education, health-care, demographics, a rising middle class, food security and private sector growth. Of the major challenges that Indian polity and governance face today include political corruption, naxalism and dirty use of religion in politics. Naxalism, like communalism and fundamentalism, has become one of the severe threats and internal security challenge ever faced by our country. It is also to note here that while the constitution envisages secularism in the sense of *dharma nirapakshita*, our politicians have conveniently interpreted it as *sarva dharma samabhava*. Going a step further all political parties use religion to gather votes. This starts from the selection of the candidates taking into account the communal character of the constituency. Vote-banks are systematically built on the basis of caste and religion and the very leaders who take advantage of these vote-banks do so in the name of secularism.

There is nothing more to say about corruption than we see in daily life and face everywhere we go. It is rampant in all walks of life, be it land and property, health, education, commerce and industry, agriculture, transport, police, armed forces, even religious institutions or so called places of spiritual pursuits. Corruption continues to exist in covert and overt ways at all three levels- political, bureaucratic and corporate sector. One can see the nexus between the politicians, the bureaucrats and the industrialists which has resulted into corruption and corrupt practices. The tentacles of corruption have affected all organs of government, including the judiciary. But among these the political corruption has specific norms and goals; it has its structure, and manifests a particular pattern of behaviour much different from other types of corruption. In the Indian context the study of political corruption is of utmost value as other types of corruption have emanated from it. Politics being the seat of power, the manifestations of corrupt politics can be observed at all levels of power hierarchy. Political corruption may not prove so damaging in developed societies but its offshoots may destroy the very fabric of a developing nation. Thus, corruption in political life in India has assumed almost criminal proportion and has ceased to provoke that amount of shock and disgust as it would have decades ago. Actually in a democracy, nothing can be more tragic, and cause greater worry than a situation where all politicians, representatives of people, are regarded as corrupt and come to be detested by people.

Next to political corruption, Naxalism and Maoism is considered as one of the greatest threats to internal security of the country. It has been started from one place and now it spreads like wild fire to make a serious impact on the peace, security and development of many Indian states. Initially the movement had its centre in West Bengal, but in later years it spread into less developed areas of rural southern and eastern India, such as Chhattisgarh, Odisha, Andhra Pradesh, Karnataka, Maharashtra, Jharkhand, Bihar and Uttar Pradesh. The growing influence of Naxalism prompted Indian Prime Minister Manmohan Singh to declare them to be the most serious internal threat to India's national security and announce a new nationwide initiative, to be called the "Integrated Action Plan" for broad, coordinated operations aimed at dealing with the Naxalite problem in affected areas. The Naxalites control over 40 per cent of India's geographical area and are concentrated in remote and densely forested areas known as "Red Corridor." The problem highlights the nation's interior weakness and revealing of interior weakness' that paves an open invitation to the external threats. However, the main culprit behind the Naxalite problem is poor governance. Until and unless, the political mess is not cleared, the issue of Naxalites can never be solved. Therefore, the real threat is not the Naxalites but the political parties and the system which has failed to contain the problem in so many years. Not only that but majority of the concerns in the country can be corrected if we can have a good leader to take up the responsibilities and handle them efficiently. The wisdom and intellect should be well blended with power and authority to handle the decade old issue.

Likewise, the use and misuse of religion in Indian politics has gained a dangerous proportion in recent decades. Although Indian subcontinent is the birthplace of some of the world's major religions; namely Hinduism, Buddhism, Jainism and Sikhism and throughout India's history, religion has been an important part of country's culture, the religious ideology, particularly that expressed by the Hindutva movement, has strongly influenced Indian politics. In the context a well known accusation that Indian political parties make for their rivals is that they play vote-bank politics, meaning give political support to issues for the sole purpose of gaining the votes of members of a particular community. Both the Congress Party and the Bharatiya Janata Party have been accused of exploiting the people by indulging in vote-bank politics. As a step further in the direction communal violence in India includes acts of violence by followers of one religious group against followers and institutions of another religious group, often in the form of rioting. It all happened despite the secular and religiously tolerant Constitution of India and broad religious representation in various aspects of society including the government. Sporadic and sometimes serious acts of religious violence tend to occur as the root causes of religious violence often run deep in history, religious activities, and politics of India. In fact, religion and politics co-exist in India. Religion can guide a politician but a politician biased in favour of one religion can never be good for all.

In reality religion enters into the official realm from the back door in the form of communalism. According to an expert analysis, the actual situation in which religion can be officially talked about only via the back door under Western-style secularism which works to aggravate the feelings of frustration and helplessness and fuels fanaticism among them. In the face of the phenomena of communalism, people of the modern era, who were taught the dangers of allowing religion into the official arena because it might be incapable of carrying on rational argument, usually think it advisable to return to the secularism that confines religion to the private realm. Because communalism, or religion as ideology, was the result of the attempt to seal off religion with Western-style secularism, dualistic approaches such as politics versus religion, or secular versus spiritual, will not work. In the circumstances, it is crucial to build a path of tolerance and harmony by attaching more importance to religion as faith that embraces the entirety of people's every day life. In the present context the issue became more complicated because Hindu nationalists are secular modernists who manipulate religion as ideology. They are like merchants dealing in packaged Hinduism as opposed to a packaged Islam, making ideology, a uniformly standardised commercial commodity. 'Religion as faith' on the other, is religion as it shaped the Indian life style before such modernisation or secularisation. Religion in that sense is not self righteous or monolithic, but pluralistic in practice. Religion in this sense is premised not upon the rigid and close-minded individual but upon the mobile and open-minded individual, and has its own principles about tolerance and intolerance. Thus, it is difficult, at least for Indian people to imagine human life that rejects the presence of religion; and the highly flexible religious tradition that once endowed human life with the meaning of life is actually abused as an ideology for secular benefits. We should devote our efforts to explore and restore the profound meaning of 'religion as faith' and re-establish religious tolerance so that all religions can respect one another.

It is quite clear from the above that the promises and commitment that India made to her people at the time of independence in different walks of life ranging from polity to the betterment of social justice, education, women status, judicial impartiality and upcoming socio-political problems remain unfulfilled and there are incomplete and urgent tasks that we have to finish soon. To identify the challenges of modern/post-modern India, it will have to clear the huge backlog of unredeemed promises. The situation, however, is not irretrievable. What is imperative is to cleanse our socio-political environment of polluting influences. Morality in public life has become a casualty and politicians are primarily responsible for this situation. The people's consciousness has to be raised in order to confront this trend. All responsible political parties should come forward to play a leading role to stop this rot. Even within the existing socio-political milieu, significant changes can be brought about, if the necessary political will is there. Today, what seems to have become our supreme task is to see how to prevent our democratic polity from becoming a government of the corrupt, by the corrupt and for the corrupt. Something has to be done and done before it gets too late.

21st January 2016
SAHARSA, Bihar

Dr Hemlata Singh
Dr Rajkumar Singh

Acknowledgements

We wish to thank the institutions and individuals for their encouragement, co-operation and good-wishes that we received and staff of the central libraries at New Delhi and other places where we got a lot of information and analytical/critical views of different subject experts. They all deserve cordial thanks.

We are deeply grateful to several persons and colleagues. Among teachers late Dr D.N. Mallik, Dr Kirtyanand Singh, Dr R.N. Kumar and Dr M.R. Kazami, retired professors of the University Department of Political Science, BRA Bihar University, Muzaffarpur, have been constant source of guide and encouragement at every stage. Colleagues Dr Dhirendra Narayan Singh, Department of Political Science, MLT College, Saharsa, Dr Chandra Prakash Singh, Department of History, Dr Kumar Jyotivardhan and Dr Usha Sinha, Department of Hindi, Dr Ram Naresh Singh, Department of Maithili, West Campus P.G. Centre, Saharsa and departmental colleagues, Dr Bijay Kumar Verma and Dr Pawan Kumar are thankful for their co-operation and good-wishes. Eldest brother, the late Suryanath Singh, elder brother Bhuvneshwar Prasad Singh, father-in-law Ramanand Singh, retired Professor and Head, University Department of Physics, BRA Bihar University, Muzaffarpur, and most revered Smt. Lalmani Devi deserve deep sense of gratitude for their sincere good-wishes. We are no less thankful to colleagues and staff of the B.N. Mandal University, West Campus, P.G. Centre, Saharsa.

We would be failing in our duty if we do not record our honest good-wishes and gratitude to the family members including our son, Aditya Priyadarshi, Senior Software Engineer at Accenture and Apurv Adarsh, Software Engineer at Tata Consultancy Service in the completion of the book.

Glossary

Absolute poverty	:	poverty as defined in terms of the minimal requirements necessary to afford minimum standards of food, clothing, health-care and shelter.
Absolutism	:	a system in which authority is absolute and unchecked.
Accountability	:	exercise of powers and discharge of duties properly.
Accused	:	the person against whom an assusation is made.
Achieved status	:	a position attained through personal ability and effort.
Adaptation	:	the ability of a socio-cultural system to change with the demands of a changing physical or social environment.
Administration	:	refers simply to the political part of the Executive branch.
Affirmative action	:	organisational policies intended to assure minorities and women of equal hiring or admission opportunities.
Age-sex structure	:	the relative proportions of different age-sex categories in a population.
Amendment	:	a change made to a bill, law, constitutional provision or regulation.
Appeal	:	a request made after a trial, asking another court usually the higher court.
Aryavarta	:	land of the Aryans.
Assemblies	:	collections of people who either directly comprise, or represent, a political or social entity.

Assimilation	:	a minority group's internalisation of the values and norms of the dominant culture.
Authority	:	power that is attached to a position that others perceive as legitimate.
Autocratic rule	:	rule by a specific leader who concentrates power in his own hands.
Bail	:	the money or bound up to secure the release of a person who has been charged.
Ballots	:	votes cast in an election contested by two or more individuals or parties.
Beliefs	:	shared ideas held by a collective of people within a socio-cultural system.
Bureaucracy	:	a way of organising the activity of any institution so that it functions efficiently and impersonally.
Cabinet	:	the name for the small body of senior politicians responsible for directing the administration of a country.
Cabinet Government	:	a collective government by a committee of individuals who are theoretically equal and bound by their collective decisions.
Capitalism	:	any economic system where there is a combination of private property, a relatively free and competitive market.
Caste system	:	a closed form of stratification in which an individual's status is determined by birth and cannot be changed.
Census	:	a count of the population, often including a detailed profile of that population.
Centralisation	:	power and authority concentrated in a few offices.
Charisma	:	a personal quality attributed to leaders who arouse fervent popular support and enthusiasm.
Citizen	:	a member of a state having both rights and duties associated with that membership.
Civil disobedience	:	a protest strategy invented and popularised by Mahatma Gandhi.
Civil society	:	a framework within which those without political authority live their lives.

Class consciousness	:	an objective awareness of the class system, including the common interest of people within one's own class.
Class	:	socio-economic differences between groups of individuals that create differences in their life chances and power.
Coalition	:	groupings of rival political units in the face of a common enemy.
Collective action	:	social action undertaken in a relatively spontaneous way by a large number of people.
Collective responsibility	:	anyone involved in the making the decision is expected to support it without reservation in public, and generally to act as though he was himself solely responsible for the decision.
Colonialism	:	the treating of another country as colony.
Communal riot	:	a riot in which the target of violence is another group based on race or ethnicity.
Congress	:	a meeting of representatives or officials for debate and discussion.
Consensus	:	agreement on basic social values by the members of a group or society.
Constitution	:	a set of rights, powers and procedures that regulate the relationships between public authorities in any state.
Constitutional law	:	the part of a legal system and legal tradition which is directly concerned with enterpreting and applying the fundamental law.
Contempt of court	:	any act which is calculated to embarrass, hinder or obstruct the court in administration of justice.
Contempt	:	failure to follow a court order.
Court	:	a legal decision made by a court that commands or directs that something be done.
Crime	:	any action that violates criminal laws established by political authority.
Culture	:	the values, norms, and material goods shared by a given group.

Democracy	: a form of government that recognises the right to citizens to participate in political decision making.
Demography	: the scientific study of human population, including size, growth, movement, density and composition.
Detention	: the holding of a person in custody or confinement.
Dictatorship	: a form of government in which one man has sole and complete political power.
Diplomacy	: an entire method of resolving international conflicts.
Direct Democracy	: direct participation of citizen in decision making and passing of laws.
Discrimination	: the denial of equal access to social resources to people on the basis of the group membership.
Education system	: the system of formalised transmission of knowledge and values operating within a given society.
Education	: the transmission of knowledge to members of society, the knowledge passed on comprises technical and cultural knowledge, technical and social skills, and the norms and values of the society.
Election	: a method of choosing amongst candidates for some post or office.
Electoral system	: a method used to translate the votes for candidates in an election into an allocation of seats.
Elite	: men and women who occupy the highest positions of the dominant institution of a society and who consequently hold enormous power.
Emergency powers	: special powers which allow normal legislative procedures or judicial remedies to be by-passed or suspended.
Evolution	: the change of biological organism by means of adaptation to the demands of the physical environment.
Executive	: the part of a governmental system which takes decision as opposed to making laws.
Federalism	: a loose alliance or union of states for limited purposes.

Feudalism	:	a social system based on fealty between a lord and a vassal.
Franchise	:	another name for the eligibility to vote.
Gender gap	:	the gap between men and women in terms of their political attitudes and behaviour.
Globalisation	:	the development of extensive worldwide patterns of economic, social, or political relationships between nations.
Government	:	formal institutional structures of the nation-state whose purpose is to regulate internal and external relations.
Gross domestic product	:	the total value of all goods and services produced within the boundaries of a particular country in any given year.
Heads of Government	:	a person appointed to head a government.
Heads of State	:	the person who exercises a number of formal and ceremonial powers and responsibilities.
Higher education	:	education beyond high school level, often in college or university.
Ideology	:	shared ideas or beliefs that serve to justify and support the interests of a particular groups or organisations.
Infrastructure	:	the interface between a socio-cultural system and its environment.
Institution	:	an established pattern of human social behaviour in a given society.
Interest group	:	a group organised to pursue specific interests in the political arena.
Judicial review	:	a method whereby a superior judicial body decides whether an executive or legislative action is constitutional.
Judiciary	:	the body of judges in a constitutional system.
Justice	:	fair trials, equality before the law and so on.
Law and order	:	the provision of a strong police force and a concern with reducing crime and vandalism.

Law	:	written rules established by a political authority and backed by government.
Leadership	:	the ability of a person or a group of persons to persuade others to act according to one's proposed course of action.
Legislature	:	the official rule-making body of a political system.
Liberal democracy	:	a form of representative democracy.
Literacy	:	the ability of individuals to read and write.
Local government	:	a system of administration for small political units, towns, counties and rural districts.
Majority system	:	a system in which a full arithmetic majority of voters (50 per cent+1) are required.
Mandate	:	vote in a fix way on some particular issue.
Middle class	:	a social class broadly defined occupationally as those working in white-collar and lower managerial occupations.
Minority group	:	a group of people who are defined on the basis of their ethnicity or race.
Mix economy	:	an economy that has major elements of both capitalism and socialism.
Modernisation	:	the capacities of countries to develop the economic and political capacity.
Multiparty system	:	a political system in which there is more than one political party contesting elections.
Nation-state	:	a modern state in which a government has sovereign power within a defined territorial area and the mass of the population are citizens.
Non-state actors	:	international agencies such as the United Nations or the World Health Organisation that play a part in the world-system.
Opposition	:	a political grouping party or loose association of individuals who wish to change the government and its policies.
Parliament	:	elected assemblies with the duty of checking, controlling and sometimes electing the executive power.

Parliamentary government	:	a system of government in which the executive is responsible to an assembly or parliament.
Party	:	an organised group of people sharing common policy preferences, a general ideological position.
Political culture	:	the totality of ideas and attitudes towards authority, discipline and other related issues.
Political party	:	an organisation of people with similar interests and attitudes established with the aim of achieving legitimate control of government and using that power to pursue specific programmes.
Political Science	:	title for the academic study of politics and political behaviour.
Politics	:	attempts to influence government activities.
Power	:	the ability to achieve aims or further the interests that one holds even when opposed by others.
President	:	a person in a Republic who can represent, legally and symbolically the entire state.
Pressure group	:	a voluntary organisation formed to defend and promote interests in society.
Privatisation	:	the transfer of public services from government control to private enterprise.
Religion	:	a set of beliefs involving symbols regarded as sacred together with ritual practices in which members of the community engage.
Representative democracy	:	a form of indirect rule by the majority of the electorate.
Republic	:	a system of government that does not entail Monarchy.
Revolution	:	a violent and total change in a political system.
Secular state	:	a secular state is one which has no official ties to any religion.
Social institution	:	a major structural entity in a socio-cultural system that addresses a basic need of the system.
Social issues	:	a problem that is the result of the institutional structure in a society.

Social justice	: the fair administration of laws without regard to ethnicity, sexual orientation, gender, religion or class.
Socialism	: a politico-economic system where the state controls the basic means of production.
Society	: a group of people who live in a particular territory, are subject to a common system, political authority, and share a common culture.
Sovereignty	: the right to own and control some area of the world.
State	: a given territory ruled by government institutions whose authority is backed by law and the ability to use force.
Status quo	: the existing state; the way things currently exist.
Structure	: in sociology, all human institutions, groups and organisations.
Technology	: the application of logic, reason, and knowledge to the problems of exploiting raw materials from the environment.
Terrorism	: the use of violence or the threat of violence to achieve political, social or economic ends.
Unemployment	: a government's measure of those who are not working but are actively seeking work.
Union	: a social organisation set up to represent the worker's interests in both the workplace and in the broader society.
Upper class	: a social class roughly composed of the more affluent members of society, especially those who have great wealth, have control over business, or hold large numbers of stocks and shares.
Validity	: the degree to which the measurement of a variable actually reflects the intended concept.
Values	: culturally defined standards held by human individuals or groups about what is desirable, proper, beautiful, good or bad.
Verdict	: the formal decision or finding of guilt or innocence made by a judge in a criminal case.
Vested interests	: an expectation of private gain that often underlies

		the expressed interest in a public issue.
Voting	:	an act of choice amongst a set of alternatives, by a free individual, and is at the heart of modern democracy.
Welfare state	:	a government system that provides a range of human services for its citizens.
World economy	:	a single division of labour that spans multiple cultures.
Zero population growth	:	population stability achieved when each woman has no more than two children.

Abbreviations

ADB	:	Asian Development Bank
BD	:	Bajrang Dal
BJP	:	Bharatiya Janata Party
CEP	:	Continuing Education Programme
CIA	:	Central Intelligence Agency
CMP	:	Common Minimum Programme
CPI (M)	:	Communist Party of India (Marxist)
CPI (ML)	:	Communist Party of India (Marxist Leninist)
CPM	:	Communist Party Marxist
CSW	:	Commission on the Status of Women
DPEP	:	District Primary Education Programme
DWID	:	Division of Women in Development
ECI	:	Election Commission of India
EFA	:	Education For All
FLAW	:	Functional Literacy for Adult Women
GAD	:	Gender and Development Approach
GIDP	:	Gender in Development Programme
GNP	:	Gross National Product
HDI	:	Human Development Index
ICSSR	:	Indian Council of Social Science Research
INC	:	Indian National Congress
ISI	:	Inter- Services Intelligence
JEG	:	Joint Expert's Group
JMM	:	Jharkhand Mukti Morcha
JP	:	Janata Party
LJPS	:	Lok Jana Shakti Party
LPG	:	Liberalisation Privatisation and Globalisation
MCCI	:	Maoist Communist Centre of India
MHRD	:	Ministry of Human Resource Development
NAEP	:	National Adult Education Programme
NDA	:	National Democratic Alliance

NEP	:	New Employment Policy
NGOs	:	Non-governmental Organisations
NLM	:	National Literacy Mission
NLMA	:	National Literacy Mission Authority
NPE	:	National Policy on Education
NREGA	:	National Rural Employment Guarantee Act
NRHM	:	National Rural Health Mission
OBCs	:	Other Backward Classes
PGN	:	Practical Gender Needs
PIL	:	Public Interest Litigation
PLC	:	Post Literacy Campaign
PPP	:	Pakistan People's Party/Public- Private Partnership
PRIs	:	Panchayati Raj Institutions
PSE	:	Public Sector Employment
PSP	:	Praja Socialist Party
PSU	:	Public Sector Unit
PWG	:	Peoples War Group
RFLP	:	Rural Functional Literacy Programme
RJD	:	Rashtriya Janata Dal
RSS	:	Rashtriya Swayam Sevak
RTI	:	Right to Information
SAL	:	Social Action Litigation
SC	:	Scheduled Castes
SCs, STs	:	Scheduled Castes, Scheduled Tribes
SGN	:	Strategic Gender Needs
SLMA	:	State Literacy Mission Authority
SP	:	Samata Party and Samajwadi Party
SS	:	Shiv Sena
ST	:	Scheduled Tribes
STEP	:	Support to Training and Employment
TLC	:	Total Literacy Campaign
UEE	:	Universalisation of Elementary Education
UNGA	:	United Nations General Assembly
UNICEF	:	United Nations Children's Fund
UNO	:	United Nations Organisation
UNSC	:	United Nations Security Council
UPA	:	United Progressive Alliance
VHP	:	Vishva Hindu Parishad
WID	:	Women In Development
ZSS	:	Zila Saksharata Samities

Chapter - 1

Indian Polity : Diagnosis with Innovative Solution

1.1 Determinants without Deterrents : Birth of India's Political Vision

At independence India felt that the national progress can neither lie in a repetition of the past nor in its denial. New patterns must inevitably be adopted but they must be integrated with the old. Of the two views-traditional and modern, the Indian modernist occupied an intermediate but quite half-way position between the modernists and the critical traditionalists. For all practical purposes they accepted the modernist assessment of traditional India and stressed the need for comprehensive modernisation.[1] The political change that took place in 1947 began to move with the existing social structure on the basis of give and take. The new institutions and the new leadership offered economic opportunity, administrative patronage, and positions of power which drew the articulate sections of society into the modernist network. In return, the political elite were provided with a basis of support that was already structured and endowed with, symbols of identification and experiential meaning. It was felt that as India is a multicultural country its society needs to find ways and means to accommodate diversity without losing its cohesiveness and unity. In the process they avoided the approach of assimilation and unbounded multiculturalism. Assimilation requires minorities to abandon their own distinctive institutions, cultures and values to merge into the prevailing culture. This way is sociologically unlikely to succeed and is morally untenable in view of the people's deep adherence to normative values such as religion. Likewise, the unbounded multiculturalism which entails giving up the concept of shared values and identity in order to privilege ethnic and religious differences presuming that a nation can be replaced by a number of diverse minorities is also unacceptable. Such a course of action usually results in an undemocratic backlash, support for extremist parties and anti-minority policies. It is morally unjustified as it does not accept the values and institutions upheld by society at large. In this background the Constitution of India ensures that all citizens have equal rights and should have an equal opportunity. In particular, the principle of secularism enshrined in our constitution is the best method to accommodate religious diversity and could be emulated across the globe. In a multicultural society, the state cannot be identified with any religious or cultural group and it should either be neutral or even-handed in its approach to all such groups. This makes it possible to survive as a nation and to move ahead as the largest democracy in the world.

Prior to the complete transfer of power on 15 August 1947 a Constituent Assembly had been set up in order to draw up a constitution for India. The Constitution enacted by the Constituent Assembly conformed the principles laid down in the 'Objective Resolution' which included, after due discussions, the word 'Republic'. It was a controversial word that was put in and withdrawn, at least thrice. The word 'Republic' first figured in the Objective Resolution moved by Pandit Jawaharlal Nehru in the Constituent Assembly on 13 December 1946. He observed, 'The Resolution states that it is our firm and solemn resolve to have a sovereign Indian republic. We have not mentioned the word republic till this time; but you will well understand that a free India can be nothing but a republic. India is bound to be sovereign, it is bound to be independent and it is bound to be a republic. It must inevitably be a republic'. In reference, to the displeasure of Rulers of Indian States he added, 'I want to make it clear personally and the House knows that I do not believe in the monarchical system anywhere, and that in the world today monarchy is a fast disappearing institution.'[2] On the other, several members of the Constituent Assembly including Sir Alladi Krishnaswami Ayyar and Sir B.N. Rau suggested the substitution of the word 'Republic' for 'State'. The general complain about the use of the word republic was that while it is suggestive of the citizens' share in the government of the country it does not necessarily connote a democratic form of government. To fill the gap, as M.R. Masani also felt that there was the need to qualify the word 'Republic' by the word 'democratic' specifically, otherwise, the republic might degenerate into an authoritarian government.[3] Pandit Nehru also supported the view of Masani and observed while speaking on the Objective Resolution pointed out that this resolution is based on democracy and that all our past bears witness to the fact that we stand for Democracy and for nothing else.[4] With the interposition of words the draft constitution finally used the 'Sovereign Democratic Republic' in the Preamble of the Constitution.

Thus, our founding fathers resolved that we, the people of India, constitute ourselves into a Sovereign Democratic Republic where all sovereign powers vested in the people with no superior internal or external, and where the people were their own masters and governed themselves through their representatives under a system they choose. The variant of democratic system chosen for us by the framers of our Constitution is that of representative parliamentary democracy where under the Legislature and the Executive are not separate centres of power. They intermingle and merge. The executive government or Council of Ministers comes out of Parliament, remains part of it and responsible to the House consisting of directly elected representatives of the people.[5] The President of India is the Head of State and is elected indirectly by a national electoral college for a five-year term. The Prime Minister of India is the head of government and exercises most executive powers. The executive branch of the Indian government consists of the President, the Vice-President and the Council of Ministers- the cabinet being its executive committee- headed by the Prime Minister. In the Indian Parliamentary system, the executive is subordinate to the legislature. The legislature of India is the bicameral Parliament. It operates under a Westminster-style Parliamentary system and comprises the Upper House called the Rajya Sabha or Council of States and Lower House called Lok Sabha or House of the People. India has a unitary three-tier indepen-dent judiciary that comprises the Supreme Court, headed by the Chief Justice of India, 21 High Courts, and a large number of trial courts. The Supreme Court has original jurisdiction over cases involving fundamental rights and over disputes between states and the centre; it has appellate jurisdiction over the High Courts. It has the power both to declare the law and to strike down union or state laws which contravene the constitution. The Supreme Court is also the ultimate interpreter of the constitution. Indian democracy is best understood by focusing on how power is distributed.

India is a caste-based society with deep-rooted social hierarchies. Here people are shaped in intensive ways through ethnic, religious and social groups. In the situation the civic culture as evolved by Almond and Verba which conceives that in a modern democracy the element of unity is dominant over the element of conflict exists merely in a rudimentary form.[6] The evolution of consensus over questions of national concern is difficult because of the heterogeneity of the society and the multitude of apparently irreconcilable interests. In this context, J.P. Nettle has rightly pointed out that cleavages based on highly divisive structures almost invariably influence the basic commitment and orientation of those who are mobilised in the electoral process.[7] In India's case the ethnological peculiarities excluded more or less the possibility of erecting a unitary state. The diversity in population could be accommodated only in a federal state and therefore the founding fathers of the constitution wanted the same, consistent with a strong government at the Centre. In addition, there was a host of princely states enclaves and exclaves whose integration was conceivable only if granted provincial autonomy.[8] The Constitution is held flexible so that there is wide scope for the play of power-politics between the Centre and the States. The system established naturally followed the multiparty system with periodic election, secular spirit of the state and representative democracy to keep the heterogeneous country together as a nation and move ahead with a prosperous life with togetherness.

Elections in a democracy can be defined as a process through which the political opinion or will of the people is shaped. They help people to crystallise their interests and to give expression to them. In the elections, it is decided who shall govern and who shall have the control over the government. The right to govern is acquired in competition with other parties. The basic theme of popular sovereignty as enshrined in the Preamble has been reaffirmed in several places in the Constitution but particularly in the chapter dealing with elections. Article 326 declares that 'the elections to the House of People and to the Legislative Assembly of every State shall be on the basis of adult suffrage'.[9] As a result the formed Governments derived their authority from the people who choose their representatives for Parliament and the State Legislatures at regular intervals. Further Section 61 of the Representation of the People Act 1951 deems that every person whose name is on the electoral rolls has the right to vote. In the representative democracy of our country this formal equality lies in the inclusion in the Constitution of universal adult franchise, with the *raison d'etre* that man or woman, rich or poor, upper or lower caste, the voter was brought through the electoral roll on to a common platform. Through this provision the age-old inequalities were, at one stroke, sought to be eliminated, or at least substantially diminished, by conferring political equality. This among other measures, reflected an enlightened and bold vision, while in many countries different groups especially women, had to struggle hard and long to obtain franchise.[10] This precious right in their hands, which ensures the democratic ideal of "one man, one vote, one value", irrespective of his wealth, education, social status and "importance" has, in fact, enhanced their self-respect as citizens of a democratic India.

True to the spirit of political system and multi-religiousness of India the framers of the Constitution made the declared country secular one although the word 'secular' was not initially incorporated in the Preamble. They denied any special treatment or preference for a particular religion and laid stress on equal approach towards all the religions of the land. Unlike the Western concept of secularism which means a total separation between the religion and the state, secularism in India is not opposed to religion as such it is opposed rather to use the religious institutions and religious motivation in the legal, political and educative processes. So long as religion does keep its own sphere secularism is religiously natural, it neither endorses nor disapproves of religiousness.[11] Under our constitution secularism has been safeguarded by providing several restrictions on the religious chauvinism and separatism as M.P. Jain writes, India is a country of religions. There exists multifarious religious groups in the country but the constitution stands for a secular state of India. No one is disabled to hold an office on the ground of religion. The essential basis of the Indian constitution is that all citizens are equal and that the religion of a citizen is irrelevant in the matter of his fundamental rights. The constitution ensures equal freedom for all religions and provide that the religion of the citizen has nothing to do in socio-economic matters.[12] Further the secular objective of the state has been specifically expressed by inserting the word 'secular' in the Preamble by the Constitution's 42nd Amendment Act 1976 and now secularism is a part of the basic structure of the constitution.[13] Again in 1976 the meaning and content of secularism was clarified which meant that the state shall not make any discrimination whatsoever on the ground of religion or community against any person professing any particular form of religious faith.[14] Thus, the Republic of India established in 1950 is the home of Hindus, Buddhists,

Jains, Sikhs, Christians, Zoroastrians, Jews and Muslims living together under the protection of a secular constitution which guarantees, by law, the absolute equality of different faiths. Secularism does not mean that one cannot practise one's religion. It means that religion is a private affair unconnected with the state, which will have no religion.[15] And secularism is the only policy which can hold our country together and take it to the path of prosperity.

Thus, after independence the strategy of nation-building in India commenced on the basis of the making of consensus and accommodation, secularism, Parliamentary democracy, federalism, democratic decentralisation and others that could make Indian republic effective and purposeful. Democracy is both a system with norms, procedures and a set of institutions; and actors, functionaries and officials who work these procedures and institutions. For the people, democracy is also a pattern of experiences. The experience of its two facets is at sharp variance. The impressions derived from its abstract side, like the norms, values, or procedures; and the concrete experiential side, like those in charge of giving these a shape, or who work them-are contrary.[16] The difference was, perhaps, due to the societal character of India at the time of independence. In the pre-modern society that India was, and largely exists— caste, religion and language are strong factors fostering sub-national identities. Horizontal and vertical cleavages have made it difficult for the civil society to develop the size and cohesion necessary to interact as an equal with the political and economic power of the state. Unless the size of the civil society enlarges to encompass most of the Indian citizenry, the psycho-cultural idea of the nation and the politico-legal concept of the state are unlikely to reinforce one another.[17] Like the plural societies of the United States, Canada, Belgium and Holland, from the very beginning, party organisations in India have had a base of support that cuts across the horizontal dispersal of caste groups, further subdivided by the sentiment of village, lineage and kin group neighbourhood, compelled the competing party organisations to build support structures for themselves across their divisions. But the Indian experience different from that of Western democracies was in the fact that, so far as social organisation was concerned, the ethnic groups in the former stood in a hierarchical relationship.[18] This difference indicated a corresponding gap in economic, political and educational attainments, particularly in the lower strata of society, which remained handicapped in their exercise of electoral choice in initial years following the independence of the country.

Each developing society like India which is struggling to modernise itself politically, registers its own peculiar, complex, and often internally self-contradictory processes. When we go in search of their 'revolutionary universal', in advance of sufficient knowledge of those processes, in the end it may prove to be a barren exercise.[19] Similar to many the Indian citizen is born to ethnicity, makes his living, by and large, in the class of his birth, and shares the perspectives of his generation. In contrast to this inherent instinct, electoral processes, party organisations, mass movements and the search for better economic returns induce or force him to take up a position and make secular decisions on issues which lie outside the primary groups to which he belongs. While he continues to live his social life within the primary groups to which he was born, the constraints imposed by such groups, on his thinking and movement, tend to become increasingly weaker in the face of his need to act effectively in conjunction with others.[20] The new challenges faced by him forced him to take a position, other than the established pattern of behaviour. The established system had hardly any match with the then shattered social, economic and cultural life of the Indian people. The introduction of Western rationalist education in India bifurcated the society's common sense and divided Indian culture in a radically different and unprecedented fashion. Traditionally, the Indian culture, which was marked by great internal inequality and distance, various inflections and articulations by divergent groups, was identified by a single common sense. The new European education was largely responsible for the ruination of this integral single common sense of traditional culture. It was done by inducting a new kind of common sense based on rationalist premises common in nineteenth century Europe. It created a strange dichotomy of inside and outside of the home and the world, of the rationalist world of politics and the sentimental one of domesticity created essentially by generalising upon the experience of the middle class.

In general, political parties are institutions of the civil society rather than the state. But they link the power structure in society with the state. The party system reflects the historical conditions of struggle in each country and is a good indicator to test this idea. It is the only one component of the political system. The others are the state structures or government institutions and the state process that links the government to the society. This interaction between state and society has three dimensions; coercive, responsive and legitimative.[21] Coercive function of the state is exercised by the police and the army and also through a framework of laws and rules to obtain obedience of the citizens. The responsive functions to the positive actions that the state takes to meet people's demands. No modern state can carry on without being responsive to social needs voiced from time to time. But coercive and responsive functions may not be adequate unless the state takes specific measures to acquire moral and voluntary support of a large number of people. Such legitimation is secured through symbolic propaganda, patriotic mobilisation and a variety of political and economic activities. The party system of a modern state is particularly relevant to the latter two functions of the state namely, responsive and legitimative. As for coercion, the state agencies are directly authorised to carry out these functions and enforce law.[22] In India, the dominant social forces operate through the major political parties in managing state power.

At the time of independence and long thereafter, the establishment of the system of Parliamentary democracy has privileged the Congress organisation at the expense of other institutions of post-colonial state. While the Congress as the premier political party was undoubtedly the main player in the new dispensation, its ability to frame a constitution and enforce central authority over diverse provinces and hitherto nominally independent princely states owed much too civil bureaucracy the military and police. Without these institutional legacies of colonialism, even an organisation like the Congress might have bulked at the tasks confronting India in the initial years of independence. Working in close concert with the Congress, these institutions engaged in a process of state consolidation where legitimacy gained from the formalisation of regular elections had frequently to be supplemented with authoritarian methods in the name of preserving law and order in the different regions.[23] The partnership between the Congress and the non-elected institutions, the civil bureaucracy and the police in particular, facilitated the establishment of a formal democracy within the barely modified structures of British India's unitary state system. The holding of regular elections lent legitimacy to a multi party system dominated by the Congress. General elections at five yearly intervals gave Indian voters the inestimable power to freely choose and depose governments.[24] With the widening of the electoral base, this is a power which a discerning Indian electorate has exercised effectively to oust discredited governments, both at the centre and states. But on the other, persistence of massive magnitude of poverty, gross social inequalities and regional disparities showed that the bulk of the Indian population was deprived of some basic human rights.

Thus, initially people's anger was held in check by their faith in the democratic system. They therefore, gave vent to their demand for accountability in the state by turning out to vote in ever larger numbers and regularly overthrowing incumbent governments.

However, to meet the economic challenges of the time, by independence, India had developed an independent economic base from which to attempt a take off into independent industrialisation.[25] India's polity had been conceptually built by Mahatma Gandhi and Jawaharlal Nehru but promotion of socialism was essentially a Nehruvian project. As the concept of socialism developed in India, the welfare facet got discarded and the central planning facet got emphasised. The 1948 industrial policy prepared the foundations for a mixed economy. The First Five Year Plan (1951-56) struck a good balance between the needs of the society and the state. It emphasised agriculture, irrigation, power and transport and its performance was impressive. The Second Plan (1956-61) was more ambitious, industry-oriented and state-centric.[26] In the year 1956 the vision of an egalitarian social order was further emphasised by Nehru and the Congress adopted the aim of ushering in a socialistic pattern of society with equitable distribution of wealth and income. In doing so it was only reiterating the instructions contained in Article 38(2) and 39(c) of the Constitution. Article 38 (2) prescribes, 'The State shall, in particular, strive to minimise the inequalities in income and endeavour to eliminate inequalities in status, facilities and opportunities not only amongst groups of people residing in different areas or engaged in different vocations.'[27] In the period rising capital intensity and worsening total factor productivity were ignored. Also ignored were the reality that agriculture must prosper and its productivity increase if it were to support industrialisation. The aims and objects of Third Five Year Plan (1961-66) faced a more fateful fortune due to 1962 war with China and 1965 war with Pakistan. In mid-1960s the country had become substantially dependent on food and financial aid from the West. Meanwhile, politics began to dominate and economic thinking became derivative. The interests of the political class and bureaucracy became the pre-eminent consideration. For democracy to be actually a system of self-governance, the substantive rights of people, that is the socio-economic rights along with political rights must be realised.

There is no doubt that Nehru felt deeply and passionately for the people; his sway over the masses was immense as was his capacity to communicate with them, to sense their feelings and to win their vote, affection and trust. It was his belief that measures like Zamindari abolition and public sector development would reduce inequalities in independent India and that through education and technological development Indian society would move in the direction of equality. Electoral politics through universal adult franchise would facilitate every individual and each group to pursue their rights. These were special safeguards in legislature and bureaucracy for representation of the most deprived sections of Indian society- the Scheduled Castes (SC) and Scheduled Tribes (ST). This was the design of socio-political change envisaged in the Indian Constitution. But Nehru's own model of development and social transformation depended on active pressure from below by the deprived, the exploited and the dominated. Such active popular participation in politics alone would enable parliamentary democracy to serve as an instrument of nation building, social change and equity.[28] And Nehru failed to help create any institutions or structures or agents through which the people or even the lower-level cadres of his own party could be mobilised and activised and politically educated. The only form of mobilisation was his extensive tours through which he communicated with the people, educated them and created popular support for his policies.

In addition, Nehruvian period did not witness greater participation by the people in the political processes except in the form of elections. Actually after independence, there was a gradual demobilisation of the people, weakening over time of the link between politics from below and the national leadership in power and also between politics and social work. He neglected party-building even after he acquired full control over it in 1951. He had never been a builder or organiser of the party before independence, but situation deteriorated after Mahatma Gandhi and Sardar Patel left the scene and Nehru became its sole leader. As a result Congress was increasingly weakened as an organisation and began to lose its role as an instrument for social change or the implementation of government policies or even education in the party ideology.[29] Mere electoral verdicts in and of themselves have not sufficiently empowered the Indian voter when it has come to shaping the state's social or economic development policies. Political privilege has been far too entrenched at various levels of the polity to permit the elimination of caste, class and gender-based discrimination. In the sense political processes in India have fallen well short of the democratic ideal and may even have served to disguise the authoritarianism inherent within the Indian political economy and state structure. Ruling configurations at the centre have been content with securing support from regional elites who are inclined to further entrench their own political and economic interests, not advance the process of democratisation.[30] With only inadequate implementation of the fundamental right provisions of the Indian constitution, the removal of widespread social inequalities and injustices has remained an unrealised ideal.

In sphere of foreign policy under the leadership of Nehru, who was the great statesman, India raised to a pedestal higher than her economic or military strength could take her,[31] but in the period the country had become heavily foreign-aid dependent during the first two decades of independence. The policy of non-alignment played the same critically decisive role. It enabled a relatively weak India to deal with the West on the basis of self-respect and equality. On a superficial view, the policy appeared to be directed against the West. In reality, it was nothing of the kind Nehru was interested not in hurting the West but improving his country's status vis-à-vis the United States and its European allies. His emphasis on rapid industrialisation, too was part of his effort to reinforce India's search for autonomy.[32] Perhaps right in his view, he stated before the Constituent Assembly on 4 December 1947 that, 'foreign policy is the outcome of economic policy and until India has properly evolved her economic policy her foreign policy will be rather vague.'[33] As a consequence, by the late 1950s, India had become the biggest aid recipient not only from the US, but also from the US-dominated World Bank. In comparison to economic interests, India's politically focused foreign policy hurts its security interests even more. A major foreign policy study conducted after 1962 and 1965 wars considered politically conceived non-alignment, unsupported by strategically structured economic and security designs responsible for the deterioration of India's ability to network globally from the late 1960s. Thus, the policy of non-alignment failed to recognise the unique configuration of world politics after the Second World War.

It all resulted in Nehru increasingly relying on government administration and bureaucracy for implementing his policies. Even the Community Development Programme and the Panchayati Raj, the two great efforts to involve the people in their own development, ended up under bureaucratic control; and the village level social worker, the kingpin in rural reconstruction, became a cog in the bureaucratic machine. He never attacked vigorously through mass mobilisation and mass educational campaigns on aspects of social structure, such as the caste system, male domination, kinship networks, economic dependence of the rural poor on the rural rich and growing corruption, which were bolstering the existing socio-economic system. While strong opposed to political opportunism and manipulation, he could replace these only with *ad hoc* political and administrative measures. This often left the field open to the manipulators. This weakness was heightened by the fact that he was a poor judge of men and women. Nehru could see the process of the political manoeuvres taking over, but could do little to counter it. He observed and denounced the corruption, careerism, bureaucratisation, and the many other emerging ills of a developing ex-colonial society but was unable, apart from exhortations, to take the necessary concrete steps to control them. Thus, the working of Indian republic for about two decades since independence had tarnished its image, in practice. The large areas of neglect which covered a wide range of subjects in this period, assumed monstrous proportions in coming years. As one of Nehru's biographers, Geoffrey Tyson has said, 'If Nehru had been a different kind of man, India would have become a different kind of country.'[34] But despite all these India's success in working a system of Parliamentary democracy, has, over time, greatly assisted the mobilisation of ever larger segments of the populace in all walks of life which decided the future course of action in Indian politics and society.

1.2 Indian Polity in Globalisation and Post-globalisation

Indian democracy has moved a long way since the country became independent and adopted a republican constitution decades ago. It has created new political arrangements as it has faced new political challenges. It has shown considerable resilience, and in some ways strengthened itself even while setting aside old arrangements and established ways of thought and action. In comparison to the dawn of independence which began with great, in today's circumstances, it is unrealistic to expect that a new leader will soon emerge, a true statesman who will combine in himself all the virtues that we expected in our political leaders at the time when the new republic came into being. The new sovereign, democratic national state that came into existence was multi-class in nature and was open-ended in the sense that the class-balance among the constituent classes could be altered. Among the most significant features of India's political development has been the commitment of its leaders to democracy, national unity and economic development, accompanied by their ability to establish the necessary political institutions, both of the state and civil society, and to root them in Indian society to create and maintain the structure of a democratic state. These institutions have been sustained despite rapid social change, with new social groups regularly entering the political arena and asserting their rights.[35] In the actual working of the system, the central government gradually acquired greater influence over the states because of the pattern of economic development adopted, which was based on planning, public sector, central funding of anti-poverty programmes, and central financial disbursement to the states from its greater tax resources. From the very beginning the Nehru-Mahalanobis strategy of growth with equity had assumed that popular mobilisation from below would be necessary to effectively implement radical measures in favour of the poor initiated by the government. But while persisting poverty has been the most important failure in India's post-independence development, the survival of the democratic structure has been its greatest success. It led to the growing demands on the state by various classes and groups including the poor. To accommodate these demands all political formations, since the late seventies, began to indulge in competitive populism using state resources to distribute largesse to the various constituent classes of the Indian state including the poor.

Apart from this for several decades the political leadership had functioned without any strategic design or perspective ideology or well thought about tactics for managing the political system. It had relied instead on *adhocism* and gimmickry for meeting the challenges in the polity and on populism, personal appeal, and use of big and black money to maintain itself in power. The major culprit for the weakening of the political institutions has been the quality of political leadership. It is the quality of political leadership which plays a critical role in nation building and development of political institutions.[36] Gradually, political parties became the weakest link in India's political system. It has developed its own distinctive party system. It is neither a two-party system nor a multi-party system with three, four or even half-a-dozen parties of the kind commonly found in continental Europe. It is a system with a multiplicity of parties. This multiplicity is a reflection of the size and diversity of our social and political order.[37] At the close of 1980s, India's economy, polity and society were strained by grave structural imbalances and distortions. The problems were challenging and the correctives required were to be complexed and painful.

The concept of globalisation began to dominate the world since nineties and it has added new dimensions to pre-requisite of success of democracy in any country. It challenges the importance of the authority and welfare function of the state, the complex implications of which are far reaching to the developing countries.[38] It is a multidimensional phenomenon comprising numerous complex and interrelated processes that have a dynamism of their own. It involves a deepening and broadening of rapid trans-boundary exchanges due to developments in technology, communications, and media. Such exchanges and interactions occur at all levels of governance and among non-state actors, creating a more interdependent world.[39] Globalisation has also affected domestic politics and thereby the capacity of governments to manage the new forces. Economic liberalisation and integration has led to greater income inequality within countries without strong welfare states as the incomes in increasingly demanded skilled workers rise while those of unskilled labour drop. The change in the nature and role of the state evoked concerns among the people at large. The relative autonomy of the state weakened and the dominant class acquired supremacy over it. The popular perception of the State as an instrument of modernisation and empowerment has also witnessed changes. In the 1990s when the market reforms shrunk the role of the State, the expectations from it did not materialise. Whenever the state found it difficult to accommodate all their demands, the discontended social groups used their identities to larger share from the State resources.[40] The basic philosophy underlying the economic reform was that the state was no longer an active agent for development, but a facilitator for corporate business.

The process of economic reforms started in 1991 when the country was at the edge of default during the premiership of P.V. Narasimha Rao. It was the result of long-term structural weaknesses of three types. The first set of problems were related to the emergence of structural features that bred inefficiency. The excessive protection to indigenous industries for long through import restrictions had made Indian industry inefficient and technologically backward. This situation was further accentuated by the so-called 'licence quota' Raj-a whole plethora of rules, regulations and restrictions which stifled entrepreneurship and innovation. The second set of weaknesses that emerged in the Indian economy was related to the continuation of the inward-oriented developmental path followed by India since independence. Especially after mid-sixties India was unable to respond adequately to the new opportunities thrown up by the changing world situation. No advantage could be taken of the internationalisation of production and of the increased international flow of funds. In the period between 1965-1991 India failed to use the opportunities provided by the changed world scenario to rapidly industrialise and transform its economy, increase levels and drastically reduce poverty levels, as did many of the East Asian countries. Even China changed track in 1978, opening up its economy, participating in the globalisation process, welcoming foreign investment, pushing up its exports, and so on.

The third set of problems which overtook the Indian economy was primarily the result of certain political imperatives, and which was related to the manner in which the Indian state structure and democratic framework evolved. Over time more and more sections emerged which made strong, articulate demands on state resources and the governments in power were increasingly unable either to meet these demands fully or diffuse the clamour for them. In the process a situation arose when macroeconomic balance, which was maintained in India, unlike many other developing countries, with great caution for the first twenty five years or so after independence, was being slowly eroded. The deteriorating situation was aggravated further by the growing political instability and political competition. The erosion in Congress Party's sole hegemony led to competitive populism with each party trying to outdo the other in distributing largesse. In the race among political parties for prestige and influence the Congress was no longer able to stand above competing groups pressing for an immediate increase in their share of the national cake and reign them in with the promise of rapid growth and a just income distribution in future.

At organisational level too with the coming of Mrs Indira Gandhi who increasingly centralised powers in her hands, democratic functioning within the Congress party declined. Consequently the party lost its organisational links with the grassroots and began political bargaining with sections of society through budgetary allocations. It paved the way for widening gap between public investment and public savings. The deteriorating fiscal and balance of payments situation had led to a mounting debt problem, both domestic and foreign, reaching crisis proportions by the end of the eighties. In earlier phase both Mrs Gandhi after her return in 1980 and Rajiv Gandhi when he took over in 1984 attempted to make economic reforms through their policies. Mrs Gandhi in 1980 tried to bring in liberalisation measures, mainly in the area of deregulation of industrial licensing and reduction of restrictions on large monopoly enterprises. Likewise Rajiv Gandhi in 1984 attempted reforms at a relatively quicker pace towards industrial deregulation, exchange rate flexibility and partial lifting of import controls. But the policy of liberalising the economy and opening it for foreign capital, private official and institutional, with wide-ranging implications for fiscal and investment priorities, income distribution and manpower management and even educational and cultural policy had been attempted to be given the shining label of modernisation to enter the twenty-first century.[41] Again the adopted policy of liberalising country's economy because of certain constraints and deficiencies succeeded in developing a dual society with a wide gap between the impoverished mass of people and a thin crust of affluence at the top. This can only result in unrest, violence and social tension and further diversion of resources away from development.

The economic reforms initiated in India in 1991 have direct impact in shaping the structural framework of our economy. A very important pillar of the new economic policies of the government, is the globalisation of the Indian economy. The government has given a firm commitment to the International Monetary Fund (IMF) to implement economic reforms and also to invite foreign capital for investment and to open many areas of the Indian market for foreign multinational corporations.[42] A developing country, wishing to move towards the goal of prosperity needs economic aid from outside the country and from world economic organisations. But the organisations and the countries, who offer economic aid, also dictate their own terms and conditions which may hamper the fulfilment of needs and requirement of aid receiving countries. This trend ultimately leads to economic imperialism which in long run, widens the gap between developed and developing nations and between rich and poor people of the country which is trying to provide and distribute all the resources to its people equally.[43] The beginning of the second stage and the new industrial policy declared, 'it involves a struggle for social and economic justice, to end poverty and unemployment and to build a modern, democratic, socialist and forward looking India. It also implies building a society wherein' India grows as part of the world economy and not in isolation.[44] However, the economic impact and the reform programmes under the process of globalisation have also affected the social and cultural life of the people in several countries including India.

Evidently, the economic issues particularly, capital, has come to acquire centre stage in the process of globalisation. Earlier the attempt by conquerors to bring the world under one system of rule was primarily related to looting the wealth and politically subjugating the conquered people. But during those days, wealth could not be converted into capital in order to buy labour power, raw materials and instruments to turn out commodities in order to amass profits. Wealth could be converted into capital only when human society entered the stage of capitalism and wealth plundered from the conquered could be transformed into capital. It led to the further rise of capitalism from the nineteenth century onwards when it emerged as a world wide system and the whole world fell into its trap. Its further advancement resulted into the search for cheap labour, raw materials and also of markets which led to the establishment of colonial rule in poor developing countries of Asia, Africa and Latin America also known as the Third World.[45] Capitalism breeds capital but also provides them sufficient leverage and opportunity to extend their mantle over poor and developing countries. These rich and industrialised capitalist countries also control and direct the international financial institutions, because of being the big contributor to it, to provide aid/capital to the needy countries and, thus, dictate their terms over them so as to suit their own economy. Their big industrial empires in the form of multinational corporations, Multi National Companies (MNCs), trade all over the world carry huge profits to their parent countries. The huge profits earned by such capitalist production, later, caused to press for export of capital as their capital cannot be invested in their domestic markets because they were already saturated. This way the problem of surplus capital came to forefront in Western /advanced countries.

In the circumstances, the developed nations wish to maintain their political-economic hegemony over developing or underdeveloped nation. They dictate such political systems and their policies to suit their own interest rather than taking care of welfare of people's living in that country. Developing countries are particularly vulnerable to global event and action and have come to depend heavily on the international community for financial and technical assistance. As a result, national policies are interlocked with global issues. 'Because poor countries generally have fragile politics and weak systems of accountability, with few autonomous institutions and little power to offset that exercised by the central government, external agencies are potentially key political players, capable of exerting considerable influence'.[46] Harold Lasswell, while writing in 1968 also maintained, 'As the globe shrinks into interdependence, relying more fully on science and technology, the policy sciences gain significance. Interdependence implies that every participant and every item in the social process is affected by the context in which it occurs.[47]

Empirical observations point out the fact that during 1960s, 1970s and 1980s, the average rate of profit and share of profit in national product of advanced capitalist had declined. The process of globalisation entered a new intensive phase in the 1980s with the gradual opening and breakdown of the communist bloc.

At the close of the eighties the intensive phase of globalisation started mainly due to the pressing needs of developed countries to outlet the growing volume of surplus capital in less developed or underdeveloped countries in spheres of manufacturing, real estates, raw material extraction, financial sector, advertising, media etc. Between 1980 and 1990, the amount of capital directly invested in foreign lands nearly tripled. Prior to this unexpected and contingent events the global capitalism had produced a whole new technology of communication which made possible a virtual leap in the level of communication and exchange. Information could now be transferred still faster in enormous quantities, and global flows of information, money and people intensified at unprecedented speed. Recent scientific revolutions, particularly in the field of information technology and economic liberalisation have contributed in accelerating the onward process of globalisation. As regards economic liberation the formation of World Trade Organisation (WTO) and MIGA are the landmark achievements towards integration of world economy which is supposed to boost productivity and elevate the living standards in all parts of the world. In addition, the electronic information technologies are part and parcel of the new financial instruments many of which have technical powers which are clearly ahead of the protocols for their regulation.[48] As a result of technological development, especially in the electronic, transport and communication sectors, there has been a proliferation of economic, scientific, technological and cultural innovations, which have greatly affected all areas of human life and particularly the development process in the third world.

India, in response to global milieu for Liberalisation, Privatisation and Globalisation (LPG), in 1990, initiated four important measures: fiscal policy reforms, monitory policy reforms, exchange rate adjustments and realistic wages and income policies. The second phase of economic reforms include: financial, social and public sector reforms, capital market, trade policy and investment reforms. These reform measures have brought about further globalisation of Indian economy with more free flow of foreign capital. Under the policy India is trying to attract foreign investment essentially from three sources. These are Foreign Direct Investment (FDI), Portfolio Investment and NRI Bonds. After the collapse of USSR, US emerged as the only super power in inter-national order based on free trade, the free movement of capital and the construction of liberal states with representative political institutions. According to Achin Vanaik, 'Neo-liberals when they talk of economic globalisation are basically claiming the following: A truly global economy is now emerging for the first time ever. It is dominance of the world market that is now the main issue. The most important economic agents are Multinational Corporations which no longer have serious national allegiance. They roam and operate worldwide.[49] Even in case of India no individual, MNC or any investing agency normally use to invest in this country for the good of the people. They do so only for their own financial benefits. This immediately keeps them aloof from certain important sectors of our national life, namely, the fields of education, health and infrastructure development. The foreign investors have confined their investment to the fields of power generation, communication, oil and gas exploration and all those fields where the returns are high and fast. In other words, the terms and conditions attached to the flow of foreign capital in India and the spheres in which it is being invested are not according to our national priorities, needs and goals, namely, the eradication of poverty, employment generation, improvement in social infrastructure relating to education, health, potable water and equitable distribution of the fruits of the development.

Thus, the process of globalisation has increased the vulnerability of the countries of the Third World which are in the process of being integrated into the world economy. As the recent financial crisis has illustrated, financial liberalisation including speculative and volatile financial flows over which the developing countries have little controls, in the absence of adequate institutional arrangements to manage the process has generated significant instability in the international economics with especially disasterous results for developing countries. It has become a new source of instability in both product and financial markets. This has already been observed by the economic crises in East Asian economies, few years ago. Scholar Robert Heilbroner comments rightly, 'The problem becomes still more complex insofar as the interconnectedness of the global economy widens the field of competition beyond national boundaries. The 350 corporations whose combined sales come to a third of the aggregate Gross National Product (GNP) of the industrial world are giant beams in the structure of world capitalism, and by that very fact, a new source of national economic instability within individual national economies. Even today there exist no effective means to protect production within a nation if the transnationals should begin to shake'.[50] As a result 80 countries containing a third of the world's population are being increasingly marginalised, and over the past 20 years developing countries' share of global trade fell from 0.8 to 0.4 per cent[51]. The fact is that 3 billion people live on less than $2 a day, and 1.2 billion live on less than $ 1 a day. This horrific level of poverty persists despite unprecedented increases in global wealth in the past century.

Indian society is drastically changing after globalisation. In this era different forms of difference have come to the foreground in relation to identity politics, gender, minorities rights, indigenous peoples, and ethnic and religious movement. The lower and weaker section of society has to be the worst sufferers as they will not get jobs. Consequently the income gap between lower and upper level of society is bound to rise and this, along with consumerism, and its demonstration over modern electronic means of communication, will lead to crimes, anarchy and destruction of social harmony and equilibrium. On the other the role of government is changing as we witness a fragmentation of policy responsibility in society in which the traditional mechanism of government control are no longer workable or even appropriate. It challenges the traditional relationship between economy and state. The globalised market system stretches beyond the political authority of any single government. Faced with a network of connections that escape their power of surveillance or regulation, national governments have become increasingly unequal to providing the legal, monetary, or protective functions that are their contribution to a well divided loyalties -on the one hand eager for its firms to maximize revenues, which are subject to national taxation, on the other hand, reluctant to see employment or research capabilities that it wants as part of its national economic strength located in a competitive national entity. Since the focus of development shifted from social goals to profit motives, the state was neither considered as a positive instrument for social transformation nor an agency for resource allocation.

The new capital flow that comes in has totally changed the class character of Indian people. Now the market products only the goods that cater the needs of those who have high purchasing power because the profits are likely to be higher in such spheres. For the time being it created the impression of growth and prosperity. But the needs of the bulk of the population are normally neglected or overlooked. C.T. Kurian mentions that globalisation usually benefits people who can play the game, but the chances are very less for those who are resourceless, uneducated and those who make livelihood through traditional production activities, will come under various kinds of pressures. So, on the one hand he talks about the marvelous technological innovations such as email and flights that convert this earth and its people into a 'global village' but at the same time he also accepts that this globe has been integrated by capital practices and ideological polarisation has largely been removed.[52] Thus, negative aspects of globalisation include the unnecessary interference of developed countries pressure to follow particular policies and programmes which are not very suitable to the people and society leading to imbalanced development and growth.

In the continuing marginalisation policy of the Government of India since independence the negative waves of globalisation added fuel to the fire. It altered the role of state as an agency for the empowerment of the socially deprived sections. Such a transition from state-oriented development to market-oriented one evoked mixed responses among the various social groups in India as different aspects of the reform processes, in one way or other threatened the very existence of these social classes and organisations. In the years following the independence the dominant classes and castes showed much enthusiasm to divert the public policies of the government for acquiring more resources from the government. Consequently the support base of the state, and its policies and programmes which were intended to empower the socially marginalised sections were tempered for attaining the ambitious target of high economic growth. The coming of globalisation and new economic reforms gave birth to a critical moment when there was an upsurge of the poor and Dalits to achieve increased shares in the allocation of economic resources and political power. It led to a change in the functioning of democracy in India in the late 1980s and early 1990s with the passage of the 73rd and 74th Amendments which gave constitutional status to two elected bodies, the Panchayats and the Nagarpalikas. As a result the political competition at the local government level witnessed crucial change of a positive nature. These constitutional reforms allowed demo-cracy to locally democratise.[53] With democracy taking root any meaningful assessment of the structure, organisation and working of political parties in India would necessarily involve an in-depth evaluation of the dynamics of party politics at the grassroots level. But in the process of globalisation, the rural poor began to experience the dislocation of their economy in its totality for the first time in the history of their existence.

However, the fiscal austerity measures, intended to bridge the fical deficit, exhausted the state capacity to meet the increasing demands on the state from various sections of the society especially the newly politicized social groups. While the fruits of the economic reform accrued to the urban elite and middle classes of the society, the traditionally backward social groups like the Dalits and the tribals were haunted by its adverse impact. Agrarian structure and Indian villages were affected negatively as seventy four per cent of India's population lives in rural areas and their livelihood mainly depends on agriculture and the related activities. The small and marginal farmers and agricultural labourers constitute the vast majority of rural society.[54] Globalisation resulted in the neglect of agriculture that adversely affected the vulnerable classes of rural society in their employment conditions, income and consumption pattern, their education and health status. Not only the village agriculture but the Indian women, Dalits, rural poor, economic organisations, media, public services, political leaders, political parties and government along with other aspects of human life registered a significant change. Under the unleashing of the market oriented economic reforms, the socially vulnerable sections became handicapped in responding to the market signals as they found their entry to the market very difficult, especially those who did not have assets or skill.[55] The benefits of the fast developing areas like information technology did not evoke much impact on the living conditions of the down-trodden sections of the people. The attack on the state by the market can be considered as a denial of the rights and livelihood to the socially marginalised sections. The measures for attaining fiscal discipline like cuts in government expenditure had a direct bearing on the welfare programmes of the SC and ST in the areas of rural water supply, poverty alleviation schemes, educational benefits, employment schemes, and other related destinations.

Post-globalisation

As a result of the globalisation and its all pervasive adverse effects society has resulted in a growing discontent and disenchantment among the people and thereby their isolation from power centres. The new middle class emerged in the era of neo-liberal policies of the government has adopted an exclusive and parochial approach that affected negatively the living conditions of the other classes and groups. It generated anomie trends in society. On the other the exclusion can be seen with the emergence of identity politics based on caste, especially among the lower strata of the society who are demanding wider power sharing in the political system. According to Rajni Kothari, "The yawning vacuum created by the alienation of people from the developmental exercise was filled by deeper pathologies like communalism and fundamentalism which found a fertile ground.[56] In contrast to the early middle class that emerged after independence, secular in outlook and sensitive to social coherence, the new middle class showed allegiance to the Hindu nationalist politics. The BJP succeeded in bringing on the loyalty of the middle class and filled the political vacuum by the decline of the Congress by providing a Hindu nationalist alternative to the Congress. The adoption of neo-liberal economic policies produced two new social groups- the loser and the winner. While the poor and the socially marginalised sections constituted the disadvantageous sections, the consumerist middle class constituted the advantageous sections. In course of time, the losers attracted to the caste-based parties, which had in fact no concrete policies and programmes for their genuine empowerment, and the gainers were mobilised towards the Hindu nationalist party like BJP. Initially, in post-independence era many promises and assets were provided by the government's of the day to different sections of the people, including the socially marginalised groups. People's expectations from the state were belied in the 1990s, when the market reforms shrunk the role of the state and hopes failed to materialise.

The waves of globalisation in India have accelerated the pace of political competition, changing structures of power and influence, and widening base of political consultation and persuasion. Although Indian policies have been subject to foreign or outside pressures since the days of the Cold War in the 1950s, yet until the mid-1980s, the decisions were accepted as being in the "long-term national interest." There were accusations in the procurement of the Jaguar aircraft also but these did not create the furore that the Bofors scam did. Since the late 1980s, as in the case of Bofors or the new economic policies in 1991 or the Indo-US nuclear deal, sectional or individual interests have become dominant.[57] In India, by and large, politics is neither suppressed nor confined to a small elite. On the contrary, politics provides the larger setting within which decision making in regard to economic development and social change, and application of pressures for redirecting development and change takes place. The Indian model of development is thus characterised by the politicisation of a fragmented social structure, through a wide dispersal and permeation of political forms, values and ideologies. The process culminates by closing the gap that has traditionally divided village society from the polity.[58] In a democracy the contest for power is never free from uncertainty and anxiety, and Indian politics is now marked by increasing turmoil. Those who make politics their career became accustomed to its turbulence and some even take a peculiar pleasure in it. These have played havoc with national politics. Pressures and counter pressures are mounted through political parties and their leaders and big bosses.

In India there is a multitude of parties based on caste, religion, ethnicity, regional affiliations, linguistic differences, and political ideology. They are frantically preoccupied with aggrandizing their own narrow interests, apathetically disregarding the larger interests of the society and the nation. The democracy in India has caused fragmentation of the society into smaller, antagonistic, belligerent segments; had led to disintegration of the states into economically inviable units plagued with adversial relationships; and has created an ambience of incessant mistrust, discord, and internecine conflicts.[59] Because of the multiplicity of parties, the politicians, propelled by expediency and opportunism, spend their time, energy, and resources in forming often transient alliances, to capture power. Each constituent element has its own agenda; hence the alliances are usually ephemeral. At present the relations between government and opposition have become increasingly acrimonious. Even where there is broad agreement over, let us say, foreign policy or economic policy, each side maintains an adversial relationship with the other, fearing that there will be a loss of face if not a loss of support from its constituents if it appears conciliatory. The habitually confrontationist conduct of both government and opposition is complicated by the fact that neither the one nor the other speaks in a single voice. This may be a good thing where it serves to defuse tension but it is not conducive to deliberations on policy.[60] Therefore, the stability of the government is precarious, and the scourge of elections always haunts the Indian electorate. Despite the advent of information age and the commencement of global interaction, the world perspective of majority of the legislators are woefully limited; and their comprehension of international issues with national and local ramifications is virtually non-existent.

In the circumstances good governance is viewed as the exercise of economic, political, and administrative authority to manage a country's affairs to all levels and as the means by which states promote social cohesion and integration, and ensure the well-being of their population. The new turmoil among Indian masses and the new forms of protest and struggle waged by a new set of actors as part of the continuing commitment to democracy, indeed to its deepening and broadening. They need to be located in the larger context of transformaion. In this context the Indian democracy witnessed two changes; First, the resurgence of the people themselves, bothin consciousness and in behaviour. They are asserting their democratic rights and challenging the established order, at local levels to begin with, but affecting the entire social and political order. Though they are by no means close to transforming it. Secondly, the emergence of a new social class of mediators in the political process and the activists. They are upper and middle class in their origin, but identify themselves with the lower orders of society - the poor, the oppressed and the segregated; social strata ranging from the untouchable and the destitude among the tribes and ethnic minorities, to the victims of sexual, ecological and generational descriminations, atrocities and violence.[61] Globalisation needs to be countered not just with decentralised and regional alternatives, or new initiatives withregard to natural resources and ecology, but also with political and ideological initiatives at the national, regional and global level.

India is currently passing through a period of many challenges in different spheres - economic, social cultural and political. Contextually, there has been a welcome shift from traditional concepts of government and politics to good governance and its attributes. Governance refers to the quality of government and manner in which power is exercised by governments in managing country's social and economic resources. Governance means, 'The process of decision making and the process by which decisions are implemented or not implemented. It also focuses on the formal and informal actors involved in decision-making and implementing the decisions made and the formal and informal structures that have been set in place to arrive at and implement the decisions. There are so many actors in governance and the government is one of them. In urban areas, the other major actors constitute political parties, voluntary organisations, research institutes, religious leaders, finance institutes, the military, media, lobbyists, international donors, multi-national corporations. While in rural areas, actors may include influential landlords, associations of peasant farmers, cooperatives and NGOs.[62] These actors, urban and rural, other than government and the military are grouped together as part of the civil society. All these may play arole in decision-making or in influencing the decision making process. The pre-requisites for quality governance are that the s system should be good and suited to the need, aspirations background and ethos of the concerned people.

The term 'Good Governance' was highlighted by the World Bank in one of its documents in 1989 in context of third world countries. It is not only confined to political governance but would include all types of governance, such as international, national, state or provincial or local. Further in 1992 the World Bank's Document on governance and development said, 'Good governance is central to creating and sustaining an environment which fosters strong and equitable development and it is an essential complement to sound economic policies. It identified three aspects of governance: the form of political regime, the process by which authority is exercised in the management of country's economic and social resources: and the capacity of governments to design, formulate and implement policies and in general, to discharge government functions.[63] But besides the World Bank indicators of good governance encompassing democracy, transparency and accountability, it may be said that the whole idea of good governance is that of a participative democratic system in which those who are called upon to govern on behalf of the people are motivated with a will to giving their best, serving and doing good to the people and in particular, solving the problems of the poor and the underprivileged and making their lives more liveable, satisfying and enjoyable. However, at large, good governance is a dynamic and value-laden concept. The values it gives importance to are eight in number. Modern concept of good governance is participatory, consensus-oriented, accountable, transparent, responsive, effective and efficient, equitable and inclusive and follows the rule of law.

In India the democratic structure of governance, which is the largest democracy of the world, badly fails on the counts of good governance. Although people have got the right to participate in governance directly as well as indirectly but peculiar situation is that this characteristic of good governance is partially realised. Especially the reforms in economic governance were started in the country under the fiscal stabilisation in early 1990s, with the World Bank/IMF loan conditional ties to improve the balance of payments and fiscal discipline, and the reorganisation of economy, polity and society, as in several other third world countries. The agenda of reforms has been clearly stated in recent official documents and reports of the government. The Indian state has adopted a largely favourable stance towards the processes of globalisation, liberalisation and privatisation.

It has embarked on the path of reorienting and restructuring its governance system. A whole new set of policies and programmes has been put in place. The canvas of reforms covers both the centre and states. It encompasses reforms in economic, social, administrative and political spheres. At present the innumerable issues regarding political economy and political sociology are surfacing that highlight the relationship that exists between development paradigms and actual development, government and governance, common people and the state. But there is no denying the fact that governments continue to play a central role in the lives of its citizens, governance came to be equated with government. Development and reform also constituted the functions of governments. Now, when one talks of governance, one refers to participatory governance which works towards development of individuals as well as the society and nation.

Earlier and in very recent the Tenth Five Year Plan (2002-2007), Eleventh Five Year Plan (2007-2012) and the Twelfth Five Year Plan (2012-2017), have focused the themes of good governance and its implementation. The Tenth Plan states, 'Governance relates to the management of all such process, that, in any society, define the environment which permits and enables individual to rise their capability levels, provide opportunities to realise their potential and enlarge the set of available choice. These processes, covering the political, social and economic aspects of life impact every level of human enterprise, be it the individual, the household, the village, the region or the national level. It covers the state, civil society and the market, each of which is critical for sustaining human development.[64] Chapter six of the tenth plan included governance issues and strategic identifies, such as people's participation, decentralisation, right to information, civil society involvement, civil service reforms, procedural reforms, judicial reforms, using information technology and empowerment of the marginalised. It was felt at the higher level that good governance is helpful in achieving human well-being and sustained development. Moreover, it is equally important to recognise that poor governance could well erode the individual capabilities as well as institutional and community capacities to meet even the basic needs of sustenance for large segments of the population. In line the new Right to Information (RTI) Act came into force on 12 October, 2005.

In fact, governance has a critical role to play in the process of development and is required as an essential tool in striking a balance between the diminishing role of government and threat of an increasingly powerful private sector. This is of great importance in the developing world where many governments appeared to have failed in performing their duties, and major changes were considered necessary for arranging new patterns of interactions between government and citizens.[65] Under the camoulage of the slogans of one world and a global village, ordinary citizens instead of being the masters in democratic polity have been increasingly reduced to being mere consumers of goods and services. The result is tremendous erosion in democratic rights and freedoms of the individual *vis-à-vis* the organs of the State substantially reducing the space for the voice of the poor and the underprivileged. Once K.R. Narayanan, the President of Indian Republic, felt the pains and said, 'We find that justice- social, economic and political-remains an unrealised dream for millions of our fellow citizens. The benefits of our economic growth are yet to reach them. We have one of the world's largest reservoirs of technical personnel, but also the world's largest number of illiterates, the world's largest middle class, but also the largest number of people below the poverty line, and the largest number of children suffering from malnutrition. He added further that there is sullen resentment among the masses against their condition erupting often in violent forms in several parts of the country. Many a social upheaval can be traced to the neglect of the lowest of society, whose discontent moves towards the path of violence.[66] Tragically the growth in our economy has been accompanied by great regional and social inequalities.

Decades passed since the globalisaion, liberalisation and privatisation have been commenced in India and now there has been a lot of debate about their impact and outcome. There are some who acclaim the results while there are others who oppose both the process of globalisation and its impact. Without doubt, globalisation has led to technological transformation which has resulted in international mobilisation. Exchange of information, technologies and methods have led to a decline in diseases, facilitated communication, made life more comfortable. But on the other the sovereign States of the time feel very uneasy, especially the developing and underdeveloped, in working within this vast array of international regimes and organisations. The rapid growth of transnational issues and problems has involved a spread of layers of political regulation both within and across political boundaries. It has been marked by the transformation of aspects of territorially-based political decision-making the development of regional and global institutions and organisations and the emergence of regional and global law. It has paved the way for rapid emergence of new forms of multilateral and transnational politic involving governments in Inter Governmental Organisations (IGOs) and a wide variety of transnational pressure groups and International Non-Governmental Organisations (INGOs). However, in the whole process poor and the deprived are the worst sufferer and therefore some consider globalisation to be a threat to a nation or society in general and to the marginalised in particular.

In the needs and aspirations of the nation and international pressure /lobbying the actual position of India exists. On the one hand the country is blessed with significant natural resources and mineral wealth; there is a complete collapse of governance that needs to be rectified soon on the other. Even today it is felt at various levels that little has been done to bring the unprivileged to the level of the privileged, to provide equality of opportunity and a life of dignity to all. In this context, a wake-up call was also given by President Pratibha Patil in her Republic Day-eve address to the nation, 'The disadvantaged too should find a place to enjoy the sunshine of the country's growth and development. Our efforts and our commitment, while pursuing the goal of high growth rates, should be to ensure that all people of our country benefit from it. Our pledge will remain unfulfilled until, as Gandhi had said, 'We have wiped every tear in every eye'.[67] In line in the 12th Five Year Plan (2007-2012) and 13th Five Year Plan (2012-2017) the Planning Commission has focused on "inclusive growth." The steps taken are expected to encourage the development of Indian agriculture, education, health and social welfare schemes through government spending.

Thus, the political vacuum created by the national and international factors paved the way for governance-related movements in India whose first target in the present is rampant corruption at all levels leading to a breakdown in the rule of law and lack of accountability all around. Although the anti-corruption movement led by Anna Hazare and Baba Ramdev's dramatic call for 'Congress-hatao' have confirmed that a movement for good governance is overdue. Earlier in the 1980s there emerged the people's movement sector-comprising farmer's movement, Dalit movements, women movements, environmental movements and the movements for information and deepening of democracy is one of the most vibrant spaces in the democratic arena. These movements are inherently political in that they seek to challenge the settled relations of power. They have quietly shifted the terms of political engagement and brought new issues to the foreground. Legislation and policies like the Right to Information, the Mahatma Gandhi Rural Employment Guarantee Act, the Forest Act and the new Land Acquisition and Rehabilitations Act are a tribute to the power and creativity of these movements.[68] Yet, these movements have not succeeded in posing a direct challenge to mainstream politics, they involved some of the finest activists and thinkers of our time. There have been many creative organisational experiments and ideological innovations, however, they remained largely invisible. At large these movements failed to translate their support in electoral terms and in order to give effect to their political agenda, remained dependent on the very political establishment they critiqued and struggled against. In post-1989 period while the idea of third space has expanded, the third force has shrunk.[69] The energy of the third space is in search of a national political vehicle, especially because the mainstream politics of UPA and NDA have become more insulated from popular struggles and movements.

However, a breakthrough appeared in the field when an anti-corruption movement was started by the Team Anna in the year 2011-12. It is after more than three decades that a movement outside the organised party sector has registered a nationwide presence and visibility. What mattered in this is that the Anna Hazare-led movement spawned smaller protests in a large number of towns and even villages. A fairly large proportion of citizens who did not participate in any protest heard about it and sympathised with it. But its success depends not so much on whether it wins an election but on how much of positive energy it releases into the political system. Even Anna Hazare's fast-unto-death organised on occasions more than one and recently in July-August 2012, which attracted unprecedented attention and adulation for the enactment of an effective Lokpal Bill to curb corruption in the top echelons of the establishment, has raised several doubts about its success. Taking important lessons from the earlier JP movement for the posterity of revolutionaries, and reformers wanting to bring macro-level change in the country, JP himself wrote for a revolution to succeed, it required a revolutionary leadership as well as a revolution organisation. In addition to JP's view, it also needs revolutionary programme of action. In this movement only one component was present: a revolutionary leadership. Apart from this there was no attempt to build a revolutionary organisation to assist the leadership and no revolutionary programme of action entailing a broad roadmap for change.[70] In addition, the movement shows that agitators are not trying to build a parallel mass base on the strength of a constructive programme as was done by Mahatma Gandhi. Team Anna lacks other tools of mass mobilisation or social reconstruction. Thus, the movement should be made holistic and there has to be a larger vision and roadmap for the country. The sooner this is understood the better it is for Team Anna and, perhaps, the country.

At present there is a widespread belief that the kind of democratic system in which we operate is failing us. Today 80 per cent of Indians are poor, and there is massive unemployment, lack of healthcare, housing and good education. In the recent period the rich have become richer, and the rich-poor divide has increased. Economic growth has benefited only a handful.[71] India is a representative democracy where people select their representatives once in five years to make laws and policies on their behalf. Limiting the participation of the people merely to voting once in five years has significantly reduced the responsiveness of the representatives to the people. One reason is that our democracy has become formalistic. Legislatures should check corruption but it would not be so if the elected are beholden to the corrupt or are themselves corrupt. The problem is political; it cannot be resolved through technical fixes or by having more laws - these are anyway being circumvented. A weak democracy presents a no-win situation; if a democracy is weak, the corrupt get elected and misuse their autonomy; if the legislator's, autonomy is curbed, democracy weakens.[72] The super-watchdog which should deliver all-round accountability, has become weak in India. The ruling class has played havoc with the watchdog institutions so as to control them for their narrow ends. That is why the demand for a strong Lokpal gained momentum.

The problem in India is not that there is too much democracy but too little. Whether the solution lies in direct democracy or devolution of powers to village councils deserves closer scrutiny. One innovative solution of direct democracy tried in numerous countries is the Referendum and Initiative. These are instruments whereby some decisions of policy and law-making are referred to a direct vote by the electorate, rather than solely being decided by their representatives. Countries that regularly practise some degree of direct democracy like Switzerland are small, homogeneous and renowned for their clockwork efficiency. Other countries that have had referendums, whether smaller ones like Sweden or larger ones like Brazil, have had them only rarely. The idea that village councils should contribute to State and national law-making is a radical one but closely related to referendums. Panchayats have existed in ancient times and have been reintroduced in modern times. But they are still struggling to find their feet, clamouring for devolution of more powers and big budgets.[73] It enjoys the same potential strengths and suffers from the same weaknesses. Unless electoral reforms can be introduced, reducing entry barriers in politics and levelling the playing field in political parties, it will be hard to keep arguing that elections are the lone remedy to unsettled issues of national importance. No such electoral reforms are on the horizon, but it is conceivable that sustained activism could put them on the agenda.

In the present scenario of Indian politics participatory democracy is being considered more and more as not merely desirable but necessary. Under conditions of globalisation, where national-level institutions of representation are being subordinated to hegemonic global power with the structure of political and economic decision-making more remote and alienated from people, the politics of participatory democracy has acquired a new relevance. Whatever be the challenges in introducing such democratic reforms the time has come to discuss such a change to ensure that our government truly represents the people.

1.3 Current Pofile and Prospect

Once a republic takes birth, it is the leaders who produce the institutions. Later, it is the institutions which produce the leaders. The success story of independent India has been its secular, federal and multi-party system. These systems have strengthened India politically, economically and emotionally. Jawaharlal Nehru played a very significant role in order to strengthen political institutions under the framework of the Indian Constitution. The adoption of the Constitution in its secular spirit during the years of strife and communal tension was itself a dashing step taken under his leadership.[74] The Indian state as it developed in the Nehruvian era, concentrated all powers of patronage in its hand. It had quickly created a progressive constitutional framework and possessed an enlightened political leadership. While the constitution and the state structures based upon it have remained essentially intact, the quality of political leadership steadily deteriorated. The inability of the state to use its political capabilities effectively, accommodating the moderate and isolating the militant, has contributed more to the spread of insurgencies in the various parts of the country.[75] Even in case of Pandit Nehru there was a clear decline in his effectiveness and glamour in comparison to pre-independence leadership, but his departure from the scene in May 1964 marked the end of an era in Indian society and politics. In the post-Nehru phase the political system of the country felt itself stressed and registered an overall decline in public morality, political leadership. Political parties were held responsible for the chaotic condition of the system. Consequently, India had ceased to be a stable society that it was in the fifties and the early sixties.

At the time Mrs Gandhi took over, the political system of the country was in deep crisis from economic points in view, in particular. It was an additional tension on the prevailing system as it had been sick politically even earlier. Hard pressed by this array of hostile economic forces, large sections of the population stepped up their demands on the system at the very moment but it was least able to meet them. It is only when relatively stable societies are sought to be changed rapidly and profoundly that they begin to undergo ferment. As a remedy to these all Emergency was declared, but this approach brought rapidly diminishing returns in terms of 'discipline', 'order' and 'stability'. Social conflict could not forever be held in abeyance, public opinion could not forever be manipulated and regulated, popular resentment could not forever be contained. At a later stage, the social ills that posed a direct threat to the political system of the country were rated high, resulting in the worsening of the quality of political management, indisputably the standards of public life have declined sharply. Our political system is the system of election and a keen observer of the Indian political scene argued that the way things are going today, it is quite possible that India might become a paradox of successful elections and a failed democracy.[76] Despite the conduct of so many elections so far, the actual exercise of power in the country has yet to reflect true democracy. This has largely been because, unlike the elites and middle class, the poor in India are unable to generate pressure. It has rightly been said, 'The very conditions which inhibit the masses from effectively organising to push their own interests, namely, their poverty, ignorance and isolation, and the hierarchical power structure of the Indian society, have made it possible for India to hold general elections based on universal suffrage, with endangering political stability.'[77] The democracy in India has lagged behind in its sacred responsibility of promoting and protecting public good.

From the mid-1960s onwards after the break of single party rule particularly in states, a beginning of political awareness was registered by the regional forces and oppressed class/caste for promotion and protection of their interests. As a result from this time the ruling establishment has shown a strong propensity to take recourse to authoritarian means to handle popular pressure. Even the declaration of internal emergency failed to mitigate the stress on system and democracy in India survives due to their pressures for a democratic polity. Simultaneously, the problems have become more pronounced with the slow erosion of the support for the Congress in post-Emergency period and its sudden decline after the 1989 Parliamentary elections. The danger to democracy comes not from the self-mobilisation of ordinary people; the threat lies in the emerging elite lacking the skill to manage to democratic institutions. There is a propensity in them to violate the rules of the game and to pay scant regard to the procedural aspects of democracy. In their haste to be empowered, they break the rules and jump the queue, indeed an unseemly sight for any established order. They also have not yet learnt to regulate, in a durable fashion, the relationship between themselves either in the social sphere or, more importantly, in the political realm.[78] Thus, unlike the earlier ritual participation, struggle is now a key form of taking part in community life for the lower castes as it always was for the working class. However, the implementation of Mandal Commission recommendation and reassertion of Hindutva ideology at the close of 1980s acted as a trigger, upsetting the ground equations of power and domination. Thereafter, groups formed around privileges and it resulted in an altogether peculiar decomposition of the consciousness of the established middle classes formed out of the upper castes. These factors remained in active consideration of Indian voters in the years to come. In the period Indian republic passed through a tough experience of coalitions and minority governments working within the traditional parameters of state without any forward movement in the direction of substantive democracy.

It is a time for the Indian republic to choose between majoritarian principles and substantive democracy. In general the failure of post-colonial states to assure equal citizenship rights and to deliver on the promise of redistributive justice has brought these entities into some disrepute. As secularism and socialism have resorted to majoritarian ideologies, religiously or ethnically defined, in attempt to prevent their own structures from being undermined. In today's polity instead of the unbending insistence on the singular loyalty of the citizen to the state, the time is overdue to rethink the relevance of multiple and shifting social identities for the cause of democracy. If it happens so it can be a boon and not a threat to democratic values and practice. The multiple identities can only flourish within a political and state system based on layered and shared sovereignties.[79] The rise of Hindu majoritarian 'nationalism' in India is tied to the defence of centralised state authority against a variety of regional as well as class-based challenges, even though it has not succeeded in dislodging the formal secular ideology of the Indian state. But over the years the social character of the BJP, as distinct from its class composition, has therefore undergone a rapid change. From a party of traders and other hidebound petty bourgeoisie, it has grown into a representative party of dominant sections of Indian society, including the ruling classes. A notable feature of the rise of right wing militant Hindu nationalism and the assumption of power by the BJP-led alliance in 1998 and 1999 elections, is the materialisation of a new alignment between the ruling classes and the social basis of political power.

While the 1990s witnessed the phenomenal growth of the BJP, the Congress registered a steady decline. The Indian National Congress- long emblematic of the ruling classes- represented a diverse social constituency earlier; consisting as much of the Dalits, and the poor and oppressed of various communities, as of the richer sections of society. It has now become more a party of the disprivileged sections of society, with the privileged moving into the BJP. In the period the vote for Congress among the rich sections of the upper castes is as low as 26.3 per cent, while the BJP boasts 57.2 per cent. Surprisingly the Congress vote 26.5 per cent was lower than that of the BJP 40.8 per cent among the rich sections of Dalits. Apart from this the Congress has also lost heavily among all sections of the Muslims and the Dalits in the Gangetic belt. The rule provided by the BJP-led alliance represents a specifically ruling-class bloc- a unification of the ruling-class interests under bourgeois leadership and bourgeois aspirations among the various strata in society. However, in a Parliamentary rule based on party competition, it is important how the social bases of support are structured. The political responsiveness of a government is partly conditioned by the social support it depends on. And in the similar class character of the two parties, their parliamentary rule cannot make any difference to the interests of the peasantry or the working class but it would have a definite setback to the democratic interests of the masses particularly in Indian context where democratic gains have been so slow and so little.

Only at this point lies the basics of Indian state- a unique situation in which the birth of our republic took place. The state became congealed in its present form in the wake of independence; in fact, the first few years were of crucial importance. It began its trajectory of consolidation by facing mass upheavals; popular struggle the like of which India never saw again. On the face of this, the state had two choices. One, it could have used the popular upheavals to start altering or restructuring its institutions. Alternatively, it could continue to rely on the inherited colonial bureaucracy, and, a host of other repressive institutions and law to subdue the popular movements. At the juncture out of fear of popular struggles, the ruling leadership chose the second alternative- a case of historical short sightedness. This choice had long-term consequences as it allowed the state institutions to become insulated from popular pressures and the need for accountability, as well as gave them permanence as necessary intermediaries to the state's exercise of power. The fluidity of the early period could have been utilised in moulding the state institutions as truly democratic structures. Given the alignment of forces in the political establishment as a whole, the first option would have had short-term destabilising consequences. But it may also have had long-term beneficial results more responsiveness to popular aspirations, anti-feudal and transformational measures such as participatory grassroots-level institutions freed of bureaucratic control, self-initiative and local mobilisation in planning and handling of poverty, health, literacy etc. Such open-ended options would surely have helped in breaking the power of the narrow-minded elite.[80] The state in India thus failed in living up to its inheritance of the values, inspirations and aspirations of the anti-colonial national movement. The state failed to materialise as the site of structural possibilities of changing social relations, of institutional initiatives, of involving people, and of normative impulses for justice and equity. Instead it pursued a narrowly conceived, western capitalist inspired modernisation under the charge of a bureaucracy that had foreclosed possibilities of an emancipatory transformation based on popular impulses.

As a result of this after more than 60 years and 15 national general elections, India's Parliament is nowhere close to being truly representative. Since the adoption of the Constitution, India has moved decisively towards a multi-party system, with laws such as the one to prevent defection restricting inner-party dissent even while curbing horse trading. Power is still concentrated in the hands of a few, with the role of the public limited to voting in governments every five years or so.[81] While the strength of Indian democracy has withstood the decades of social, economic and political developments, there are numerous challenges to democratic governance. The social and economic progress achieved by the deepening of democracy in many societies has been shaped by their efforts to successfully protect the rule of law. Despite various attempts to enforce and institutionalise the rule of law in Indian society, the intended results have not been achieved. While the normative framework of constitutional governance is established through the Constitution of India and the various institutions established under it, deeply embedded values constitutionalism have not taken roots in the Indian society.[82] In between the period, huge social expectations have been generated by institutions that are responsible for checking abuse of power. But given that the capacity for dealing with abuse of power is disproportionate to the demands imposed upon them by the sheer size and magnitude of the country, there have been numerous unfulfilled promises. Urgent steps are needed to establish a rule of law society in India, without which our fundamental credentials as a democracy will seriously be undermined.

Even the national general elections held in 2004 and 2009 failed to make an impression quite different to the earlier, it however, registered a voting structural adjustments contrary to the decade of 1990s. The verdict of the 2004 Parliamentary elections showed that Indian democracy is not just the largest in the world, it is also becoming one of the most vibrant. The defeat of the BJP is not only a mark of the vibrancy of Indian democracy, it also removed a major paradox from politics. It brought a much closer correspondence between the social forces which took shape in the 1990s and political power. As such, this lends greater coherence to Indian politics, and in this there is an opportunity for democratic forces to strength the secular and pluralist foundations of Indian republic as cherished by the framers of Indian Constitution. In 2004 elections there was a subtle shift in the social profile of voters. By the late 1990s, the Congress had become a party whose support base was a mirror image of its opponent in different parts of the country. The party did not have a vote of its own and was excessively dependent upon the residual support it got from the marginal sections of society. This time the Congress regained something of its famous rainbow coalition. It has improved its standing among the urban middle classes and educated voters. It has done so while retaining the bottom of the pyramid that constitutes its core voting bloc.[83] In the last three elections the seat/vote multiplier for the

Congress has gone up from 0.74 in 1999 to 1.01 in 2004 and 1.34 in 2009 and every one per cent of the vote gave the Congress four seats in 1999, 5.5 seats in 2004 and 7.2 seats in 2009.[84] Though there was nothing like a national wave, strong or mild, there appeared to be a nationwide trend working to the Congress' advantage.

On the other in both these elections the BJP posted its lowest vote share since it first exploded in 1989. This is the third successive election that its support base has shrunk since the high watermark of 1998. The BJP's rise to power through the 1990s involved three kinds of expansions, all of which faced reversal in 2009 elections. First of all it involved extending the party's support base to new States. The big strides that the party made in the South and East in the early 1990s soon came to a point of stagnation. Secondly, the BJP expanded its bandwidth on the political spectrum by acquiring new allies. The NDA of 1999-2004 represented the pinnacle of the BJP's political expansion. Since then it has been downhill for the party. From the peak of 41.1 share of the national vote, the NDA slipped to 35.9 per cent in 2004 and has fallen to just 24.1 per cent in 2009. Thirdly, The BJP attracted new social groups during its phase of expansion. It expanded from urban to the rural areas. From being an upper caste party, it cultivated a major base among the lower OBC's. It took major strides towards capturing the adivasi vote in middle India and started securing some vote among non-Hindus. In 2009 election, the BJP's hitherto upward trend among adivasis and Muslim voters has been reversed and its expansion among the lower OBC's halted.[85] It suffered a negative swing in nearly every State. It needs to reflect not so much on the election campaign and strategies as on its overall political direction.

In totality the recent trends of election results and experiences show that the underprivileged and vulnerable people have displayed an unanticipated capacity to exercise their voting power against the privilegensia's insensitiveness to their sufferings and misery. These are the people who make the economy work and therefore feel they ought to have right to say that some investments should directly benefit them so that they come to possess some assets, get enhanced opportunity for credit, secure employment, and have access to education and health. The formation and consolidation of this section of society is not in haste, but ever since the anti-Emergency wave of 1977, people have learnt to mobilise themselves in terms of their experiences. It also appeared that in these elections, emotional issues and primordial sentiments were set aside. The everyday life of ordinary people with their myriad small problems became foregrounded. The everyday life that is lived in different contexts is also a reflection and expression of the religious, cultural, social and regional diversities of Indian society. The vote, therefore, in essence, is also for the plural traditions and the secular way of life of Indian society. Separation of religion and politics is the means to make politics autonomous of substantive commitments and fulfil the unfulfilled desires of Indian republic.

The due time for 16th national general election is the year 2014 but the post-2009 general elections phase in India continued to remain a crucial one. It witnessed the anger in the minds of the people which was steadily built up as scams of huge proportion burst one after another; the 2-G spectrum scam, Commonwealth Games scam, Aadarsh Society scam in which high level politicians, civil servants and military officer were found to be involved with government looking the other way failing to take swift and decisive action, and moving only under the direction of the Supreme Court. Public confidence in the willingness and ability of government to act against corruption was shaken and India came to be known as one of the most corrupt countries in the world.[86] The large scale all pervading corruption compelled Anna Hazare to launch fast in April 2011 at Jantar Mantar, New Delhi. At the time the people were so outraged by scandals after scandals of large proportion coming out, that they responded in a big way when Anna and his associates gave a call for fight against corruption. Corruption exists at the 'culturing edge level' the day-to-day engagement of people with lower level of administration as also big corruption at the highest level.[87] There is no doubt that the entire political system and public life including government needs to be cleaned. It is a deeply-entrenched, systemic problem that is corroding the nation, widening the gulf between ordinary citizens and those with access to power and privilege, and under-mining the faith of people in democratic institutions.[88] However, President Pratibha Patil in her Republic Day address on 26 January 2012 warned the reformers not to shake the tree of state so hard in their drive to remove bad fruit that the tree itself is brought down. In the context nobody can disagree with the idea that India's democratic system must be safeguarded while introducing reforms in its political institutions.

In the forthcoming general elections to the members of Lok Sabha the ruling Congress Party and the main opposition Bharatiya Janata Party with their allies and associates is likely to face each other in a straight way. In the election if the Congress party wants to worm its way back into middle class respectability, it has to raise its own decency index. At the very minimum, the country needs to see for itself that the Congress has respect for constitutional and political institutions. As the oldest and the most responsible political party, it is the Congress's historic burden to inculcate good manners in the polity.[89] On the other is the BJP and its associates, but equally for both, winning the coming elections in India is not easy. The Party's enthusiasm in the BJP's third consecutive triumph in Gujarat's 2012 state assembly elections is understandable. It has, at large, began to think this victory in terms of national context and with analysis, it is hopeful about the prospect of 2014 Parliamentary election. In party's expectations the viability of Chief Minister Narendra Modi as a Prime Ministerial candidate and the electoral appeal of Hindutva is rated high. For the past decade, most observers of Indian politics have believed the electoral appeal of Hindutva to be on the decline. In the current electoral strategy the party is not sure whether the continuing decline of Hindutva can be a arrested, or even reversed or the Party can only succeed by emphasising claims of "development" and "good governance."[90] In any case the BJP should avoid easy generalisations about Hindutva advocacy in facilitating the party's dominance. As per general assumption Modi's success has accrued from a "post - Hindutva" strategy based on "development." However, the central problem for the Congress and the BJP would be to face regional parties in which most have taken the form of dynasty. Each one of those now has a strong, proprietary vote-bank and total ownership of its party. In earlier elections these regional parties had been the greatest game changer in our politics. Each one has learnt the art of leveraging his regional power to grab a share of the national pie.[91] These regional parties may be limited by geography but cannot be challenged by a national party.

Today the people are in a mood which comes rarely in the life of a country. They are looking forward starry eyed, to a new direction, a new era, a life. Despite the conduct of so many elections so far, the actual exercise of power in the country has yet to reflect real democracy. To the extent that democracy in India has lagged behind in its sacred responsibility of promoting and protecting public good, it has certainly failed. It is the state that needs to accommodate the interests of different stakeholders on important issues by building political consensus and by being transparent in the way it functions. The tardy functioning of democracy since independence has produced in India a vast college of political leaders at various levels but there has been a failure to develop political capabilities to deal with expanding pressures in empowering society, to broaden the social base of nationalism, and to find political cover for pragmatic actions. The government will certainly have to do a lot more in achieving sustainable, socially equitable growth. For that, the country needs a strong popular movement that puts pressure on the administration. If the Indian republic is to flourish and prosper, it cannot be left to the mercy of politicians alone. The national conscience has to be aroused to such a degree that it would cease to tolerate falsehood and dishonesty in public life. India's people need to be an active part of the political process before they can be the agents of change, and the masters of their own destiny.

References

1. Dr Rajkumar Singh, *India and Pakistan - Social, Political and Military Perspectives* (New Delhi: Regal Publications, 2009), pp. 33-34.
2. K.C. Markandan, *The Preamble - Key to the Mind of the Makers of the Indian Constitution* (New Delhi: National Publishing House, 1984), pp. 109-10.
3. *Ibid.*, p. 114.
4. *Constituent Assembly Debates*, Vol. 1, 15 December 1946. p. 93.
5. Subhash C. Kashyap, 'Democratic Governance - Space for the Under - Privileged', *South Asia Politics*, Vol. 7, No. 8, December 2008 (New Delhi: 2008), p. 6.
6. Gabriel A. Almond and Sidney Verba, *The Civic Culture* (Princeton: 1963), p. 5.
7. J.P. Nettle, *Political Mobilisation: A Sociological Analysis of Methods and Concepts* (New York: 1967), p. 271.
8. Durga Das Basu, *Introduction to the Constitution of India* (Calcutta: 1966), p. 38.
9. M.V. Pylee, *India's Constitution* (Bombay: Asia Publishing House, 1974), p. 19.
10. Navin Chawla, 'Towards a Level Playing Field', *The Hindu*, 5 January 2012.
11. M.V. Pylee, *Our Constitution Government and Politics* (Delhi: Universal Law Publishing Co. 2000), p. 53.
12. M.P. Jain, *Indian Constitutional Law* (Agra: Wadhwa & Company, 2000), p. 9.
13. Bommai Vs. Union of India, AIR, 1994, SC. 1998, as quoted in Ganesh Prasad and Anand Kumar, 'The Concept, Constraints and Prospect of Secularism in India', *The Indian Journal of Political Science*, Vol. LXVII, No. 4, October - December 2006 (Meerut: 2006), p. 795.

14. *Ibid.*, p. 794.
15. Markandey Katju, 'Rid Our Body Politic of Communal Poison', *The Hindu*, 11 October 2012.
16. Javeed Alam, *Who Wants Democracy - Tracts for the Times* (New Delhi: Orient Blackswan, 2012), p. 12.
17. Verghese Koithara, *Society State and Security: The Indian Experience* (New Delhi: Sage Publications, 1999), p. 28.
18. Dr Rajkumar Singh, *India and Pakistan - Social, Political and Military Perspectives*, p. 33.
19. Talcott Parsons, 'Political Development: Times Sequences and Rates of Change', in Finkle and Gable (eds.), *Political Development and Social Change* (New York: 1971), p. 456.
20. A.H. Somjee, *The Democratic Process in a Developing Society* (Delhi: 1979), p. 6.
21. Manoranjan Mohanty, 'The Contemporary State', *Teaching Politics*, Vol. VIII, Nos. 1-2, 1992.
22. Manoranjan Mohanty, 'Party and Polity', in G.P. Deshpande and Alka Acharya (eds.), *50 Years of India China - Crossing a Bridge of Dreams* (New Delhi: Tulika Publications, 2001), p. 136.
23. Sugata Bose and Ayesha Jalal, *Modern South Asia - History, Culture, Political Economy* (New Delhi: Oxford University Press, 2004), p. 169.
24. *Ibid.*, p. 170.
25. Aditya Mukherjee and Mridula Mukherjee, 'Imperialism and the Growth of Indian Capitalism in the Twentieth Century', *Economic and Political Weekly*, 12 March 1988.
26. Verghese Koithara, *Society, State and Security: The Indian Experience*, p. 43.
27. As quoted in Vivek Katju, 'Herald a National Vision That Little Resembles the Old', *The Hindu*, 16 November 2012.
28. Bipin Chandra, Mridula Mukherjee and Aditya Mukherjee, *India After Independence 1947-2000* (New Delhi: Penguin Books, 2002), p. 182.
29. *Ibid.*, p. 183.
30. Sugata Bose and Ayesha Jalal, *Modern South Asia - History, Culture,, Political Economy*, p. 170.
31. S.K. Sinha, 'Nehru - Gandhis in Indian Politics', *The Hindustan Times*, 30 June 1991.
32. Girilal Jain, 'Gandhiji and Mr Nehru - Two Different Moral Universes', *The Times of India*, 16 November 1980.
33. Verghese Koithara, *Society, State and Security - The Indian Experience*, p. 61.

34. Geoffrey Tyson, *Nehru: The Years of Power* (London: 1966), p. 173.
35. Bipin Chandra, Mridula Mukherjee and Aditya Mukherjee, *India After Independence 1947-2000*, p. 471.
36. *Ibid*., p. 472.
37. Andre Beteille, 'Politics Without Policy', *The Hindu*, 28 June 2012.
38. A.K. Ojha, 'Globalisation and Liberalisation-Propects of New World,' *Third Concept*, August 2002, p. 13.
39. V.N. Vishwanathan, 'Human Rights in a Globalised World-The Indian Experiences,' *IJPS*, LXIX, No. 1, January-March 2008 (Meerut: 2008), p. 51.
40. Suditpa Kaviraj, 'The Modern State in India', in Zoya Hasan (ed.), *Introduction: The Political Career of the State in Independent India* (2000), p. 56.
41. Balraj Mehta, 'India: Perspective and Prospectives'; *Employment News*, 7-13 April 1990, p. 3.
42. Y. Gurappa Naidu, 'Globalisation and Its Impact on Indian Society', *IJPS*, Vol. LXVII, No. 1, January-March 2006 (Meerut: 2006), p. 68.
43. Geeta Chaturvedi, 'Democracy in Global India', *Ibid*., Vol. LXIX, No. 4, October-December 2008, p. 849.
44. K.S. Thakur, 'Indian Economy After Globalisation', *Third Concept*, June 1997, p. 51.
45. Sudhanshu Tripathi, 'Globalisation and Its Consequences,' *South Asia Politics*, Vol. 9, Nos. 3 and 4, July-August 2010 (New Delhi: 2010), pp. 32-33.
46. Pierre-Landell-Mills and Ismail Serageldin, 'Governance and the External Factor,' *World Bank, Proceedings of the World Bank Annual Conference on Development Economics, 1991* (Washington: World Bank, 1992), p. 309.
47. H.D. Lasswell, 'The Policy Sciences', *Encyclopaedia of the Social Sciences, Vol. 12*, (Newyork: Macmillan, 1968), p. 184.
48. Sudhanshu Tripathi, 'Globalisation and Its Consequences', p. 33.
49. Achin Vanaik, *Economic Globalisation: Myth or Reality* (New Delhi: People's Publication House, 2001), pp. 2-3.
50. As quoted in Sudhanshu Tripathi,'Globalisation and Its Consequences,' p. 34.
51. R.K. Sapru, *Development Administration*, 2nd edition (New Delhi: Sterling Publications, 2002), p. 275.
52. Sakhi Athyal, 'Globalisation, Youth and Religion in India', p. 1.
53. Shastri Sandeep, 'Local Democracy and Political Parties' in India in Ajay K. Mehra, D.D. Khanna and Gert W. Kueck (eds.), *Political parties and party systems* (New Delhi: Sage Publications, 2003), p. 384.

54. A. Maria Alphousal and J. Belphine Prema Dhanaseeli, 'Strategy Against the Threat to Rural Poor, '*Eubious Journal of Asian and International Bio Ethics* (2003)', p. 2.
55. V. Biju Kumar, 'Post-Colonial State: An Overview', *IJPS*, Vol. LXVI, No. 4, October-December 2005 (Meerut: 2005), p. 948.
56. Rajni Kothari, '*Growing Amnesia: An Essay on Poverty and Human Consciousness*' (New Delhi: Penguin, 1993), pp. 121-22.
57. Arun Kumar, 'Why Fears of a Foreign Hand are Real', *The Hindu*, 22 June 2012.
58. Moumita Ghosh, 'Democracy in India-Background and Emerging Challenges', *South Asia Politics*, Vol. 9, No. 8, December 2010 (New Delhi: 2010), pp. 25-26.
59. C.L. Sharma, 'State of Democracy in India,' *IJPS*, Vol. LXVII, No. 1, January-March 2006 (Meerut: 2006), pp. 11-13.
60. Andre Beteille, 'Politics Without Policy.'
61. Moumita Ghosh, 'Democracy in India-Background and Emerging Challenges', p. 27.
62. Subhash C. Kashyap, 'Democratic Governance-Space for the Underprivileged', *South Asia Politics*, Vol. 7, No. 8, December 2008 (New Delhi: 2008), p. 7.
63. Deepali Singh, Nafees A. Ansari and Shaifali Singh, 'Good Governance and Implementation in Era of Globalisation,' IJPS, Vol. LXX, No. 4, October-December 2009 (Meerut: 2009), pp. 1110-11.
64. *Ibid.*, pp. 1114-15.
65. Harish Chandra Behera, 'Political System and Governance in South Asia,' *South Asia Politics*, Vol. 8, No. 11, March 2010 (New Delhi: 2010), p. 23.
66. As quoted in Subhash C. Kashyap, 'Democratic Governance-Space for the Underprivileged,' p. 13.
67. V.R. Krishna Iyer, 'Needed, a Renewed Socialist Concern', *The Hindu*, 5 Feburary 2008.
68. Yogendra Yadav, 'Imagining a New National Politics,' *Ibid.*, 12 August 2012.
69. *Ibid.*
70. P.K. Siddharth, 'Revolution Without Idea,' *The Times of India* (Nagpur), 1 August 2012.
71. Markandey Katju, 'Four People's Principles', *The Hindu*, 11 January 2012.
72. Arun Kumar, 'The Corrupt Rule the Roost', *Ibid.*, 7 January 2012.
73. Aijayant 'jay' Panda, 'Choosing Between Reform and Referendum,' *Ibid.*, 11 January 2012.
74. Dr Akhileshwar Singh, *Political Leadership of Jawaharlal Nehru* (New Delhi: 1986), p. 266.

75. Verghese Koithara, *Society, State and Security - The Indian Experience*, p. 307.
76. Dr Rajkumar Singh, *India and Pakistan - Social, Political and Military Perspectives*, pp. 71-74.
77. Gunnar Myrdal, *Asian Drama: An Inquiry into the Poverty of Nations* (London: 1968), p. 295.
78. A.K. Sen, *Inequality Reexamined* (New Delhi: Oxford University Press, 1995), as quoted in Javeed Alam, *Who Wants Democracy - Tracts for the Times*, pp. 43-44.
79. *Ibid.*, pp. 204-05.
80. *Ibid.*, pp. 106-14.
81. *The Hindu* (editorial), 15 May 2012.
82. C. Raj Kumar, 'Democracy and the Rule of Law in India', *Ibid.*, 21 September 2007.
83. *Ibid.*, 26 May 2009.
84. *Ibid.*
85. As quoted in Ibid.
86. P.R. Dubhashi, 'Hazare's Fast and Its Aftermath', *South Asia Politics*, Vol. 10, No. 1, May 2011 (New Delhi: 2011), p. 11.
87. P.R. Dubhshi, 'End of Anna Team's Fast and Its Aftermath', *Ibid.*, Vol. 11, No. 5, September 2012, pp. 17-18.
88. *The Hindu* (editorial), 28 January 2012.
89. Harish Khare, 'Time for House - cleaning in the Congress,' Ibid., 4 April 2012.
90. Tariq Thachil, 'Can Hindutva Win Votes?', *The Indian Express*, 25 February 2013.
91. Shekhar Gupta, 'One Dynasty Dimming', *Ibid.*, 23 February 2013.

Chapter - 2

India : Strategy of Social Justice and Reservation

2.1 Dimensions of Human Mind

Society is the product of relationship, the relation between the individuals. The society and the individual are not two separate entities. They are interrelated. The society in which we live is a replica and is the outward expression of what we are inwardly. Despite all the outward dissimilarity, there is a strong inward resemblance. Whatever may be the superficial differences of race, colour, creed, caste and sex, inwardly we are shaped more or less on the same lines. We are conditioned by fear, beliefs, ideas, hopes, despair, pain and pleasure which we project out into our relationship. It is a circular movement like the tide that moves in and moves out. The force that is sent out returns. Although the behaviourist school of phychologists has gone a long way to prove that man is the outcome of his environment and have tried to establish the influences of environment on the mind of man and the operation of the vicious circle, its action and interaction. But it is only partly true.

From the very beginning the environmental influences play on the mind of man. But as we grown up our mind becomes dull and loses its sensitivity to respond directly to the environmental forces. It is due to the fact that the moment we are born we are labelled as Indians, Brahmins, Christians, Hindus, Muslims etc., and as such some ideology - values, ideas, beliefs etc, - is imposed upon us. Our whole upbringing, training and education is in accordance with this ideology. The society makes us conform and fit into its established patterns of life, social, ethical, religious, moral and so on. If we had been transplanted at a very young age to some other parts of the world, our social morality, social ethics and behaviour patterns would have been completely different. So, it is the environmental factors that condition us to think, act and behave as Hindus, Muslims, Catholics, Russians etc. It is a habitual response to a habitual pattern. The whole process of life, all our thoughts, feelings and actions become mechanical and repetitive.[1] In other words, we become conditioned beings. The society, thus, moulds our mind almost cuts out a groove within which thought is allowed to function.

Political systems and social organisations often do try to reform and regulate the outer form. Everyone of us wants to bring about change, a new way of life, a new approach that can give life a new meaning because the old culture has failed to respond to the challenges of the new. But treatment of peripheral issues and surface solutions hardly make any difference and are not able to bring about a fundamental change. While remaining a Brahmin, a Christian, a Hindu, or a Russian within, revolt has very little meaning as the society continues to be static. The cultures of various countries are apparently very different, but underneath, the movement is the same. Systems and formulas have failed us because the root cause of the problem lies in man's mental construction which has to be understood and dealt with religion, nationality, caste etc. are specialised influences which create divisions and separations. It is the mind that gives importance to race, caste, and colour. Conflicts and frictions can be solved only when an attempt is made to see all the factors which go to compose the situation. It is the spirit of enquiry that can take the individual beyond the mandate of traditions and patterns.

None but the development of individual's capacity, who is capable of attaining a different level of perception, free of accumulation, should be evolved. It gives the mind a creative quality of seeing with absolute objectivity things as they are in the right perspective. It can change life's relationship between man and environment. An education that will not confine itself to the development of intellect alone can awaken the right perception of right values which would bring about the spirit of concern and commitment to the well being of humanity as a whole. It would, apart from enabling man to earn his livelihood, help them to develop a universal outlook that will enhance the quality of life, taking larger interests of the community in view.

2.2 Meaning and Measurement of Social Justice

Social justice is a revolutionary concept which provides meaning and significance to life and makes the rule of law dynamic. When Indian society seeks to meet the challenge of socio-economic inequality by its legislation and with the assistance of the rule of law, it seeks to achieve economic justice without any violent conflict. It is closely related with social equality and social rights and these are dependent on economic equality and rights. It also meant that if any group in society has suffered from structural inequalities inherent in the social system special care should be taken to remove such structural inequalities. The Preamble and various provisions of the Constitution of India ensure to all citizens justice- social, economic and political. In today's India policies and politics of social justice have reached a dead end and some concrete proposals are needed for the just realisation of social justice.

Meaning and Dimensions of Social Justice

Different societies, at different times and places, and at different stages of social, cultural and technological development have shaped the essential dimensions of social life in different ways. The variations in policies result in different outcomes for people's circumstances of living, for their relative power, for the quality of their relations and for the overall quality of life. Systems of social policies are always results of human choices. However, these choices in any generation, tend to be influenced and constrained by traditions and beliefs that reflect choices of prior generations. Nevertheless, since people originated all social policies, people, in any generation, can act collectively to change prevailing social policies in order to achieve more desired outcomes. People have struggled for, and achieved, such changes throughout history, in spite of social classes interested in preserving established ways of life. In the past at different times throughout social evolution human groups have actually created policy systems conducive to meeting the needs of all people, facilitating thus everyone's development. Societies that created such institutional systems in the past did practice "social justice" in accordance with the perspective.

Classically, especially corrective or distributive justice referred to ensuring that individuals fulfilled their societal roles[2] and received what was due from society. "Social Justice" is generally used to refer to a set of institutions which will enable people to lead a fulfilling life and to be active contributors of their community.[3] The goal of social justice is generally the same as human development. The relevant institutions can include education, healthcare, social security, labour rights, as well as broader system of public services, progressive taxation and regulation of markets, to ensure fair distribution of wealth, equality of opportunity and no gross inequality of income.

In ancient Western philosophy after examining various current definitions of the term "Social Justice" Plato came to the conclusion that justice consists in each individual discharging the function for which he is best fitted; and that everyone does this, the inherent constitution of the individual and also of society is such that the happiness of individuals as well as goodness of the society will both be assured.[4] While Aristotle believed rights existed only between free people and law should take account in the first instance of relations of inequality in which individuals are treated in proportion to their worth and only secondarily of relations of equality. Especially in context of distributive justice Aristotle held the view that people were distributed goods and assets according to their merit.[5] During the middle ages, religious scholars, such as Thomas Aquinas continued discussion in various ways, but ultimately connected to being a good citizen for the purpose of serving God.

Alike, in ancient India social justice functioned in accordance with *Dharmasastras*. Under its influence the monarchy was inclined to follow the rules set by the texts or scriptures. These texts set the yardstick to dispense justice. Texts such as *Manusmirti*, *Arthasastra* provided the guidelines to the discretion of monarchs. These texts were created through the rishis, gurus or sacred persons for the purpose of divine revealation and bypassing these men and scriptures were viewed as injustice or *adharma*. Though the practice of social justice seems simply, it reflects varying degree of social discontent as the perception of equality goes beyond the clutches of scriptures. In the prevailing system the very first blow was generated by Buddhist texts. They countered the ethical basis of varna system and its inhuman elements. The Buddhist texts disclosed the injustice in its contents of social justice. For the first time the concept of social justice was swing between the texts and counter-texts. Though the respective heritage and identity were defined in terms of religion, both the monarchs and the citizens were divided on these two tracks.[6] The Hindu texts upheld varna system for social justice and the Buddhist texts upheld casteless system.

In medieval India with the coming of Mughals the state witnessed an addition of Islamic texts in executing social justice. In the period social identity was dominated in terms of religious scriptures as the big rulers belonged to Islam. However, Hindu rulers in the era followed their own scriptures, the royal patronage of certain groups helped to accumulate more wealth. The perception of inequality between Hindus and Muslims was the concern when the farmer was levied higher tax. Moreover the system of reward and punishment assumed discrimination between social groups. In this phase the downfall of old Hindus values started. Hinduism and its system turned inwards. The conscious effort to preserve its identity, indigenous culture, values and honour under foreign rule made people to follow rules and rituals rigidly and blindly. Many social evils, disparities and discriminatory practices took birth.[7] Also, as a result of continuous invasions by Turks, Afghans, and Mughals and their draining out nation's wealth to foreign lands earlier and feudalistic attitude, arbitrary rule and extravagance and luxurious life style of Mughal rulers and those at the helm of authority increased the disparity between the rulers and the ruled. However, before British rule, the image of India as a whole, was of "a vast, mighty and magnificent empire, brilliantly organised and culturally unified which dominated a massive swath of the earth."

The British domination in India started with the rule of British East India Company and in line by 1670s , King Charles gave enormous powers to East India Company through five Acts without responsibilities like maintaining its own army, acquiring new territories on their own terms and impose its own civil and criminal law. The rule of East India Company was heavily guided by market forces and it badly affected all segments of society. Lower segment of society like peasants suffered due to heavy taxation and indebtness at heavy rates, skilled craftsmen due to Company's policy to promote British goods and discourage handicrafts, and upper segments due to the loss of their source of income due to British policies of annexation and expansion, who became unable to work, ashamed to beg and condemned to poverty. Further apathy of British rulers towards indigenous skills, knowledge and occupations and the process of modernisation and industrialisation has made many traditional occupations absolete or less paying or were regard more hazardous and more time consuming. It pushed millions of rural artisans, craftsman and small scale farmers, for whom work was essential for survival, back-wards in a very subtle manner. It resulted in discrediting many traditional occupations and in destruction of Indian handicrafts and cottage industry. It scattered efforts, sense of direction and manufacturing skills of millions of artisans, craftsman, weavers etc. The economic exploitation, economic drain and repressive attitude submerged the masses in ignorance, enfeebled by diseases and oppressed by wants.

Social Justice and Independent India

"Social Justice" means availability of equal social opportunities for the development of personality to all the people in society, without any discrimination on the basis of caste, sex or race. No one should be deprived, because of these differences, those social conditions which are essential for social development.[8] The issue of social justice is associated with social equality and at the time of independence, the constitution-makers were highly influenced by the feeling of social equality and social justice. For the same reason, they incorporated the words, like Socialist, Secular, Democratic and Republic in the Preamble. Especially the word justice in the Preamble is explained as justice, social, economic and political. The term justice is secured in the constitution through various provisions of Fundamental Rights and Directive Principles. Social justice denotes the equal treatment of all citizens without any social distinction. It means absence of privilege being extended to any particular section of the society, and improvement in the conditions of backward classes (SCs, STs and OBCs) and women. In line economic justice denotes on the non-discrimination between people on the basis of economic factors. It involves the elimination of glaring inequalities in wealth, income and property. A combination of social justice and economic justice denotes what is known as "distributive justice." While political justice implies that all citizens should have equal political rights, equal voice in the government. The Preamble secures at all citizens of India equality of status and opportunity.

The Indian Constitution is unique in its content and spirit. Though borrowed from almost every constitution of the world, the Constitution of India has several salient features that distinguish it from the constitution of other countries. However, social justice is the foundation stone of Indian Constitution. Indian Constitution-makers were well known to the use and minimality of various principles of justice. They wanted to search such form of justice which could fulfil the expectations of whole revolution as Jawaharlal Nehru reminded the Constituent Assembly, 'First work of this assembly is to make India independent by a new constitution through which starving people will get complete meal and clothes and each Indian will get best option that he can progress himself'.[9] Social justice was found useful for everyone in its kind and flexible form. Although social justice is not defined anywhere in the constitution but it is an ideal element of feeling which is a goal of constitution. Feeling of social justice is a form of relative concept which is changeable by the time, circumstances, culture and ambitions of the people.[10] But the inclusion of the word "Socialist" in the Preamble by the 42nd Amendment Act has strengthened the constitutional ethos of social and economic justice.

Under Indian Constitution the use of social justice is accepted in wider sense which includes social as well as economic justice. According to Chief Justice Gajendragadkar, 'In this sense social justice holds the aims of equal opportunity to every citizen in the matter of social and economical activities and to prevent inequalities. The Constitution of India does not completely dedicated to any traditional ideology and it is embedded in progressive concept of social justice and various rules of justice such as- quality, transaction, necessity, options etc are as its helping organs. In fact, dedication of the constitution is in such type of social justice which can fulfil the expectations of welfare state according to Indian conditions. Keeping in view the value of equality our constitution boldly mentions that the state shall not deny to any person equality before the law or the protection of the laws within the territory of India.[11] The original principle of equalitarian justice is propounded/ derived by Aristotle that is equal behaviour in equal matter. If there is unequal behaviour between equal, there will be injustice. On the issue of "Equality" the Supreme Court of India delivered several judgements defining the concept itself and in the context recently in the case of E.P. Royappa vs. State of Tamil Nadu.[12] Justice P.N. Bhagwati has held that equality is movable concept which has many forms and aspects. It cannot be tightened in traditional and principled circle. Equality with equal behaviour prohibits arbitrariness in action.

Democracy, as we know, is not only a form of government but focuses on human rights and human dignity in turn implies rule of law, equality, liberty and freedom from oppression, exploitation and arbitrary interference. The Constitution of India has accepted right to equality as an essential element of justice and sought to realise the various components of social justice. In addition, to make the principle of equality more effective, the system of special provision for backward classes of society several provisions have been made in the constitution. Under Article 15(4) the state shall make any special provision for the advancement of any socially and educationally backward classes of citizen or for the Scheduled Castes and Scheduled Tribes (SCs and STs), and in the same manner by accepting the opportunity of equality to employment under state in Article 16(1), it has excepted the principle of equalisation under Article 16(4). If it is in the opinion of the state that any class of citizens has not adequately representation under state employment, state shall make any provision for the reservation of appointments. Likewise, according to Article 46, the state shall promote with special care the educational and economic interests of weaker sections of the people, and in particular of the scheduled castes and scheduled tribes and shall protect them from social injustice and all forms of exploitation.[13] In a very important case of Indra Shahni vs. Union of India[14] the Supreme Court of India declared 27 per cent reservation legal for socially and economically backward classes of the society. Basically protective discrimination is used to fulfil those lacks which arise due to a long time deprivation. It is a part of corrective and compensatory justice. It has been told that peoples of backward class of society have been bearing injustice for generation to generation. Some peoples of the society made supremacy on the benefits of the society and made deprived to others. So this provision of protective discrimination has been made for those deprived people who are living in unbeneficial circumstances.

At large, apart from the Preamble which ensures social justice in multi-dimensional direction Part III and IV of the Constitution provide detailing of social justice under the titles of Fundamental Rights and Directive Principles of State Policy respectively. Article 23 relates to the prohibition of traffic in human beings and forced labour and Article 24 forbides the employment of children in factories under which no child below the age of fourteen years shall be employed to work in any factory or mine or engaged in any other hazardous employment. In line in Articles 37, 38, 39, 39A and 46 of the Directive Principles of State Policy the states were given a large number of governing guidelines relating to promotion of welfare of the people in society. It includes certain principles of policy to be followed by the State, providing equal justice and free legal aid and promotion of educational and economic interests of Scheduled Castes, Scheduled Tribes and other backward classes. Thus, realising that the masses had suffered for long and recognising the reality of prevailing social inequalities, the founding fathers placed the mandate of social equality at the helm of Constitution and attempted to create a system where every member is empowered to participate in the liberties and the freedom provided under the Constitution.

After the adoption of our Constitution, large scale social and economic changes have taken place. It is true that in many areas, we could not achieve the desired results, but even then the powers of law and legislation have tremendous impact in society. Law is essentially marginal to the process by which society changes; law is an effect rather than a cause. Legislation is always based on the quintessence of the public opinion. But inevitably, it often lags behind the real life and Goethe once said of law as the rule of dead over the living. This is too a conservative view and sees laws as passive and reactive, something that accommodates change rather than causes it.[15] India after attaining independence by a series of social welfare legislations based on the mandate of our Constitution proved that law could be active and dynamic. No longer was the State seen as standing to one side of the society and performing the role of a night watchman, but as a manager of social and economic interests. The State has become the centre of political and economic power and source and distributor of basic legal rights and material standards. Society is constantly in motion, economies strengthen and fail technology moves on, new social institutions emerge, even there is fundamental alteration of the structure of society. In the process the Courts have taken recourse to these provisions often, in their crusade to bring justice to the poor. Through innovative and creative strategies, they have expanded the scope of the Fundamental Rights, in order to render justice to women, children, bonded labourers and other oppressed sections of society.

Justice is called a total value. This is why the fathers of our Constitution stressed that the positive/constructive aspect of political freedom has to be instrumental in the creation of a new social order, based on the doctrine of socio-economic justice.[16] A number of practical measures have been taken from the beginning, to create more favourable social conditions for the millions of downtrodden. First of all, the Constitution had been amended when experience with its working made such change necessary. In 1950 itself, arising out of the Supreme Court decision in the State of Madras vs. Champakam Dorairajan, clause (4) was added to Article 15, dealing with prohibition of discrimination on grounds of religion, race, etc. The new clause said that nothing in Article 15, nor in clause 2 of Article 29, nothing in either shall prevent the State from making any special provision for the advancement of any socially and educationally backward classes of citizens or for the SCs and STs.[17] Similarly, when it was found, on the basis of ten years' progress in respect of the conditions of Scheduled Castes and Tribes, and also Anglo-Indians, that the reservation of seats for the former and the provision for nomination in respect of the latter, for a period of ten years prescribed in Constitution of 1950 was inadequate, a clause in the 8th Amendment, passed in 1960, extended both to 20 years. In many other way best possible was done to improve the conditions of the weaker sections of the community. Politically too, these weaker sections of the community have been able to make their influence felt as, for example, in the composition of Cabinets both at the Centre and in the States.

In the years following independence of the country, India planned for a welfare State and attempted several welfare schemes in general. Especially for Jawaharlal Nehru, the ideal was to be not only all-round national economic development, with its associated characteristics of a more general social progress, but also more specifically, the improvement of the lot of the poorer sections of the population and of the rural areas which Gandhiji had always emphasised.[18] The Harijans, in particular, are in most areas in a social situation for which there is no parallel in the world. Gandhi realised that, if our national movement was to become a mass movement, these sections of our society which constitute the large majority of our population have also to be brought into it. And they will not come into it unless the historic injustices, negative and positive, things undone and things done, are rectified, and even more important, they feel that they are being rectified and justice done to them at last. In this connection two important protective legislations in operation for people belonging to SCs are the Protection of Civil Rights 1955 and the Scheduled Castes and Scheduled Tribes (Prevention of Atrocities) Act, 1989. However, despite these constitutional position, atrocities and crimes on members of SCs, especially the women, continue to occur in all parts of the country in varying degrees. As per the National Crime Records Bureau Report 2005, the crimes against SCs in the last few years were mainly atrocities followed by hurt and rape.

Social Justice Planners: Gandhi and Ambedkar

Earlier with the rise of Gandhi who combined the fight for independence with a radical social reform agenda through his constructive programme, these concerns acquired a new dimension in coming years. The Gandhi-Ambedkar debate on the best way to tackle the old caste divisions in the Indian society provides good evidence of this. The two opposite frameworks of Gandhi and Ambedkar in advancing the cause of group rights find an echo in the contemporary India. Ambedkar's basic contention against the Congress under Gandhi's leadership was that the Congress claim of representing the entire population of India was false as the Muslims, except for once during the Khilafat agitation and the untouchables have stood outside the movement. Individuals in the movement under Gandhi's leadership joined only for personal gains. The overwhelming majority of the untouchables, asserted Ambedkar, stayed out of the freedom movement for some valid reasons. He thought that the Gandhian movement for India's independence was both unnecessary and injustified. Ambedkar's position was nullified by the election results of 1937 in which the Congress did extremely well in the seats reserved for Harijans. However, they both- Gandhi and Ambedkar, fought to eradicate India's internal apartheid manifested in the pernicious caste practice of untouchability and was committed to a vision of modernised India free of caste and colonial oppression. Both were champions of untouchables or dalits, both considered untouchability the most shameful smear on the Indian social fabric and both thought that social reform in India ought to precede political freedom.[19] Both were also highly charismatic national leaders who carried the masses with them. But the two- Gandhi and Ambedkar-held different opinions on many issues including the social justice.

On his notion of social justice Gandhi was more influenced by the Indian tradition than by Western liberal ideas. In fact, it is difficult to categorise him as a liberal or as a socialist thinker, but in his concept of social justice he included the ideas of both positive liberalism and democratic socialism. For example, he accepted the view that every individual should have the means to secure his freedom and to develop his personality; and he also believed that means of livelihood should not be monopolised by any one section of society. But Gandhi unlike the supporters of positive liberalism and of democratic socialism, did not look towards the state to achieve these ends.

Unlike Gandhi, Ambedkar's concept of social justice was influenced by the Western liberal ideas and the conditions that prevailed in the Indian society. His stay in America for three years (1913-16) and in England for two years (1920-22) enabled him to come into direct contact with the ideas of liberal thinkers. He had also personal experience of the curse of untouchability which prevailed in the Indian society. Naturally, it became the first concern of his life to fight against it at all levels, social, economic and political in order to establish in India a society based on social justice.[20] Thus, Ambedkar's circumstances forced him to be a revolutionary and simultaneously put his foot in the door of the establishment whenever he got a chance to. But Dr Ambedkar's vision did not end at the horizon of Dalit Power; rather, he envisaged an India liberated from caste consciousness, a futuristic society no longer trapped in the feudal binaries of master and slave, privilege and privation.[21] Unfortunately, Ambedkar's vision has been negated by the perpetuation of caste attitudes in an electoral democracy whose political dynamics are fuelled by group antagonism. With group identity and interest raised to cornerstone of political struggle, India now faces the long running scenario of caste war fought out on various social and economic fronts, at varying intensities.

Socially Gandhi believed in *varnashrama vyavastha* in the Vedic sense and not in the present popular sense in which it is divided into innumerable castes. The four varna system, according to Gandhi, was based on scientific principles. It is inherent in human nature and Hinduism has simply reduced it to a science. It does not attach to birth...The division, however into innumerable castes is an unwarranted liberty taken with the doctrine.[22] As a result the four divisions, he believed, defined a man's calling, but did not restrict or regulate social intercourse. They defined duties but referred no privileges. He, therefore, thought that inter-dining or even inter-marriage did not deprive an individual of his status that his birth had given him. On the basis of this opinion Gandhi thought that though a Brahman was born to serve God's creation with his knowledge, he was not absolved from bodily labour. Similarly, though a Shudra was born to serve a God's creation with bodily labour, there was nothing to prevent the Shudra from acquiring all the knowledge he wished. He admitted that a Hindu who refused to dine with another from a sense of superiority misrepresented his dharma. And in the sense there is no place for untouchability in Hinduism. Untouchability is repugnant to reason and to the instinct of mercy, pity or love- Hindus will certainly never deserve freedom nor get it, if they allow their noble religion to be disgraced by the retention of the taint of untouchability.[23] In essence, Gandhi also opposed any claim of privileges by any of the four varnas and condemned particularly the curse of untouchability which, though not an essential part of Hinduism, had continued in tradition.

Educated at the London School of Economics and Columbia University, New York, Dr Ambedkar was one of the most highly educated members of his generation. Heir to the traditions of rationalism and liberalism, he was a believer in constitutional means but also deployed the threatre of public protest to considerable strategic effect.[24] In society, Ambedkar wanted to reorganise the society on equality and rationality and therefore, opposed the caste-based social structure which, he thought was characterised by graded inequality. He considered Indian society made up of four classes- the Priestly class (Brahmins), the military class (Kshatriyas), the merchant class (Vaishyas) and the artisan and the minial class (Shudras). It was an open class system in which individuals, when qualified, would change their class. In course of development over the years, these classes lost their open door character and became self-enclosed units called castes and brought with it unequal distribution of privileges and benefits.[25] With the development of untouchability, the Shudras had to suffer discrimination and oppression unparalleled in human history. He said that in order to reorganise society on the basis of equality and fraternity the caste system must go. There was a close relation between the caste system and untouchability. It was, therefore not possible to abolish one without abolishing the other.

However, in the context, Ambedkar fundamentally departed from the liberal paradigm of rights and justice. On the issue Ambedkar sought to accomplish two unusual results. First, his theory of rights was addressed more to civil society than to the state; rights do not just appear as constraints and limits on the power of the state. Rather, they emerge as legal entitlements casting corresponding obligations on the members of civil society, rights, atypically, in Ambedkar's thought legitimate an interventionist state, even the dominant colonial formation. As one scholar puts it, 'Ambedkar's essential justice strategy was to innovate jural relations : the Depressed Classes had a right, and the state a duty, to eradicate obdurate discriminatory practices in civil society; and the State had the power and members of civil society were under a liability to have their cultural practices redefined.'[26] And secondly, Ambedkar presented the problem of rights and basic needs. The basic human needs were both material and non-material. The later comprise dignity and fraternity while the former include immunity from bodily and psychic aggression, access to public facilities, a share in resources and participation in government employment.[27] It is considered a unique theory of representation; political representation goes beyond legislative reservations and extends to reservation in administration.

From the beginning Mahatma Gandhi was very much concerned with the economic well-being of the weaker section and for the purpose, he, even transformed the character of Indian National Congress. Prior to Gandhi's emergence as national leader the party was dominated by the middle class interest but under Gandhi became identified with the masses. Throughout his life Gandhi sought to develop ways to fight India's extreme poverty, backwardness and socio-economic challenges as a part of his wider involvement in the Indian independence movement. His championing of Swadeshi and non-cooperation were centred on the principles of economic self-sufficiency. He was opposed to the exploitation of one class by another but wanted to put an end of such an exploitation by peaceful means.[28] Contextually, Gandhi espoused the notion of "trusteeship" which centred on denying material pursuits and coveting of wealth, with practitioners acting as "trustee" of other individuals and the community in their management of economic resources and property.[29] He laid equal emphasis on the moral development of individual and he opposed large scale industry because it hurts the moral well-being. According to him, the value of an industry should be gauged less by the dividends it pays to shareholders than by its effects on the bodies, soul and spirits of the people employed in it. The first basic principle of Gandhi's economic thought is a special emphasis on 'plain living' which helps in cutting down your wants and being self-reliant. He vehemently opposed the economic that ignored considerations of social justice and as Gandhi said it could never be regarded as good economics.

In sphere of economic justice Dr Ambedkar was a strong proponent of land reform and of a prominent role for the state in economic development. He recognised the inequities in an unfettered capitalist economy. He was not oblivious of the fact that economic injustice was a major factor in social injustice. In order to secure the interest of the weaker section of society he emphasised the role of the state. In the 'States and Minorities' Ambedkar stated that industries which were key industries should be owned and run by the state or by corporations established by the state, insurance should be a monopoly of the state and agriculture should state industry.[30] He thought that in order to provide for the equitable distribution of wealth it was necessary to put an obligation on the state to plan the economic life of the people. Such an obligation should not be left on the will of the legislature but should be prescribed by the law of the constitution. Thus, in order to establish a society on the principle of social justice he emphasised that the economic structure should be based on the principles of democratic socialism. He categorically stated, 'State socialism is essential for the rapid industrialisation of India. Private enterprise cannot do it and if it did, it would produce those inequalities of wealth which private capitalism has produced in Europe and which should be an warning to Indians.'[31] He strongly pleaded in favour of his economic thinking and argued that the individual should not be required to relinquish any of his constitutional rights as a condition precedent to the receipt of a privilege and that the state shall not delegate powers to private persons to govern others. He points out that the system of social economy based on private enterprise and pursuit of personal gain violates these requirements.

Gandhi believed politics a part of human nature and for him all life was one piece. A man who aspired to attain Truth or God which was the ultimate end of human life could not ignore any field of life. Different fields of life were necessarily related to each other. Politics and religion were, therefore, inseparably related to each other and could not be divorced. He was dedicated to the attainment of Swaraj but Swaraj for him did not merely signify replacement of the foreign rule by Home Rule. He wrote in the *Hind Swaraj* in 1908, 'We do not want the tyranny of either English rule or Indian rule. He was emphatic that Swaraj did not mean English rule without the Englishmen. In fact, Swaraj of his dream was the poor man's Swarajya in which the common man will be guaranteed all necessities of life, in which everyone will have freedom of religion, faith and worship, in which the landlord and capitalist will cease to exploit the tenant and the labour. "Justice" and "equality", wrote Gandhi, 'mean the establishment of just and equitable relations between capital and labour, between the landlord and the tenant'.[32] According to him the state's functions and powers should be decentralised. As such he favoured participation by all in the governance of the country and supported, therefore, adult sufferage. The authority symbolising the state must not be a privilege of the few at the cost of the many. If there was abuse of authority it must be resisted with the soul force- Satyagraha. He viewed untouchability as basically a social problem and was opposed to its solving by special representation. Throughout his life he was commited to remove the blot of untouchability from the society and preserve the unity of Hindu society. At best, he wanted to establish in India an egalitarian society based on social justice.

In sphere of political justice, in contrast to Gandhi, Ambedkar believed that a centralised polity with a strong Central Government was necessary for India to ensure building up of Indian nation and also to protect the interest of the weaker section of society. It was from this point of view that he supported a unitary government for India at the Round Table Conference. 'I am a strong believer in the unitary form of government and the thought of disturbing it- does not please me very much...However —I shall be prepared to consider federal form if it can be shown that in it local autonomy is not inconsistent with central unity.[33] Although he favoured adult suffrage and in his opinion every section of society should participate in it. On the issue of representation he argued in favour of joint electorates with reserved seats as stated before the Simon Commission, 'Territorial electorates and separate electorates are two extremes which must be avoided in any scheme of representation that may be devised for the introduction of a democratic form of government in this most undemocratic country. The golden mean is the system of joint electorates with reserved seats.[34] In the context he strongly pleaded adequate representation in legislature, executive and public services. For him the cause of weaker section of society was upper most, particularly of the Scheduled Castes, to enable them to lead a life with dignity in the Indian society. He provided them protective discrimination because they had suffered from structural inequality inherent in the Indian social structure.

The two undisputed leaders- Mahatma Gandhi and Dr B.R. Ambedkar believed in social justice and endeavoured throughout their life to establish in India an egalitarian society based on the principle of equality and rationality. They dreamt a India, free from evils such as untouchability and inequality in social, economic and political spheres.

Social Justice : Factfile and Prospect

Justice, social, economic and political is the spirit and vision of our Constitution, implemented on 26 January 1950. Now it became the duty of the State to secure a social order in which the legal system of the nation promote justice on a basis of equal opportunity and in particular ensure that opportunities for securing justice are not denied to any citizen by reason of economic or other disabilities. In essence social justice means a way of life with monumental liberty, equality and fraternity as the principles of life. A true essence of social justice cannot be established without removing the inequalities in income and making endeavour to eliminate inequalities in status through the rule of law. Social justice is a core constitutional objective. Without social justice the constitution would not be able to secure economic and other justice to the people. In addition, the social justice ideas of Gandhi and Ambedkar have left its imprint on the social tapestry of the country after independence, and shaped the socio-political fabric of India today. As a result of their opinion and role the independent India attempted to forge India's moral and social foundation as a new and strove for a political order of constitutional democracy that is sensitive to disadvantaged, inherited from the past or engendered by prevailing social relations.

However, policies and politics of social justice have reached a near dead end in contemporary India. In post-independence era India's bold experiment with politics of social representation and policies of affirmative action in the twentieth century is among the largest and more successful examples of social engineering across the globe. The system of reservations for Scheduled Castes and Scheduled Tribes in government jobs and legislatures continues to yield positive outcomes, better than anything that existed earlier or any scheme that seeks to replace it. After independence, though the context changed, the justification did not. The presence of a middle class outside the upper castes and its rise among dalits further strengthened the search for representational basis of affirmative action policies. The principle of proportionality of representation requires singular identities and thus reinforces the obsession with caste. Competitive politics furthered the drive towards seeking political representation.[35] From the valid argument that political representation is necessary to serve the interest of the disadvantaged, there was a leap into believing that political representation was sufficient.

Especially with the coming of globalisation which has affected all aspects of human life, the social institutions, protecting and expansioning the concept of social justice, underwent a significant change. It operates in an uneven and unequal manner. The neo-liberal economy with liberalisation, privatisation and globalisation, has further compounded the unevenness and inequality in society. The small minority of world's population holds maximum resources and majority of people are grapple in poverty. The state, as an institution guarantees social welfare and social justice to the marginalised groups but globalisation has not only threatened but it also made it weak. It has now retreated back from its welfare role. In the contemporary context social justice agenda is taken over by non-state organisations that is critical. The older theories of social justice, which are either inadequate or inapplicable, today cannot cover the new developments that have taken place in the era of globalisation and therefore they have to be reviewed specifically in Indian context.

Even after the general elections to the 16th Lok Sabha held in April-May 2014 the long simmering discontent has not come down. This election was not fought on traditional grounds of inherited loyalties that demand obeisance- caste, religion and ethnicity- but around two issues that have never been in serious contention before: the economy and social justice. These have cracked the mould of Indian politics wide open and out of the fissures new lines of conflict are emerging day after day.[36] Having got clear and strong majority after a long gap in Indian politics Narendra Damodardas Modi became the 15th Prime Minister of India on the evening of 26th May 2014. The ferocity with which the champions of Secular, Socialist and Democratic values sought to destroy him politically and the manner of his poised retaliation gaining strength and credibility with each passing day reiterates that 'an idea whose time has come cannot be resisted'; that nothing is stronger than an idea whose time has come; that the day has come when there will be no battlefields but market openings to commerce and minds opening to space...[37] With the opening of mind and market the role of government is also changing as we witness a fragmentation of policy responsibility in society in which the traditional mechanism of government control are no longer workable or even appropriate. It challenges the traditional relationship between economy and state. The globalised market system stretches beyond the political authority of any single government. Faced with a network of connections that escape their power of surveillance or regulation, national governments have become increasingly unequal to providing the legal, monetary or protective functions.[38] Since the focus of development shifted from social goals to profit motives the state was neither considered as a positive instrument for social transformation nor an agency for resource allocation.

2.3 Politics of Reservation: Retrospect and Prospect

The reservation system has received a mixed response from Indians since its inception. It has been praised for diminishing the gap between the upper and lower castes by allowing the latter to enjoy the further increased opportunities as the former in jobs, education and governance by alloting seats exclusively for them. It has also been criticised for discouraging a merit-based system and encouraging vote-bank politics. From centuries, India is the homeland of people who are different to each other on the basis of language, religion, caste, race and community. The exploitation and deprivation of one section by other is the outcome of strict social division and prejudice. As a result, a large section of Indians have been identified as under privileged, backward and deprived.[39] Reservation in India is the process of setting aside a certain percentage of seats in government institutions for members of backward and under-represented communities. It is governed by constitutional laws, statutory laws, and local rules and regulations. Initially the system of reservation was put in place by the British over the objection of the nationalist movement, but in time it was embraced by Congress and virtually by all political parties in India. Subsequently, the reservation provision was incorporated into the Indian Constitution along with a constitutional commitment to ensure more adequate representation to deprives, socially and educationally in particular. [40]

Pre-independence Tradition of Reservation

From time immemorial, the most common form of past discrimination in India is the practice of untouchability. An untouchable person is generally considered "impure" or a "lesser human" at the earliest, in Vedic period, the Varna system was used but it was based on the profession one chose rather than on the birth. The system consists of four ranked varnas. At the time a person's varna was defined by his or her socio-economic duties, broadly classified into four classes or varnas. These duties were either voluntarily performed or were assigned by the local administrator when one's varna was initially not defined by one's birth into any particular family. Over the centuries, especially during the eleventh century onwards, the system has changed so that one is born into a varna based on lineage.[41] In the seventh century, Hiuen-tsang found the sudras constituting the agricultural class. Devala quoted in the Mitaksara prescribes that the sudra should serve the twice-born and may engage in agriculture, rearing cattle, carrying loads, sale of commodities, drawing and painting, dancing, singing and playing on musical instruments.[42] In the tenth century, the Arab traveller Ibn Khurdadha also made a general statement that the sudras were husbandmen by profession. Al Idrisi too remarked that they were labourers and agriculturists.[43] But inspite of the general trend of improvement in the status of the sudras in many spheres, the relative bondage of the lower sections of the sudras may be further noticed in a religious ideology which acquired considerable force during the early medieval period. In this phase gradually the spirit of exclusiveness and ideas of ritual purity were carried to extremes and many more sudras became untouchable.[44] In the context further the Bhakti movement was characterised by the protest of lower classes against the higher classes and witnessed the rise of a number of saints from lower castes. The saints of the time endeavoured to educate and elevate the people through their teachings and also succeeded in creating a space for sudra class in general in almost all the spheres of life, religious, social, economic, etc.

In modern age after coming of the British to uplift the socio-economic conditions of these large sections of people and to end the exploitation from their lives, social reformers and leaders of the country organised several social and legal movements. Although the concept of untouchability was not practised uniformly throughout the country and therefore the identification of oppressed classes was difficult. In general, the practice of segregation and untouchability prevailed more in the southern parts of India as opposed to in the northern India. Furthermore, certain castes or communities, considered untouchable in one province were not in other provinces.[45] In the North Mahatma Jyotirao Phule made a demand of free and compulsory education for Smrti along with proportionate representation in government jobs. In 1891, there was a demand for reservation of government jobs with an agitation against the recruitment of non-natives into public service overlooking qualified native people. In 1901, reservations were introduced in Maharashtra, in the Princely State of Kolhapur, by Shahu Maharaj. He introduced reservation in favour of non-Brahmin and backward classes as early as 1902. The Maharaja provided free education to ensure everyone got suitable employment no matter what social class they belonged. The notification of 1902 created 50 per cent reservation in services for backward classes/communities in the State of Kolhapur. This is the first official instance of government order for providing reservation for depressed classes in India.[46] Further in 1908, reservations were introduced in favour of a number of castes and communities that had little share in the administration by the British.

In sphere of reservation, the British, years before independence in 1932 tried a new type of political engineering to divide and deflect the nationalist challenge. The British Prime Minister Ramsay MacDonald announced the Communal Award on 16th August 1932, specifying representation in elected bodies for various communities, which gave separate electorates to the depressed classes.[47] The Communal Award granted separate electorates in British India for the Forward Caste, Lower Caste, Muslims, Buddhists, Sikhs, Indian Christians, Anglo-Indians, Europeans and Untouchables then also known as Dalits. It was the result of discussions held during Second Round Table Conference and the Award provided a number of seats of untouchables to be filled by election from special constituencies in which voters belonging to the untouchables only could vote. It proved highly controversial as it was planned to be an extension of divide and rule policy of the British. On the one hand the

Communal Award was supported by many among the minority communities, most notably the Dalit leader Dr B. R. Ambedkar but it was vehemently opposed by Mahatma Gandhi on the other who began his fast in Yervada prison on 20 September 1932. Gandhi's main objection to the arrangement was that the separate electorates were harmful for the Depressed Classes and for Hinduism; the separate electorate would simply 'vivisect and disrupt Hinduism'. On the issue of two votes for Depressed Classes under the proposal Gandhi said clearly, 'does not protect them or Hindu society in general from being disrupted. Such a system was tantamount to the injection of poison that is calculated to destroy Hinduism and do no good whatever to the depressed classes. A statutory separation even in a limited form, from the Hindu fold, will be harmful for them 'as it would arrest the marvellous growth of the work of Hindu reformers who have dedicated themselves to the uplift of their suppressed brethren in every walk of life'.[48] Even the clarifications made by the British Premier Ramsay MacDonald failed to satisfy Gandhi who was adamant in his opposition.

In context B.R. Ambedkar, while favouring the British proposal, sharply criticised Gandhi's patronising attitude towards the lower castes, reacted violently to Mahatma's fast programme and pointed out that Mahatma's arguments were strange and incomprehensible to the Depressed Classes. Commenting on Gandhi's fast Ambedkar complained, 'he has staked his very life in order to deprive them of little they have got. He charged Gandhi with releasing uncontrollable reactionary forces and widening the gulf between the depressed classes and the Hindus.'[49] Unlike Gandhi Ambedkar maintained that the untouchables were an element separate from Hinduism. He grasped the root of the matter when he said that the Hindus had much to lose by the abolition of untouchability, though they had nothing to fear from political reservation leading to this abolition. He considered untouchability an economic system which is worse than slavery. In reference to Gandhi's statement of the marvellous work of Hindu reformers, Ambedkar's response was blunt and cold, but true and memorable, 'There have been many Mahatma's in India whose sole object was to remove untouchability and to elevate and absorb the Depressed Classes, but everyone of them has failed in his mission. Mahatmas have come, Mahatmas have gone. But the untouchables have remained as untouchables.[50]

The deadlock between Gandhi and Ambedkar ended with the signing of a compromise called 'Poona Pact'. It was an agreement between

Dr Ambedkar and Mahatma Gandhi held on 24 September 1932 at Yervada Central Jail in Pune. The nine-point terms of the Poona Pact provided for reservation of seats for the Depressed Classes out of general electorate. Election to these seats was to be held by joint electorates and all members of the Depressed Classes registered in general electoral roll of a constituency will form an electoral college which will elect a panel of four candidates belonging to the Depressed Classes for each of such reserved seats by the method of the single vote and four persons getting the highest number of votes in such primary elections shall be the candidates for election by the general electorate. Provision was made in the Poona Pact regarding representation of the Depressed Classes at the Central and Provincial levels and this arrangement shall continue until determined otherwise by mutual agreement between the communities concerned in this settlement. This apart, viewing the importance of education it was mentioned that in every province out of the educational grant and adequate sum shall be ear-marked for providing educational facilities to the members of Depressed Classes. Electorates for other religions like Muslim and Sikh remained separate. Gandhi won on separate electorates; there were to be none. The rest of the terms of the Poona Pact show that Ambedkar made the best of a bad bargain.

The Poona Pact no doubt gave more seats as Ambedkar accepted a total of 148 reserved seats in all legislatures, while the Award had given them only 78 separate electoral seats. Despite this Ambedkar repented this decision bitterly all through his remaining life. As he himself put it, 'increase in seats could never compensate for the priceless privilege of the second vote given to the untouchables. The value of such a vote 'as a political weapon was beyond reckoning'. The conflict between Ambedkar and Gandhi on the issue of the separate electorates for untouchables and the depressed classes, and the way in which it was resolved, has affected very fundamentally the nature of political participation by the scheduled castes and tribes in contemporary India.[51] Whatever be the merits of the actual electoral proposals, Gandhi's victory represented, for him and others, the victory of the idea that the problem of untouchability was a social problem and not a political one; and that it was a problem of Hindu religion and not of the Hindu economy. In 1935, the British passed the Government of India Act 1935 in which the reservation of seats for the Depressed Classes was incorporated into the Act. The Act introduced the term Scheduled Castes, defining the group as such castes, races or tribes or parts of groups within castes, races or tribes. In line, the Constitution of independent India recognised the Scheduled Castes and Scheduled Tribes as the two groups of historically disadvantaged people and promised an all-out war against untouchability. It abolished, as a matter of fundamental right, untouchability and bonded labour. The practice of bonded labour was declared by the Constitution as an offence.

Reservation and Constitutional Provisions : SCs/STs

The Constituent Assembly of India formed before Independence debated in detail the issue of reservation under the new Constitution. The vision of the formulators of the Indian Constitution was to develop India into a socialist state. A socialist state is the state that protects and uplifts its weaker sections. It strives to reduce the social and economical inequality between the people. To achieve this goal our constitution has incorporated several provisions that are in the benefit of the weaker sections. In the context the Constitution has adopted the principle of Compensatory Discrimination to uplift the weaker sections. Under this principle the constitution has made provisions that compensate these sections by discriminating in favour of them for past wrongs. 'Our constitution explicitly permits certain forms of affirmative action and it has always been a public policy choice that enjoys extensive support. In a country with as acute forms of backwardness as ours thing should hardly be otherwise.'[52] Affirmative action or positive discrimination known as employment equality in Canada, reservation in India, and positive action in the United Kingdom is the policy of providing special opportunities for, and favouring members of, a disadvantaged group who suffer from discrimination.[53] The nature of positive discrimination policies varies from region to region. In India we use a quota system, whereby a certain percentage of jobs or school vacancies must be set aside for members of a certain group. The term affirmative action was first used in the United States of America and it was intended to promote the opportunities of defined minority groups within a society to give them equal access to that of the privileged majority population.

The primary stated objective of the Indian reservation system is to increase the opportunities for enhanced social and educational status of the underprivileged communities and thus enable them to take their place in the mainstream of Indian society. In this connection the establishment of Indian democratic republic is not enough as B.R. Ambedkar expressed in Constituent Assembly, 'We must make our political democracy a social democracy as well. Political democracy cannot last unless there lies at the base of it social democracy. As to what does the social democracy mean, he adds, 'It means a way of life, which recognises liberty, equality and fraternity as the principles of life. These principles of liberty, equality and fraternity are not to be treated as separate items of trinity. They form a union of trinity in the sense that to divorce one from the other is to defeat the very purpose of democracy.[54] Undisputedly, Dr Ambedkar was ardent social activist and he remained ever fighting at all levels for cause of social justice and economic equality amongst all sections of Indian society. As a result, Indian constitution envisages a state where everybody is treated equally. Even in the Preamble, the constitution strives to provide equality in opportunity. Further the constitution adopts the concept of "like should be treated alike" as the basis of equality. There can be several ways through which the condition of underprivileged can be improved and reservation is one such way. In such a situation it can be said safely that although reservation is not guaranteed by the constitution or it is a constitutional right but it is certainly protected by the constitution as a mechanism to uplift the underprivileged classes.

Reservation in the Constitution of India has been provided for weaker sections of the society which includes, Scheduled Castes, Scheduled Tribes, Backward Classes, Women and other groups of people who are severely disadvantaged are older people (senior citizens) and people with disability. In the prevailing caste system of India the sudras have been exploited for ages. They were denied the right to education and thus were left languishing behind, socially and economically. Such people have been categorised into Scheduled Castes. Tribal communities, who never mixed with the main society, are similarly challenged and are categorised into Scheduled Tribes. As to the Backward Classes the constitution does not define the term. It is up to the centre and the states to specify the classes that belong to this group. But it is understood that classes that are not represented adequately in the services of the state can be termed backward classes. Further the President can, under Article 340 constitute a commission to investigate the condition of socially and educationally backward classes. Likewise, the condition of women in India has also been very bad. They have always been treated as a second class citizens and did not have any decision-making power and lacked in education. Accordingly provision for weaker sections have been amply incorporated in Article 15, 16 and 340. The provisions regarding reservation have been interpreted and guided by the different landmark decisions of the Supreme Court of India right from the days of the promulgation of the Indian Constitution.

Although the constitutional provision for reservation of SC and ST was incorporated in Article 15 (4), the era of reservation started in 1951 after a judgement of the Supreme Court of India in the case of Champakam Dorairajan vs. State of Madras AIR 1951. The said judgement simply says, 'Nothing in this article or in Article 29(2) shall prevent the state for making any provision for the advancement of any socially and economically backward classes of citizens or for Scheduled Castes and Scheduled Tribes.[55] On the other Article 15(1) and 16(1) specifically prohibit any discrimination on grounds of religion, race, caste, sex and place of birth or any of them. This position is more explicit from whatever has been said by both the responsible functionaries of the relevant time. So, it would not be within the scope of the state to list out socially and educationally backward classes on any consideration of religion or castes in view of specific prohibition under the Articles 15(1) and 16(1).[56] In view of the provision Articles may have to be interpreted in relation to the aims and objects recited in the Preamble.

In fact, the provision in Articles 15(4) and 16(4), has the main consideration of enabling socially and educationally backward class- the depressed and downtrodden classes of people to join the mainstream of Indian society and to provide them facilities to create ability by affirmative means but not at the risk of any discrimination on merits and efficiency. So, it is undisputedly clear that the elite class of families within the reservation class may not find any place for any preferential benefits; because they have already reached normal and sometimes even high economic and social status. The founding fathers were amply clear that such benefit should be extended for a limited period of time to provide an opportunity for growth up to a level.[57] It was given for the time being as Nehru wrote in his letter to Chief Ministers of States on 27 June 1961, 'We should get out of old habits of reservations and particular privilege being given to this caste or that group. The recent meeting we held here at which the Chief Ministers were present to consider national integration, laid down that help should be given on economic considerations and not on caste. It is true that we are tied up with certain rules and conventions about helping Scheduled Castes and Tribes. They deserve help but, even so, I dislike any kind of reservation, more particularly in services.[58] Nehru was strongly against anything which leads to inefficiency and second rate standards. He favoured the opportunity for good education for which he advocated universal free elementary education. He laid stress on bright and able boys and girls because it is only they who will raise our standards. George Washington, the first President of USA, alike had advocated in 1790 free and compulsory education at primary levels by mentioning that in the newly formed Democratic Republic of US education was not meant merely to provide employment but a team of able and devoted citizens to protect the interests of future generation.

The Scheduled Castes and Scheduled Tribes are two groups of historically disadvantaged people recognised in the Constitution of India. The Constitution (Scheduled Castes) Order, 1950 lists 1,108 castes and the Constitution (Scheduled Tribes) Order, 1950 lists 744 tribes in the First Schedule of the country.[59] According to the 2011 census, the Scheduled Castes and Scheduled Tribes comprise about 16.6 per cent and 8.6 per cent respectively of India's population. After independence the Constituent Assembly continued the prevailing definition of Scheduled Castes and Tribes, giving President of India and governors of the states a mandate to compile a full listing of castes and tribes with power to edit it later as required. The Constitution provides a three- pronged strategy[60] to improve the situation of SCs and STs. (i) *Protective arrangements* : Such measures as are required to enforce equality, to provide punitive measures for transgressions, to eliminate establish practices that perpetuate inequalities, etc. (ii) *Affirmative action*: Provide positive or preferential treatment in allotment of jobs and access to higher education as a means to accelerate the integration of the SCs and STs with mainstream society. Affirmative action is popularly known as reservation; and (iii) *Development*: Provide resources and benefits to bridge the socio-economic gap between the SCs and STs and other communities.

This apart, to ensure that the problems faced by SCs/STs are appropriately addressed, it is imperative that first those problems be highlighted and brought to the attention of the law-making bodies by themselves, the makers of the constitution provided for the adequate representation in the constitution. Accordingly under Article 330 seats have been reserved in the House of People for SCs/STs. The number of seats reserved in a state for them is proportional to the population of SCs/STs in that state. Based on the demographics reflected by census, certain constituencies are reserved and only SCs/STs can contest election from such seats. In the election there is only one electoral roll and there is no separate electorate for SCs/STs. Further, it is important to note that SCs/STs still can contest election in unreserved constituencies as well.

Under Article 332 seats have been reserved in state legislatures for, SCs/ STs. The number of reserved is proportional to the population of SCs and STs in that state. However, Article 334 put a time limitation on the reservation of seats in legislatures, Lok Sabha as well as state legislatures. Initially, seats were reserved only for 10 years but it has been increased for 10 years regularly. Recently in August 2009 the Parliament has adopted the Constitution (109th amendment) Bill, 2009 for providing reservation of seats for Scheduled Castes and Scheduled Tribes in the Lok Sabha and the State Legislative Assemblies for another 10 years beyond January 25, 2010. As per the Bill, of the 543 seats in the Lok Sabha, SCs had 79 and STs 41 seats. Similarly, of the 3,961 seats in the Legislative Assemblies SCs had been reserved 543 seats and STs 527.[61] The nomination provision for Anglo-Indians to the Lok Sabha and Legislative Assemblies has been extended for another 10 years with this amendment. Today, in 2014 out of 543 seats in India's Parliament, 84 (18.42 per cent) are reserved for SC Dalits and 47 (8.66 per cent) for STs.

Likewise the reservation for SCs and STs in direct recruitment in government services is not new. Even at the time of foreign rulers India was having reservation for SCs (8.33 per cent) in government services. This percentage was increased to 12.5 per cent for SCs and at this time STs given five per cent reservation in government after independence in 1950 in direct recruitment. Further the percentage increased to 15 per cent for SCs and 7.5 per cent STs in light of the population of these communities. In a further development in1982 the Constitution specified 15 per cent and 7.5 per cent of vacancies in public sector and government-aided educational institutes as a quota reserved for the SC and ST candidates respectively for a period of five years after which the quota system would be reviewed. This period was routinely extended by the succeeding governments. Also, gradually Articles 16(4A) and 16(4B) were incorporated in the Constitution as a result of 77th and 81st Constitutional Amendment Acts in 1995 and 2000 respectively which further strengthen the position of SCs and STs.[62] Article 16(4A) states, 'Nothing in this article shall prevent the state from making any provisions for reservation in the matter of promotion to any class or classes of posts in the services under the State in favour of SCs and STs which in the opinion of the State are not adequately represented under the State. Clarifying the provision Article 16(4B) states, 'Nothing in this article shall prevent the State from considering any unfiled vacancies of a year which are reserved for being filled up in that year in accordance with any provision for reservation made under Clause (4) or Clause (4A) as a separate class of vacancies to be filled up in any succeeding year in which they are being filled up for determining the ceiling of fifty per cent reservation on total number of vacancies of that year. The Supreme Court of India, in a landmark judgement, ruled that reservation cannot exceed 50 per cent.[63]

The most important stated aim of the Indian reservation system is to boost the opportunities for improved social and instructive position of the underprivileged communities and, thus, allow them to take their equitable place in the conventional Indian society. There is an additional provision in Article 46 which states that state shall promote with special care, the educational and economical interests of the weaker sections of the people, and in particular of Scheduled Castes and Scheduled Tribes, and shall protect them from social injustice and all forms of exploitation. In addition to these several Acts/Constitutional Amendments and judicial judgements were made to give preferences to SCs and STs interest in society. For example, Article 335 allows relaxation in qualifying marks for admission in educational institutes or promotion for SCs/STs. In the case of State of Madhya Pradesh vs. Nivedita Jain AIR 1981, the Supreme Court held that complete relaxation of qualifying marks for SCs/STs in Pre-Medical Examinations for admission to Medical Colleges is valid. Other Articles which directly relate to the interests of SCs/STs include, 19(5), 40, 164, 275, 330, 332, 338, 338A, 339 and 340.

Women and children also come in the purview of weaker sections of society and several provisions have been made for them to uplift their position/status in the country. Article 15(3) allows the state to make special provisions for women and children. Several Acts such as Dowry Prevention Act have been passed including the most recent one of Protection of Women from Domestic Violence Act 2005 and under Article 23, under the fundamental right against exploitation, flesh trade has been banned. Article 39 ensures equal pay to women for equal work and in the case of Randhir Singh vs. Union of India 1982, the Supreme Court held that the concept of equal pay for equal work is indeed a constitutional goal and is capable of being enforced through constitutional remedies under Article 32. Apart from Article 40 which provides 1/3 reservation in Panchayat and 42 which provides free pregnancy care and delivery, Article 44 urges the state to implement uniform civil code, which will help improve the condition of women across all religions. It has however, not been implemented due to politics. In the case of Sarla Mudgal vs. Union of India AIR 1995, the Supreme Court has held that in Indian Republic there is to be only one nation, the Indian nation and no community could claim to be a separate entity on the basis of religion. In the latest development the President of India has given assent to Antirape Bill, Criminal Law (Amendment Bill-2013) with an aim to provide a strong deterrent against crimes like rapes. It provides for rigorous imprisonment for a minimum of 20 years and even death sentence for rape victims.[64] The passed Act amended various sections of the Indian Panel Code, the Code of Criminal Procedure, the Indian Evidence Act and the Protection of Children from Sex Offences Act.

According to Article 19A education upto 14 years has been made a fundamental right and the state is required to provide school education to children. In the case of Unni Krishnan vs. State of Andhra Pradesh AIR 1993, the Supreme Court held that right to education for children between 6 to 14 years of age is a fundamental right as it flows from right to life. After this decision, education was made a fundamental right explicitly through 86th Amendment in 2002. Whereas Article 24 provides children a fundamental right against exploitation and it is prohibited to employ children below 14 years of age in factories and any hazardous processes. Decades earlier in the case of M.C. Mehta vs. State of Tamil Nadu, AIR 1991, the Supreme Court has held that children cannot be employed in match factories or which are directly connected with the process as it is hazardous for the children. Further in case of Lakshmi Kant Pandey vs. Union of India AIR 1984, J. Bhagwati has laid down guidelines for adoption of Indian children for foreigners. In a specific case Article 41 urges the state to give assistance in the matter of employment, education, and public assistance in cases of unemployment, old age, sickness. Thus, no doubt, reservation, in principle, is an effective means of improving the condition of socially and economically backward classes.

Constitution and Reservation of OBCs

Article 46 which comes under the Directive Principles of State Policy contained in Part IV of the Constitution of India, are although not enforceable by any court, but the principles laid down therein are considered fundamental in governance of the country, making it the duty of the State to apply these principles in making laws to establish a just society in the country. The principles have been inspired by the Directive

Principles given in the Constitution of Ireland and also by the principles of Gandhism; and relate to social justice, economic welfare, foreign policy and legal and administrative matters. In particular Article 46 states, 'The State shall promote with special care the educational and economic interests of weaker sections of the people, and, in particular, of the Scheduled Castes and Scheduled Tribes, and shall protect them from social injustice and all forms of exploitation.' At the earliest in the case of Srimathi Champakam Dorairajan vs. The State of Madras the Apex Court held that admissions to the college is not invalid, because under Article 46 of the Constitution, the State is bound to promote and carry out the principle adopted by the Constitution. In the purview of weaker section Other Backward Class (OBC) is a collective term used by the Government of India to classify castes which are educationally and socially disadvantaged. In the Indian Constitution, OBCs are described as socially and educationally backward classes and the Government of India is enjoined to ensure their social and educational development. Further according to Article 340 the President may by order appoint a commission, consisting of such persons as he thinks fit to investigate the conditions of socially and educationally classes within the territory of India.

In line, First Backward Classes Commission was established by a Presidential Order on 29 January 1953 under the chairmanship of Kaka Kalelkar and it submitted the report on 30 March 1955. It had prepared a list of 2,399 backward castes or communities for the entire country, of which 837 had been classified as the "most backward." Some of the most notable recommendations of the commission were:

(i) Undertaking caste-wise enumeration of population in the census of 1961;

(ii) Relating social backwardness of a class to its low position in the traditional caste hierarchy of Indian society;

(iii) Treating all women as a class as backward;

(iv) Reservation of 70 per cent seats in all technical and professional institutions for qualified students of backward classes;

(v) Reservation of vacancies in all government services and local bodies for other backward classes.

The commission in its final report recommended "caste as the criteria to determine backwardness. The report was not accepted by the government, which feared that the backward classes excluded from the caste and communities selected by the commission might not be considered and those in most need would be swamped by the multitudes, thus receiving insufficient attention. The first backward commission observed that although untouchability or tribal character may not be found, the backwardness persists."[65] Finally, this report was rejected by the Central Government on the ground that it had not applied any objectives tests for identifying the Backward Class and thus there was a need of second backward classes commission.

After a long gap in 1979 the Janata Party government under the Premiership of Morarji Desai established Mandal Commission to identify the socially or educationally backward.[66] It was headed by Indian Parliamentarian B.P. Mandal to consider the question of seat reservations and quotas for the people to redress caste discrimination, and used eleven social, economic and educational indicators to determine backwardness. In between the years, since the formation of first commission in 1953, a great many things have in fact changed both in our political perceptions and in social reality. The leaders of the nationalist movement who successfully fought for India's freedom from colonial rule believed that India may have been a society of castes and communities in the past but would become a nation of citizens with adoption of a new republican constitution. They were too optimistic. The Constitution did create rights for the citizen, but it did not eradicate caste from the hearts and minds of the citizens it created.[67] India's historical failures aborted land distribution, neglected agriculture, except during the period of Green Revolution 1960s-70s and a soft approach in attacking caste iniquities, have helped to maintain these structures. By the time universal franchise has brought into the political fold groups which for centuries existed on the peripheries of the Indian political order.

While identifying the Mandal Commission adopted various methods and techniques to collect the necessary data and evidence. In order to identify who qualified as an "other backward class", the commission adopted eleven criteria which could be grouped under three major headings: social, educational and economic. In sphere of each several points were made considerable. All the social indicators were given a weightage of three points each, educational indicators were given a weightage of two points each and economic indicators were given a weightage of one point each. Economic, in addition to social and educational indicators, were considered important as they directly flowed from social and educational backwardness. Thus, the Mandal Commission judged classes on a scale from 0 to 22. These 11 indicators were applied to all the castes covered by the survey for a particular state. As a result of this application, all castes which had a score of 50 per cent of 11 points were listed as socially and educationally backward and the rest were treated as "advance." The commission estimated that 54 per cent of the total population belonging to 3,743 different castes and communities, excluding SCs and STs were "backward." It used 1931 census as base because beyond that no caste-wise data to calculate the number of OBCs was available and it finally concluded the population of OBCs to be 52 per cent.[68] In identifying the backwardness, the commission thoroughly assumed that a child from an advanced class family and that of a backward class family had the same intelligence at the time of their birth, it is obvious that owing to vast differences in social, cultural and environmental factors, the former will beat the latter by lengths in any competitive field. It was of the view that what we call "merit is an amalgam of native endowments and environmental privileges.[69] Even if an advanced class child's intelligence quotient was much lower compared to the child of backward class, chances are that the former will still beat the latter in any competition where selection is made on the basis of 'merit'.

The report of the commission was submitted in December 1980 which stated, 'It may appear the upliftment of Other Backward Classes is part of the larger national problem of the removal of mass poverty. This is only partially correct. The deprivation of OBCs is a very special case of the larger national issue: here the basic question is that of the social and educational backwardness and poverty is only a direct consequence of these two crippling caste-based handicaps. As these handicaps are embedded in our social structure, their removal will require far-reaching structural changes. No less important will be changes in the perception of the problems of OBCs by the ruling classes of the country.[70] The submitted report called for reserving 27 per cent of all services and public sector undertakings under the Central Government and 27 per cent of all admissions to institutions of higher education for Other Backward Classes over and above the existing 22.5 per cent reservation for SCs and STs. The basis of this recommendation was a 1963 judgement of Supreme Court in which it held that total reservation, inclusive of the quantum for the SCs and the STs, could not exceed 50 per cent. It became the basis for fixing the OBCs quota at 27 per cent with totalling at 49.5 per cent. However, the recommendation was kept in cold storage for subsequent nine years when Congress was at the helm of affairs and its implementation was announced in August 1990 when V.P. Singh was the Prime Minister of India.

The announcement of V.P. Singh government to implement Mandal Commission's report met with large scale protest especially in colleges across the country. It sparked a series of self-immolations starting with Rajiv Goswami, a student of Delhi University. Allocating quota's on the basis of caste is a form of racial discrimination, and contrary to the right to equality. If at all, quotas should be based on economic hardships, which can be changed, not on race. Basing them on an unchangeable factor makes them unfair and useless. Despite the improvement in lower caste socio-economic status, the presence of caste will still be felt and administered officially. In between the violent movements and large scale protests, a writ petition was filed in the Supreme Court against the implementation of the Mandal report. The Court in its judgement in the case of Indira Sawhney vs. Union of India delivered on November 16, 1992 upheld 27 per cent reservation for OBCs subject to the exclusion of socially advanced persons/sections (creamy layer) from amongst the OBCs and directed the government to evolve criteria for identification of this creamy layer. The government appointed a committee to address the issue. As per the recommendations the rule of exclusion applied to children of holding different constitutional positions, class-1 officers and defence officers who hold the rank of colonel or above. Children of persons with annual income greater than rupees 1 lakh were also to be excluded. The limit was later revised to rupees 2.5 lakh in 2004.[71] The recommendations were accepted and circulated among all ministries/departments of the Central and State governments in September 1993, allowing reservations to come into force.

Decision of the V.P. Singh government to implement the job reservation plan of Mandal Commission at the time and even today appeared the scheme designated to divide the Hindu community by caste and thereby undermine the Bharatiya Janata Party's (BJPs) electoral project of mobilising support by playing the Hindu majoritarian card.[72] In response, the Hindu movement led by the BJP and others, such as RSS, VHP and Bajrang Dal became active and left a decisive effect on party system. Its leader responded by undertaking a *rath yatra* and threatened to arrive in Ayodhya and start building the temple. It resulted in the polarisation of Indian politics on communal line. By doing this the BJP had taken on not only its political rivals but had also challenged one of the main ideological foundations of the Indian state.[73] The powerful political currents unleashed by the Mandal politics including the vandalism by the upper caste youths with the connivance of powerful organised forces too brought significant changes in the character of the political participation of the oppressed class. Two things have been occurring simultaneously within these vulnerable communities. First there was a long period of capitalist development, especially in agriculture, which followed by the land reforms, after independence.[74] Many of the OBCs became propriety peasants. The long chain of dependance and bondage on the landlords was snapped. Education, employment etc. among the OBCs slowly expanded. New modern classes were slowly emerging among them. Among the Dalits reservations as quotas in education and employment and other meekly implemented affirmative action also led to similar results though on a smaller scale.[75] As a consequence of all this, class and income differentiation has been taking place, however, uneven, among these castes-communities and therefore a dispersal of earlier forms of power with their traditional leadership.

The present caste-based reservation system of Union Government is as follows:

Category as per Government of India	*Reservation percentage as per Government of India*
Scheduled Castes (SC)	15 per cent
Scheduled Tribes (ST)	7.5 per cent
Other Backward Classes (OBCs)	27 per cent
Total constitutional reservation percentage	49.5 per cent
General (Open all including SC/ST and OBC)	50.5 per cent

Further in a major policy decision taken in 2005 the Union Government decided to provide 27 per cent reservation for OBCs in educational institutions like IITs and IIMs. This was done in response to a public interest litigation- Ashoka Kumar Thakur vs. Union of India. The Court held that the 1931 census could not be a determinative factor for identifying the OBCs for the purpose of providing reservation. The Court also observed, 'Reservation cannot be permanent and appear to perpetuate backwardness.'[76] On 10 April 2008 the Supreme Court of India upheld the government's initiative of 27 per cent OBC quota in government-funded institutions. It categorically reiterated its prior stand that those considered part of "creamy layer" should be excluded by government-funded institutions and by private institutions from the scope of the reservation policy. The creamy layer is a term used in Indian politics to refer to the relatively wealthier and better educated members of the Other Backward Classes who are not eligible for government sponsored educational and professional benefit programmes. The income ceiling for creamy layer has been gradually raised from rupees one lakh in 1993 to six lakh in May 2013 and so they are excluded from being categorised as "socially and educationally backward" regardless of their social/ educational backwardness.[77] The verdict produced mixed reactions from supporting and opposing quarters. However, the leaders, parties and governments should not use reservation as food but only as a medicine for overcoming the illness that Hindu society caused among sections of its own people.

Review and Remittance of Reservation

After independence, India committed itself to a socially just and an egalitarian social order. The Constitution promulgated in 1950, recognised the SCs and the STs as two of the most marginalised social groups needing special protections. A number of provisions, therefore, were specifically incorporated for the two social groups with a view to abolish all forms of discrimination, untouchability and social exclusion emanating from the caste system and to alleviate the peripheral position of these social groups. The system of reservations meant to uplift the weaker sections, has in fact, succeeded in the creation of creamy layer within the marginalised social groups to the extent that the percolation of the benefits have been marginal and differentially accessed.[78] On the other the Indian Government's approach towards these social groups has been primarily shaped by the provisions in the Constitution, which guarantee equality before the law, and empowers the state to make special provisions for the promotion of the educational, social, political and economic interests of the SCs/STs, and to further, protect them from any form of social discrimination and exclusion.

For the purpose the government has used a two-fold strategy for the empowerment of the SCs/STs which includes firstly, the provision of legal safeguards against discrimination and secondly, pro-active measures in the form of reservation policy for the public sector and state supported sectors. Reservation for the SCs/STs in the government services, educational institutions and political bodies like the Central and State legislatures also fall under pro-active measures. These measures have been incorporated to ensure the proportional participation of the SCs/STs in the public domain-democratic decision-making bodies. However, in private sector, wherein, more than 90 per cent of the SC/ST workers are engaged is excluded and therefore, remains outside the purview of the reservation policy and open to possible discrimination.[79] In addition, the policy of reservation has further reduced the scope of employment available in the public domain, since the public sector is in itself being disinvested. It has also been noticed that the decline in Central Government jobs for the SCs and STs was at a rate higher than that for the non-SCs/STs.

Definitely in public sector undertakings the positive impacts of the reservation policy were visible. The representation of the SCs and the STs was found to have improved both in terms of absolute numbers and percentage share. However, the majority of SCs and the STs in public sector undertakings were concentrated in Group D followed by Group C categories of jobs. In Group A and Group B categories of jobs, the representation of the SCs and the STs was found to be unsatisfactory and at levels below the stipulated quotas (except for the STs in Group B category in 2004, whereby, their representation stood at 7.84 per cent). Further, the adverse impacts of the New Employment Policy (NEP) were also visible in the Public Sector Employment (PSU) as the absolute numbers and the percentage share of the SC and ST employee declined after its inception. There is no doubt the reservation policy has contributed immensely towards the representation of the marginalised social groups in public sector employment. Concomitantly, much needs to be done to fairly represent the marginalised social communities- their representation especially in the higher echelons of jobs seems to be lower. Despite improvements there is still a gap of more than three per cent in Group A jobs and 3.18 per cent in Group B jobs in 2003. Therefore, it is desirable that the reservation policy in public sector jobs be implemented in its entirety so as to realise the social justice and egalitarian aims of the government.

In sphere of reservation of the SCs/STs and the OBCs Indra Sawhney (1992), the Supreme Court generously endorsed the use of caste to determine backwardness, though caste could not be the sole factor. Deference to the state on the determination of backwardness continued in later cases as the Court permitted the same treatment for Other Backward Class (OBC) and Scheduled Castes and Scheduled Tribes (SC/ST). But Indra Sawhney made two important normative points. The first was the 50 per cent cap on reservations, ground in the rationale that backwardness does not exist in the abstract; it depends on the average on society. Secondly, the Court held that reservation in public employment could only exist at the entry level. The reasoning was that reservations exist to create a level-playing field, to remedy unequal starting positions, thereby removing the justification for promotion quotas.[80] To overcome the decision of a nine-judge bench in Indra Sawhney and other judgements that disallowed reservation in promotions and consequential seniority. Parliament enacted three constitutional amendments, in 1995, 2000 and 2002. But while upholding the constitutional validity for the amendments, the Supreme Court in the case of M. Nagraj vs Union of India (October 2006), made it very clear that Article 16(4A), which was inserted through these amendments, was only an enabling provision. In essence, every time a government or the legislature sought to provide reservation in promotions under Article 16(4A), it would have to pass constitutional muster. While justifying each attempt to provide reservation in promotions, the state would have to demonstrate backwardness, inadequacy of representation and maintenance of efficiency.[81]

In the context it should be remembered that Article 16(4A) permits reservation in promotion only for the SCs/STs and not for the OBCs. Secondly, the test of creamy layer is not applicable to SCs/STs. The settled position of law is that all members of recognised SC/ST groups automatically satisfy the condition of backwardness and there is no burden on the state to further establish the backwardness of these individuals benefiting from reservation. While this requirement exists for the OBCs in terms of the 'creamy layer' test. Thus, even now, there is no bar on reservation in promotion. In the 2006 judgement on the extent to which reservation is permissible, the constitution bench had noted that the ceiling of 50 per cent, a concept of creamy layer and the statement of compelling reasons were all constitutional requirements without which the structure of equality of opportunity in Article 16 would collapse.[82] Recently in August 2012 the Central Government has decided to amend the constitution (117th Constitution Amendment Bill) to provide for reservation for Scheduled Castes and Scheduled Tribes in promotion in government services. The SCs and the STs are grossly under-represented in the upper echelons of government - as indeed they are in upper management elsewhere and every effort must be made to undo this injustice brought about by centuries old practices of social discrimination.[83] Reservation in promotions has been a sphere of intense disagreement between Parliament and the Supreme Court.

Reservation of 27 per cent jobs in public sector undertakings for Other Backward Classes (OBCs) was based on the central premise of the Mandal Commission that India should proceed from an ideology that rested upon hereditary hierarchy to an ideology that emphasised equality of outcomes not equality of opportunity. "If a tree is to be judged by its fruits", wrote the commission, "equality of results is obviously the most reliable test of our aspirations and efforts to achieve a just and equitable order. A formidable task under any circumstances, it becomes particularly so in a society which has remained segmented in a finely graded caste hierarchy for centuries."[84] Until 1985, the affairs of the Backward Classes were looked after by the Backward Cell in the Ministry of Home Affairs. A separate Ministry of Welfare was established in 1985, renamed in 1998 to the Ministry of Social Justice and Empowerment, to attend to matters relating to Scheduled Castes, Scheduled Tribes and OBCs.[85] The Backward Classes Division of the Ministry looks after the policy, planning and implementation of programmes relating to social and economic empowerment of OBCs and matters relating to two institutions set up for the welfare of OBCs, the National Backward Classes Finance and Development Corporation and the National Commission for Backward Classes.

The 400 caste enumerated in the Mandal Commission report were to be given reservation. The annual number of jobs in government service to be set aside was small estimated at 50,000 annually but the government's announcement triggered large scale violence across northern Indian, especially in the universities. Though many of the opponents of reservation, did so because they were excluded, there was also a growing sense that a moral injustice was being committed, that equality of opportunity was being eroded, that appointments would be made on the basis of membership in a caste irrespective of whether the individual was economically or socially handicapped, and that the government had extended the benefits for political reasons. The issue of reservation presented before us the extreme polarisation of positions between these groups suggests the failure of social revolution, wherein annihilation of caste has not been accomplished. Instead we have a situation where the "upper castes" believe that only the "lower castes" are stuck with a premodern identity while they have transcended it. The Court's ruling too seems to endorse this belief when it suggests that excessive reservation would have the effect of discriminating against the socially advantaged classes.[86] Discrimination is now regarded as a problem that the "upper castes" have to grapple with. Within this scheme, what continues to be conceded to the "lower castes" is their "deprivation" or "backwardness." In this context the court's approach has taken a observable shift in the discourse on caste-based reservation, from the idea of discrimination to deprivation.[87] In a country like India once a system of group preferences was introduced, leaders of political parties regarded support for preferences as a strategy for winning political support. Reservation based religion and caste is divisive and disintegrative in the long run. Recently and in earlier phase the Andhra Pradesh High Court has declared reservation for religious minorities constitutionally invalid.[88] The government of the day had demonstrated by providing that minority backward classes forming part of the sub-quota were more backward than the other backward classes.

Even of the prevailing caste system and social polarisation political parties take full advantage. They know that reservations are no way to improve the lot of the poor and the backward. They support them because of self-interest of the "creamy layer", who use the reservations to further their own family interests and as a political flag of 'achievement' during election campaigns.[89] Several studies show that the OBC class is comparable with the general caste in terms of annual per capita consumption expenditure, and the top strata of OBC is ahead in a host of consumption areas.[90] Most often, only economically sound people from the so-called lower castes make use of most of the reserved seats, thus countering the spirit of reservation. Especially in this era of globalisation and privatisation multi-national companies will be deterred by this action of the government and foreign investment in India may dry down, hurting the growth of the Indian economy.

Recently in September 2012 when Parliament was discussing the reservation for SCs/STs in promotion in the light of a judgement given earlier by the Supreme Court of India, in which the apex court had made backwardness, adequate representation and administrative efficiency as mandatory criteria for giving promotion quota to SCs/STs, members of political parties including the Indian National Congress raised the issue of OBC reservation in promotion. V. Hanumantha, a Congress MP in Rajya Sabha and prominent leader from Andhra Pradesh said, 'There is a sizable backward class in the country and it should be given reservation in promotion as is proposed to be done for the SCs and STs.[91] Further in response to the statement of DMK's chief M. Karunanidhi, who supported the demand for "promotion quota" for OBC on par with the one proposed for SCs and STs, other chieftains of the cause, Lalu Prasad Yadav, N. Chandrababu Naidu and Mulayam Singh Yadav demanded the promotion quota for OBCs. In a further development members of OBC Parliamentary Forum, headed by V. Hanumantha Rao, demanding that the Centre bring a law to institute promotion quota for backward, submitted a formal demand to Prime Minister Manmohan Singh.[92] The issue was again raised on March 8, 2013, and in reply of Lok Sabha question Minister of State in the Ministry of Personnel, Public Grievances and Pensions and Minister of State in the Prime Minister's office, V. Narayanswamy has submitted that government should consider extending reservation to the members of other backward classes in promotion also and bring an amendment to the constitution to give effect to this proposal.[93] This view was also supported in a Department related Parliamentary Standing Committee's report in the year 2004 which observed that to meet the constitutional obligation to provide adequate representation to OBCs the government should consider extending reservation to the members of other backward classes in promotion.

Today the demand for reservation is coming from various sections and groups. There are demands that reservation be extended to women and to Muslims. The private sector and military have been excluded from the reservation system, but there are already demands that both be included. Even the Christians are demanding reservation as well. In the situation anxiety is deepened by the realisation of the fact that in addition to our old enemies in the form of castes and creeds we are going to have many political parties with diverse and opposing political creeds. Implementation of any reservation/promotion policy on ad-hoc considerations under pressure of political mobs without rational classification as required under the law may prove to be discriminatory. Thus, it is high to expect that the government would take proper measures to honour the basic mandates of accountability at appropriate levels so as to avert any possibility of unconstitutional functioning and possible cause of contempt of constitution.

References

1. R. Padmini, 'Individual and Society,' *The Political Elites of Pakistan and other Sociological Essays*, Dr Sheo Kumar Lal (ed.) (New Delhi : 1983), pp. 103-7.
2. Aristotle, *The Politics*, available on en.wikipedia.org/wikisocial_justice0.
3. John Rawls, *A Theory of Justice* (1971), p. 4.

4. V.K.N. Menon, *India Since Independence From the Preamble to the Present* (New Delhi: S. Chand & Co., 1970), p. 27.
5. *Nicomachean Ethics*, Vol. 3. It is the name normally given to Aristotle's best known work on ethics.
6. Subramaniam Chandran, 'Endorsing Social Identity for Social Justice: Transition from Ancient to Contemporary Constructions in India,' available at: http:/ssm.com/abstract.
7. 'Social-Structure in India- Is It Highly Stratified?', available at latasinha. Wordpress.com/stratification-of... .
8. S. Waseem Ahmad and M. Ashraf Ali, 'Social Justice and the Constitution of India,' *The Indian Journal of Political Science*, Vol. IXVII, No.4, October-December 2006 (Meerut: 2006), p. 767.
9. For detail see, *Minarva Mills vs. Union of India* (1980), 3 SCC 625.
10. V.R. Krishna Iyer, *Social Justice-Sunset or Dawn* (1987), p. 53.
11. Article 14 of the Indian Constitution.
12. *All India Reporter* (AIR), 1974 SC 587.
13. Article 46 of the Indian Constitution.
14. For detail see, *Supreme Court Judgement*, 1992 Supp. (3), SCC 217.
15. 'Problems of Social Inequality and Possibilities of Judicial Intervention,' The First Annual Dr K.R. Narayanan Memorial Lecture, held at Jamia Millia Islamia University, (New Delhi), 13 November 2007.
16. Dr Anil Kumar Mohapatra, 'Basic Objectives and Values of the Indian Constitution', *Orissa Review*, January 2011, p. 33.
17. V.K.N. Menon, *India Since Independence-From the Preamble to the Present*, p. 32.
18. *Ibid.*, p. 33.
19. Debjani Ganguly, 'Convergent Cosmopolitics in the Age of Empire: Gandhi and Ambedkar in World History,' *borderland, e-journal*, Vol. 4, No. 3, 2006.
20. Shailendra Kumar Tiwari, 'Social Justice: Gandhi and Ambedkar,' *The Indian Journal of Political Science*, Vol. LXX, No. 2, April-June 2009 (Meerut: 2009), pp. 430 and 434.
21. Ranjit Hoskote, 'Ambedkar's Legacy,' *The Hindu*, 10 December 2006.
22. M.K. Gandhi, 'Hinduism,' *Young India*, 6 October 1921.
23. *Ibid.*
24. Ranjit Hoskote, 'Ambedkar's Legacy'.
25. B.R. Ambedkar, *Caste in India: Writings and Speeches*, Vol. I, pp.17-18.
26. Upendra Baxi and Bhikhu Parekh (eds.), *Crisis and Change in Contemporary India*.
27. *Ibid.*, p.145.

28. Shailendra Kumar Tiwari, 'Social Justice: Gandhi and Ambedkar', p. 432.
29. Jagannath Swaroop Mathur, *Industrial Civilisation and Gandhian Economics* (1971), p.165.
30. B.R. Ambedkar, *States and Minorities, Writings and Speeches*, Vol. I, pp. 396-97.
31. As quoted in Dr Venkatesh Athreya, 'Reappraisal-A New Resonance,' *Frontline*, Vol.19, Issue 15, July 20- August-2, 2002.
32. Nilanjana Jain, *The Problem of Justice in Political Theory and State Practice* (New Delhi: Anamica Publishers & Distributors), p.134.
33. *Dr Baba Saheb Ambedkar Writings and Speeches*, Vol. 2, pp. 507-8.
34. *Ibid.*, p. 357.
35. Yogendra Yadav, 'Rethinking Social Justice', 5 January 2012, available on www.countercurrents.org
36. Prem Shankar Jha, 'Dance of Democracy on A Razor's Edge', *Tehelka*, Vol. II, Issue 16, 9 April 2014, available on Tehelka.com
37. B.B. Dutta, '2014: The End of Nehruvian Republic,' *South Asia Politics*, Vol. 13, No. 3, July 2014 (New Delhi : 2014), pp. 1-3.
38. Rajkumar Singh, *Be Update and Face to Face With Indian Republic* (Delhi: Kalpaz Publications, 2014), p.140.
39. Hema Banerjee, 'Reservation Policy: A Controversial Affair in Island's Society', *The Indian Journal of Political Science*, Vol. LXX, No. 3, July-September 2009 (Meerut: 2009), p. 813.
40. Munin Baruah, 'Caste Reservation in India,' *South Asia Politics*, Vol. 6, No. 5, 2007 (New Delhi: 2007), p. 47.
41. 'Verna, Caste and other Divisions', *US Library of Congress*, 20 August 2013.
42. Meenakshi Jha, 'Locating the Space for Sudras in Medieval Bhakti (A.D. 600-1400)', *Proceedings of the Indian History Congress*, 66th Session (Indian History Congress, Delhi, 2006), p. 379.
43. B.N.S. Yadav, *Society and Culture in Northern India in Twelfth Century* (Allahabad Central Book Depot), p. 41.
44. Meenakshi Jha, 'Locating the Space for Sudras in Medieval Bhakti (A.D. 600-1400)', p. 381.
45. 'The Untouchables of India' *Praxis*, 20 October 2011.
46. As quoted *in History of Bahujan Samaj Party*, 20 October 2011.
47. Sugata Bose and Ayesha Jalal, *Modern South Asia-History, Culture, Political Economy* (New Delhi: Oxford University Press 2004), p. 124.
48. Upendra Baxi, 'Emancipation as Justice: Babasaheb Ambedkar's Legacy and Vision', in Upendra Baxi, Bhikhu Parekh (eds), *Crisis and Change in Contemporary India*.

49. B.R. Ambedkar, *What the Congress and Gandhi Have Done to the Untouchables* (Bombay: Thacker & Co.,1945), p. 327.
50. *Ibid.*, p. 326.
51. Upendra Baxi, 'Emancipation as Justice: Babasaheb Ambedkar's Legacy and Vision,' p. 31.
52. Madhav Khosla, 'Promotion Quota Seeks Equality of Outcome,' *The Hindu*, September 2012.
53. Terry H. Anderson, *The Pursuit of Fairness: A History of Affirmative Action* (Oxford University Press, 2004).
54. As quoted in Prahladrai L. Avasathi, 'Caste Based Reservation in Employment and Promotion,' *South Asia Politics*, Vol. II, No. 5, September 2012 (New Delhi: 2012), p. 21.
55. Durga Das Basu, *Introduction to the Constitution of India*, (New Delhi: Prentice- Hall of India, 1983), p. 87.
56. *Ibid.*, p. 89.
57. Prahladrai L. Avasathi, 'Caste Based Reservation in Employment and Promotion,' p. 23.
58. *Ibid.*, p. 22.
59. *Text of the Constitution* (Scheduled Tribes) Order 1950, as amended.
60. '*Scheduled Caste Welfare-List of Scheduled Castes*' 16 August 2012 (New Delhi: Ministry of Social Justice and Empowerment, 2012).
61. *The Hindu*, 5 August 2009.
62. Dr Sunil Kumar Jangir, 'Reservation Policy and Indian Constitution in India,' *American International Journal of Research in Humanities, Arts and Social Sciences*, 3(1), June-August 2013 (USA, 2013), p.126.
63. *Ibid.*, p.127.
64. *The Times of India*, 3 April 2013.
65. From the text of *First Kaka Kalelkar Commission* on Identification of Weaker Sections in Indian Society.
66. Amit Bhattacharya, 'Who are the OBCs', *The Times of India*, 8 April 2006.
67. Andre Beteille, 'India's Destiny not Caste in Stone,' *The Hindu*, 21 February 2012.
68. Ramaiah A., 'Identifying Other Backward Classes,' *Economic and Political Weekly*, 6 June 1992 (Mumbai: 1992), pp.1203-07.
69. *Mandal Commission Report*, Vol. I, p. 23.
70. *Mandal Commission Report*, Vol. I, Chapter XIII, Recommendations, pp. 57-60.
71. *The Times of India*, 8 April 2006.
72. Rajkumar Singh, *Be Update and Face to Face with Indian Republic*, p. 45.

73. *Ibid.*
74. Utsa Patnaik (ed.), *Agrarian Relations and Accumulation-The Mode of Production Debate* (Bombay: Sameksha Trust Publication,1993), as quoted in Dipankar Sinha, Kaberi Chakrabarti (eds.), *Democratic Governance in India-Reflections and Refractions* (Delhi: Kalpaz Publications, 2007), p. 36.
75. *Ibid.*, pp. 36-37.
76. *Supreme Court on OBC Quota in IITs/IIMs*, 29 March 2007.
77. Visit: http://www.obcguru.com
78. Sukhadeo Thorat and Chittaranjan Senapati, 'Reservation Policy in India-Dimension and Issues,' *Indian Institute of Dalit Studies*, Vol.I, No. 2, p. 7.
79. *Ibid.*, p. 8.
80. Madhav Khosla, 'Promotion Quota Seeks Equality of Outcome.'
81. Anup Surendranath, 'Winning the Case on Promotion Quotas,' in *Ibid.*, 6 September 2012.
82. 'Tread Carefully' (editorial), *Ibid.*, 28 August 2012.
83. *Ibid.*
84. Munin Baruah, 'Caste Reservations in India,' p. 48.
85. Visit: socialjustice.nic.in
86. Rekha Pappu, M. Madhava Prasad, K. Satyanarayana and Susie Tharu, 'Reservation or Affirmative Action?', *The Hindu*, 12 December 2006.
87. *Ibid.*
88. K. Vivek Reddy, 'Lessons on How Not to Pitch a Quota,' in *Ibid.*, 21 June 2012.
89. L.S. Rao, 'Too Many Bosses-The UPA has a Cabinet with Many Insubordinate Ministers,' *The Telegraph*, 5 June 2006.
90. Shailesh Dobhal, 'In Consumption, OBC are no Longer Backward,' *The Economic Times*, 2 June 2006.
91. *Firstpost*, 4 September 2012.
92. *The Times of India*, 7 September 2012.
93. *Lok Sabha Debates*, 8 March 2013.

Chapter - 3

Education and Literacy in India: Modern and Post-modern

3.1 Education : Meaning and Role in Social Change

Education is undoubtedly a process to lead and guide a man well and continuously on the pathway to development. It plays a vital role in human development and the progress and growth of any country depends to a large extent on the quality and number of trained manpower available in different areas. It is an instrument as well as a catalyst of social transformation and is expected to bring qualitative change in man's perception, attitudes, habits, priority and goals. With the development of society educational system develops and with the development of education society develops. In the sense education and society are inter-dependent. It is a two-way traffic in which while education preserves, transmits and stimulates the wholesome culture, the society also, according to its changed conditions expects the school to review and plan its work as per demands and aspirations of the changing society. The whole planning of the school, including the curriculum, should reflect the changes in social values, norms and patterns.[1]

Education: A Dynamic Concept

The word 'Education' currently used in English is, in fact, derived from the Latin word Educare, which is further originated from Educere and in its basic spirit, is the manifestation or expression. In further depth it will become apparent that it reveals the inner capability of man that guides him continuously throughout at various levels in all walks of life. In this context, as to the meaning of education even there is no contradiction between the Western and Indian viewpoints. In the West, the two great Greek Philosophers- Socrates and Plato remained identical from the meaning and purpose of education. Socrates has categorically said that education is to draw out what are already within while Plato states that it is the acquisition of virtue by child.[2] In particular, Plato has written extensively on education and his views, despite being relevant in circumstances of his own time have importance more or less, in one way or the other, in current perspective all over the world. His views on education occupied a significant role in his vision of the ideal Republic, wherein the individual could serve the best by being subordinated to a just society. Plato saw the development of an individual in a just society and therefore focussed on his plan of education accordingly. However, after Plato, Aristotle gave new dimension to education in theoretical perspective and stressed that education must not serve any mean or vocational activity as these activities are the functions of slaves. He laid emphasis on obedience and responsibility for those who are designated to rule in times to come. For the purpose he stressed on the curriculum of the Academy to impart the four type of education- basics, related to natural science, physical and humanities. In his view the development of character-building right from the childhood is an important aspects of personality and for the purpose he advised to censor that aspect of education, which could, obstruct the way to character building. Even at the time the dimensions of education could not be confined to Plato and Aristotle and throughout the West thinkers, philosophers, scholars and educationists accorded new horizons from time to time through their ideas, suggestions and works.

Likewise, in the East and India in particular, the education systems existed in the Vedic and later Vedic periods were different to one-another. During the time of Tirthankar Mahavira and Siddhartha Gautama the education system seemed to be receiving a new dimension. Again at the time of Chanakya when in the Mauryan Empire the world renowned universities like Takshila, Vikramshila and Nalanda were flourishing, the basic spirit of education was imparted liberally to an extent among women and common people by Jainism and Buddhism. Even at the time Kautilya- the great scholar declared education to be the best friend and says further, 'An educated person is respected everywhere and education beats beauty and the youth. In modern India several contemporary thinkers- Vivekananda, Rabindra Nath Tagore and Sri Aurobindo have mentioned that education is the manifestation of the perfection already in man. Tagore while describing the scope of education includes the high head, free knowledge, truth coming from the depth, tireless striving stretching arms towards perfection....within it.[3] In line Aurobindo has talked about the integral education which must help flourish the very best in a human being- the unique and exquisite, something, which every individual is born to offer to the world. Further, Aurobindo has also pointed out that education is meant to bring out the best in man, to develop his potentialities to the maximum, to integrate him with himself - his surroundings, his society, his country and humanity to make him the complete man - the integrated man.

However, the blueprint of educational system given by Mahatma Gandhi, the father of the nation, is more relevant as it is job-centred, value-based and mass-oriented. It provides for manual work along with intellectual exercise a central place in the curriculum at all stages. From the beginning Gandhi realised that education is the pivotal activity on which not only the progress of the individual but moral, economic and political progress of the entire society depends. In his own words, 'Education must be of a new type for the sake of the creation of a new world.'[4] Elaborating the idea he added, 'Our system of (Basic) education leads to the development of the mind, body and soul. The ordinary system cares only for mind.'[5] His educational theory is "original", "new", and epoch making. 'By education I mean an all round drawing out of the best in child and man's body, mind and spirit....I would therefore begin the child's education by teaching it a useful handicraft and enabling it to produce from the movement it begins its training.'[6] The aim of education in society is determined by the nature of society and man we cherish. Gandhi's education aims apart from its social and economic bearing, transformation of the individual as well as the whole society. For him education is a means for the upliftment not only of the individual but of the entire society.

The new scheme of education which Gandhiji launched in 1937 and avocated widely in India was named "Basic Education", "Nai Taleem" or "Wardha Scheme." Inaugurating the Wardha Conference on 2 October, 1937 Gandhiji said, 'I am convinced that the present system of primary education is not only wasteful but positively harmful.'[7] Basic stands for fundamentals and means that this scheme of education was based on the national culture and civilisation of India. Its important features includes: (i) Free compulsory education, (ii) Craft as the centre of education, (iii) Self-supporting aspect of education, (iv) Cult of non-violence,

Education for democratic values, etc. Thus, basic education as conceived and explained by Mahatma Gandhi is an education which aims at creating a social order free from violence and injustice.[8] Therefore, creative, socially useful and productive work in the schools in which all boys and girls may participate, irrespective of any distinction of caste and class is placed at the core of basic education. The fundamental objective of basic education is nothing less than the development of the child's total personality in totality which includes productive efficiency as well.

Hence, each time in history, education got a new different dimension. As per requirements it obtained refinement in prevailing situations of time and space, to become more or less welfaristic.

Role of Education in Social Change

Apart from set definitions, education can also be defined both as a process and as a social institution. In the broadest sense the process of education occurs whenever any influence produces change in the physical or mental behaviour of a person. In this sense, the mass media political speeches and labour unions exert educative influences and as a social institutions we may consider education as the sum total of this schools and the people who in some way interact with them.[9] In the context, the impact of education on the society in relation to its development may be seen both as a cause and consequence. High level of education contributes to the growth of individual and society but the development of education depends to a certain extent on wealth. As the family income increases, children demand higher education and parents feel pleasure in fulfilling the demands of the children. Similarly, as national income increases, it becomes possible to earmark larger sums for education.[10] Education contributes its vital input in the growth and prosperity of a nation. In fact it is the backbone of all national endeavours. It has the power to transform human beings into human resources.[11] Education stands for March of the human race towards even higher objectives.

At large social change is a sociological term which covers a wider area and by social change we mean the change in social structure whatever its reasons may be. The theories of society stem not from education directly but from the characteristics of individual. That is why the mode of development of each society differs from others. In this context Stephen Cotgrove observed, 'Many theories of societies have, in fact, stemed from certain assumptions about the characteristics of the individuals who compose it. Theories of economic behaviour, for example, have assumed that man is motivated primarily by the desire to maximise his material satisfaction. And especially in developing countries modern society is passing through an age which demands good performance for the fulfilment of its requirements. Education helps the society in this task and at the juncture society must provide some concrete organisational means by which it is possible for individuals to enter into a social system and find social and economic rewards in commensurate with their desires. Certain organisations have traditionally been crucial to the upward social movement of individuals. Schools have been the foremost of these, particularly during previous generations when higher degrees were scarce and difficult to earn.[12]

Education played a significant role in social stratification. Society is an organisation of individuals. But men hold different views on a certain issue. And with the development of their personality they seek power, prestige, property and popularity. With the passing of time they all develop different qualities. All this brings about stratification in the society. As Coleman has rightly said, 'the rulers always expected the educational system to serve as a major channel of rapid social mobility, but in the period after World War II education began to show signs of functioning more and more as an instrument of social stratification.[13] In fact, on the one hand education makes stratification of society and brings about intergroup conflict due to unequal development but on the other hand, it seeks the way to solve such type of problems.

Especially in democratic society education is all the more valuable. For, it is the first condition for the successful working of democratic government that the electorate should be educated. In a country like India education has become a source of prestige and a symbol of higher social status. The families which achieve higher economic status but do not correspondingly get their children highly educated are not held in high public esteem.[14] In addition, education brings about a tremendous change in the political structure of the society by educating the individual and awakening them about their rights. If we compare the present system of the society with the past we would realise how greatly different the present system is from the past. Earlier people were little conscious of their rights and freedom. They only did their own work and spent their life. They believed in obeying the order of their administrators and elders. But now the situation has been changed because of the impact of education which inspires and encourages people to think independently and to acquire resources for the development of their personality.[15] The mass awakening to a large extent paved the way more or less for people's participation in one way or the other especially in social and political spheres. Resultantly, situations started changing rapidly.

However, despite the constant refinements and so many dimensions in education process much more has still to be done to achieve the real object, to make education all welfaristic. Education is, to repeat, an endless process. To struggle with problems and come out of obstacles on the way is unavoidable; rather, it is essential part of this process. That is why it continues. To conclude, so many dimensions are to be added in this process in the prevailing situations of space, and as per the demand of time. Effective and worthy efforts have always been tried to make the system momentous and welfaristic. If education process has not brought fruits as per the expectations, it is definitely due to lack of sincere, effective and appropriate efforts. This equally applies to the present and will be so in future.

3.2 Literacy in India: An Overview

In a country like India literacy is a key for socio-economic progress. It is defined as the ability to identify, understand, interpret, create, communicate, compute and use printed and written materials associated with varying contexts. The earliest system of gurukul declined gradually and in British India a large number of English primary schools grew and correspondingly the literacy rate in India rose from 3.2 per cent in 1881 to 12.2 per cent in 1947. In independent India the provision of universal and compulsory education for all children in the age group of 6-14 was cherished as a priority in the Directive Policy in Article 45 of the Constitution. In a major breakthrough the Parliament passed 86th Amendment Act, 2002 to make elementary education a Fundamental Right for children. In order to provide more funds for education an education cess of two per cent was imposed on all direct and indirect central taxes through the Finance Act, 2004. Despite government programmes and efforts slow increase in literacy rate and wider gender disparity in the literacy rate continued to be an unhealthy sign for literacy prospect in the country.

Wider Meaning of Literacy

Originally derived from the Latin word "Letter" literacy is the ability to read and write in at least one language. Literacy is a human right, a tool of personal empowerment and a means for social and human development. The notion of basic literacy is used for the initial learning of reading and writing which adults who have never been to school need to go through. In this context the term functional literacy is kept for the level of reading and writing which adults are thought to need in modern complex society. Use of the term underlines the idea that although people may have basic levels of literacy, they need a different level to operate in their day-to-day lives.[16] In a clearer term it may be said that to acquire literacy is more than to psychologically and mechanically dominate reading and writing techniques. It is to dominate those techniques in terms of consciousness; to understand what one reads and to write what one understands. It is to communicate graphically. Acquiring literacy does not involve memorising sentences, words or syllables - lifeless objects unconnected to an existential universe- but rather an attitude of creation and recreation, a self-transformation, producing a stance of intervention in one's context.[17] It is at the heart of basic education for all, and essential for eradicating poverty, reducing child mortality, curbing population growth, achieving gender equality and ensuring sustainable development, peace and democracy.

Several international agencies including the International Council for Adult Education, notes literacy as learning to read and write, reading and writing to learn and developing these skills and using them effectively for meeting basic needs.[18] Universal access to quality education in developed countries has helped to shape this concept of literacy. According to it true literacy encompasses much more than just basic skills. It includes the ability to analyse things, understand general ideas or terms, use symbols in complex ways, apply theories and perform other necessary life skills, including the ability to engage in the social and economic life of the community. This broader concept of literacy is also called functional literacy and opposite to it is the basic literacy concept which focuses on acquiring skills, functional literacy deals with how people actually use such skill to live and work in society. Recent research in fields such as sociology, the cognitive sciences, linguistics, anthropology and education have contributed to an even broader, more inclusive view of literacy, called plural literacy. According to the United Nations Education Scientific and Cultural Organisation, 'A plural view of literacy recognises that there are many literacy practices that are embedded in social, political and cultural processes, personal circumstances and socio-economic structures.[19] This view of literacy sees it as an evolving set of skills, with less of an emphasis on a fixed set of generic skills, as in basic literacy, or measurable technical and life skills, as in functional literacy.

Similarly, in addition, there are studies of multiple literacy that focus on encouraging students to take meaning from, and to understand how, literacy can help them in different social contexts. However, both these views- plural and multiple are important because they highlight the many different ways we use language in our homes, workplaces, schools, communities and social groups. What we use literacy to do varies in different settings. But the way of defining literacy affects how problems are identified and what is done to solve the problem. For instance, government literacy policies intended to create employment and develop work-related skills reflect a functional view of literacy.[20] A plural or multiple literacy approach seeks to achieve more communal results. The exclusive use of functional literacy policies would have little impact on multiple or plural literacy objectives- such as better health outcomes, expanded adult learning and more civic engagement. Therefore, the creation of literacy policies needs to address functional and plural/multiple literacies.

In this circumstances we need a radical redefinition of literacy, one that includes a recognition of the vital importance that morality plays in shaping literacy. We need a radical redefinition of what it means for society to have all the appearances of literary and yet to abandon the book as its dominant metaphor. We must understand what happens when the computer replaces the book as the prime metaphor for visualising the self... It is to remember that those who celebrate the intensities and discontinuities of post-modern electronic culture in print write from an advanced literacy. That literacy provides them the profound power of choosing their ideational repertoire. No such choice or power is available to the illiterate young person subjected to an endless stream of electronic images. In general on the basis of definitions, literacy has got four levels; (i) *Below Basic Literacy*- It indicates no more than the most simple and concrete literacy skills; (ii) *Basic Literacy*- It indicates skills necessary to perform simple and everyday literacy activities; (iii) *Intermediate Literacy*- It indicates skills necessary to perform moderately challenging literacy activities and (iv) *Proficient Literacy*- It indicates skills necessary to perform more complex and challenging literacy activities.

In today's world literacy is about more than just words and meaning. It is important because the world is rapidly changing. The effects of globalisation and free trade, better communication and information technologies and the rise of societies that use knowledge and information to create wealth, have resulted in a growing demand for highly skilled workers. This global competition for skilled, literate workers explains why literacy has become so important.[21] It is important because it affects people's lives directly, impacting their chances of employment, level of income, and type of occupation.[22] Research shows that higher literacy skills can lead to better jobs, increased incomes and greater productivity.[23] Literacy skills also affect social status, level of political participation, opportunities for cultural expression, health, survival of language, access to social services and opportunity to learn.[24] Having good literacy skills enhances a country's quality of life by reducing poverty, lowering unemployment, lessening the need for public assistance and encouraging better parenting.[25]

Thus, the word "literacy", while at first glance seem to be a term that everyone understand, at the same, the concept has proved to be both complex and dynamic, continuing to be interpreted and defined in a multiplicity of ways. People's notions of what it means to be literate or illiterate are influenced by academic research, institutional agendas, national context, cultural values and personal experiences. In the academic community, theories of literacy have evolved from those focused solely on changes in individuals to more complex views encompassing the broader social contexts that encourage and enable literacy activities and practices to occur. As a result of these and other developments, understanding in the international policy community have expanded too: from viewing literacy as a simple process of acquiring basic cognitive skills, to using these skills in ways that contribute to socio-economic development, to developing the capacity for social awareness and critical reflections as a basis for personal and social change. Besides these international views of literacy, there are a number of regional and national definitions of literacy and most of the countries define literacy as the ability to read and/or write simple statements in either a national or native language.

Literacy in India as defined in census operations, is the ability to read and write with understanding in any language. A person who can merely read but cannot write is not classified as literate. Any formal education or minimum educational standard is not necessary to be considered literate. The Indian Constitution has recognised the significance of education and literacy for social transformation. The Preamble affirms a determination to secure liberty of thought, expression, belief, faith and worship and equality of status and opportunity. Literacy forms the cornerstone for making the provision of equality of opportunity a reality. The objective specified in the Preamble contains the basic structure of the Constitution, which cannot be amended, and the preamble may be invoked to determine the ambit of Fundamental Rights and Directive Principles of State Policy. There are several articles of the Constitution which provides for its citizens better opportunities relating to education-the key vehicle for literacy. In Fundamental Rights Articles 12, 14, 19, 21, 29 and 30(1) while Articles 39(A), 41, 45, 46, 51A(h) in Directive Principles of State Policy, directly or indirectly ensure the provisions/ rights of citizens to get education and literacy. In addition, there have been specific amendments 42nd, 73rd, 74th and 83rd to the Constitution affecting education. These amendments pertain to provisions to enable education being included in the Concurrent List, devolution of powers to the local bodies and making elementary education a Fundamental Right formally.

Similar to UNICEF's definition the Indian government defines literacy as the ability to read and write for a person aged seven or above. A nation's literacy rate is determined, to a great degree, by the definition of literacy and the method used to measure it. Countries struggling to achieve higher rates often tend to lower definitional bars which then makes progress that much easier. India is no exception. However, even in case of India, the definition of literacy as given by our policy-makers needs a revision. *The Hindu* wrote, 'Without addition of any values and qualification for employment, mere ability to read and write is not sufficient. We need to channelise more funds on educational sector to improve the quality of education imparted to Indians, not only in terms of technology and employ ability but also moral values which would make them a responsible citizen of India.[26] Education is not all about knowledge of alphabets, it is much more than that. Education, in its true sense, is when people understand the meaning of development and become aware about the important issues. When they become able to grow themselves and can contribute in nation's growth. This requires information and potential to understand the repercussion of events, which come by proper basic education. 'Recently the increment in literacy rate is really good for a developing country. But apparently the definition of being literate in India would not suffice to meet the educational status'.[27] India's literacy rate has increased six times since the end of the British rule from 12 per cent to 74 per cent in 2011 but still India has the world's largest population of illiterates and at the current rate of progress it will take until 2060 for India to achieve universal literacy.

Expansion and Increment of Literacy

In pre and post India's independence the main information on literacy was collected from censuses. In all the censuses besides data on literacy, additional information was also collected. In 1872, the information about youths upto age 20 attending schools, college or under private tuition was recorded. In 1881 Census, the information was collected whether the individuals were under instruction or not, if not, whether they were able to read and write. In 1891 Census, besides the information regarding the language in which the person was literate the foreign language known was also recorded. From 1901 to 1941 Censuses, there was an additional question whether the literate knew English or not. Information on the standard of Education was collected for the first time in 1941 census after that it was asked in every subsequent census. In fact, Indian idea of education is historically based on what had been cultural literacy, an age-old folkloristic phenomenon, rarely found in subaltern societies elsewhere. The colonial educational set up, for long divergent, and latter parallel to the local community-based systems, has now been taken to be the only viable system of educating the child for the post-modern socio-economic model. The gradual growth rate of free India reflects the significant steps, independent India has taken to create a more literate society. For example, in 1901, the crude literacy rate was an insignificant 5.35 per cent. In 1951, this was still dismal 16.67 per cent. In contrast with a 11.32 percentage point increase between 1901 and 1951 but the crude literacy rate rose by 48.22 points between 1951 and 2011 with the 1991-2001 decade registering the highest growth rate of 11.67 percentage point.

Thus, post-Independent India inherited a system of education, which was characterised by large scale and intra-regional imbalances. The system educated a few, leaving a wide gap between the educated and illiterate. The country's literacy rate in 1947 was only 14 per cent and female literacy was abysmally low at eight per cent. Only one child out of three had an opportunity for enrollment in primary schools. Educational inequality was aggravated by economic inequality, gender disparity and rigid social stratification. In order to remove illiteracy a number of significant programmes have been taken up since Independence to eradicate. Every issue that our society faces is like a link of chain. Each issue is connected to another, either directly or indirectly. The chain of issues in this society that we live in, the strongest link of that chain is illiteracy. Illiteracy is the mother of all issues as it gives birth to many other issues like poverty, unemployment, child labour, female foeticide, population burst and many more. India is developing but at a very slow rate, this is not the fault of a corrupt government; it is this problem of illiteracy only. Literacy enables a person to think rationally, to be understanding, to be more responsible and to make his/her own decisions. A literate person is aware of all his fundamental rights and duties. Literacy is the ultimate solution to fight problems like communalism, terrorism and under development. Our government is of the people, for the people and by the people, but what is the use if people cannot even make the right choice? Illiteracy can bring down even the most powerful nations down, so if we are to become a developed nation, the government should first remove the problem of illiteracy by introducing effective programmes with proper implementation and budget.

Eradication of illiteracy has been one of the major national concerns of the Government of India since Independence. The need for a literate population and universal education for all children in the age group of 6-14 was recognised as a crucial input for nation building and was given due consideration in the Constitution as well as in the successive five year plans. Some of the important programmes have included:

(i) **Social Education**: The main elements were literacy, extension, general education, leadership training and social consciousness. The programme was implemented in the First Five-Year Plan (1951-56).

(ii) **Gram Shikshan Mohim**: Movement for literacy in rural areas was started in 1959 in Satara district of Maharashtra, and was later extended to other parts of the state. The programme aimed at imparting basic literacy skill within a period of about four months and by 1963, it spread to all the districts of the state. The programme, however, suffered from a lack of systematic follow up and consequently relapse to illiteracy was massive.

(iii) **Farmer's Functional Literacy Project**: Started in 1967-68 as an inter-ministerial project for farmers' training and functional literacy, the project aimed at popularisation of high yielding varieties of seeds through the process of adult education. The programme was confined to 144 districts of the country where nearly 8,640 classes were organised for about 2.6 lakh adults.

(iv) **Non-formal Education**: In the beginning of the Fifth Plan, a programme of non-formal education for 15-25 age-group was launched. Although the scope, content and objective of the non-formal education was clearly spelt out, its understanding in the field was very limited and the programmes actually organised indistinguishable from the conventional literacy programmes.

(v) **Polyvalent Adult Education Centres**: Workers' Social Education Institutes and Polyvalent Adult Education Centres were reviewed by a group in 1977, which recommended adoption of Polyvalent Education Centres in the adult education programme for workers in urban areas. In pursuance of this decision, Shramik Vidyapeeths were set up in states.

In the years 1964-66, the Government of India appointed a Education Commission to examine the prevailing conditions of education in India and suggest measures for its improvement. In its report the Commission recognised the importance of providing stimulating conditions of work and equate opportunities for professional advancement in educational institutions.[28] The favourable condition does support the creative work like teaching and research as well as help retain the quality teachers in the system. The benchmark of the conditions for educational institutions is to enable teachers to function at their highest level of efficiency.[29] The Commission's report, among other things, stressed on the need of appointing women teachers at all levels, opportunities for part time employment of women teachers, residential accommodation for women teachers particularly in rural areas, introduction of condensed course for women, promotion of private study in women through corresponding method and special allowances for women teachers. In the light of Education Commission's Report the Government set up Functional Literacy for Adult Women (FLAW) in the years 1975-76. The aim of the FLAW scheme was to enable illiterate adult women to acquire functional skills along with literacy, to promote better awareness of health, hygiene, childcare practices and to bring about attitudinal changes. The target age group in the scheme was 15-45, with greater attention to those in the 15-35 age group. It was gradually expanded along with expansion of ICDC up to the year 1981-82 but soon the Planning Commission decided to stop the expansion of FLAW scheme in ICDC project areas mainly due to a constraint of resources.

Till the close of 1970s overriding priority was given to primary education on the assumption that the expansion of primary education would automatically take care of problems of illiteracy. It was only in 1977-78 that the government decided to accord due weightage to adult education along with the programme of Universalisation of Elementary Education (UEE) and the National Adult Education Programme (NAEP) was launched on 2 October, 1978. For the first time Adult Education was put on the educational agenda of the nation and thereby made central to the development approach that was pursued. However, the NAEP was not very successful because it was traditional, honorarium-based, hierarchical and government-funded and controlled. Further, the Sixth Five Year Plan (1980-1985) emphasised minimum essential education to all adults, irrespective of their age, sex and residence. This was to be achieved by flexibility, inter-sectoral cooperation and inter-agency coordination.[30] These efforts were to be supported by post-literacy, continuing education through a network of rural libraries as well as instructional programmes conducted through mass communication media. Non-Formal Education for adults particularly in the productive age group 15-35 years, was to receive priority in the Sixth Plan, in view of its potential for immediate impact in raising the level of productivity in the economy. In addition, the programme was designed to give priority to a lot of weaker sections like women, Scheduled Castes, Scheduled Tribes and agriculturer labourers as well as slum dwellers.

During the Seventh Five Year Plan (1985-1990) and Eighth Five Year Plan (1992-1997) emphasis on eradicating illiteracy and development of national adult education programmes continued. In the Seventh Plan the Planning Commission's objective was to address the needs of 90 million people, ages 15-35, in the Adult Education Programme. The network of libraries was to play a role in the development of literature for neo-literates. Library systems were to be strengthen with specific attention given to improvement of facilities at the national-level institutions. The strategy to achieve the goal was through a mass movement involving social institutions, voluntary organisations, students, teachers, employers and the community.[31] Likewise, in the Eighth Five Year Plan universalisation of elementary education, eradication of illiteracy in the 15-35 year age group, and strengthening of vocational education in relation to emerging needs in rural and urban settings were the major thrusts of the plan. These goals were to be achieved by using formal, non-formal and open channels of learning. Book promotion in various forms was also emphasised in this plan.

In the Ninth Five Year Plan (1997-2002) the emphasis was on restoring the lost momentum of the adult education programme and making it more effective by clarifying the administrative and financing roles of the Centre, the States, Zila Saksharata Samiti (ZSS), Panchayati Raj Institutions (PRIs), other local bodies and non-governmental organisations (NGOs). Other steps included increasing the range and depth of NGOs involvement in literacy campaigns; meeting the special needs of Scheduled Castes/Scheduled Tribes (SCs/STs) and reducing rural-urban and male-female disparities in literacy through the campaign mode. In this plan period the National Literacy Mission (NLM) programme was revamped in 1999. In coming years the National Literacy Mission became an important agency for eradicating illiteracy in India.[32] After the launch of NLM in 1988 between 1988 and 1990, the Mission tried to consolidate the earlier centre-based programme to make its implementation more effective through the campaigned-based approach. Provision was also made for the devolution of power from the National Literacy Mission Authority (NLMA) to the State Literacy Mission Authority (SLMA) for financial sanction to projects under the Total Literacy Campaign (TLC) and Post Literacy Campaign (PLC) and empowerment of PRIs and urban/local bodies to achieve universal literacy.

The goal of the National Literacy Mission is to attain full literacy, at a sustainable threshold level of 75 per cent by 2005. The mission seeks to achieve this goal by imparting functional literacy to non-literates in the 15-35 age group. This age group has been the focus of attention because they are in the productive and reproductive period of life. The total literacy campaign offers them a second chance, in case they missed the opportunity or were denied access to mainstream formal education. The mission also takes into its fold children in the 9-14 age group, in areas not covered by non-formal education programmes to reach the benefits of literacy to out-of-school children as well. The major thrust of these programmes is not on the promotion of literacy among women, scheduled castes and tribes and backward classes.[33] Besides, the National Literacy Mission eventually aims at ensuring that the total literacy campaigns and their sequel, the post-literacy campaigns, successfully move on to continuing education, which provides life-long learning and is responsible for the creation of a learning society. In line the National Literacy Mission had scheduled the strategy to achieve the set goals:

(i) Adopted a national strategy in mission mode to take care of the need of diversity of approach and inter-regional variations.

(ii) Stress on proper environment building and active participation of the people, especially women.

(iii) In course joint efforts by Government and Non-Governmental organisations.

(iv) Preparation of local specific primers in local languages.

(v) Integrated approach to total literacy and post-literacy programmes to tackle the problem of residual illiteracy and to reduce the time gap between TLC and PLC.

(vi) Stress on vocational training of neo-literates to facilitate linking literacy with life skills.[34]

As a result of different literacy schemes/programmes run by various governmental and non-governmental agencies, the rate of literacy had increased in the country from 18.55 per cent in 1951 to 65.38 per cent in 2001. In the last five decades the literacy per cent had grown by 47.05 per cent or by an average of 9.41 per cent. The National Literacy Mission had covered 96.64 million persons under various adult literacy schemes upto December 2001. Out of 593 districts in the country, 160 districts were covered under Total Literacy Campaign, 264 under Post Literacy Campaign, including 30 under the Rural Functional Literacy Programme and 152 under the Continuing Education Programme. The NLM at the time, was engaged in the task of imparting functional literacy to persons in the 15-35 age group and had set a medium term goal for itself to achieve a sustainable threshold literacy level of 75 per cent by 2005.

Because India was lagging behind in sphere of literacy rate the Tenth Five Year Plan (2002-2007) and Eleventh Five Year Plan (2007-2012) set their targets to get the desired results through various agencies. In the field of education, the National Literacy Mission was in place with clear focus and medium term goals. In the Tenth Plan Period the target of adult education included; (i) To achieve full literacy that is a sustainable threshold of 75 per cent by 2005; (ii) To cover all left over districts by 2003-2004; (iii) To remove residual illiteracy in the existing districts by 2004-2005; (iv) To complete Post Literacy Campaign in all districts, and (v) To launch Continuing Education Programmes in 100 districts by the end of the Plan Period.[35] In fact, illiteracy is largely a problem of social groups among whom literacy rates are low and who also suffer from other handicaps which make it difficult for them to participate in the adult education programme. It is, therefore, most important to ensure greater participation of these groups in future adult education programmes. This requires a focused attention to their needs and problems and to the adoption of specific measures to suit their requirements. The focus in the Tenth Plan was to shift to residual illiteracy and cater to difficult segments of the population. This means that all the left over districts and the left over harder-to reach groups were to be targeted specifically. In the circumstances, a firm view needs to be taken on the content and the reach of the Adult Literacy Programme. Through the schemes of continuing education and vocational training to enable them to earn a living after they have achieve literacy.

In line the Eleventh Five Year Plan (2007-2012) witnessed the outlay for Adult Education, fixed at 1.5 billion dollars, which was a very significant enhancement over the combined outlays of 715 million dollars for the Eighth, Ninth and Tenth Plan periods. The 11th Five Year Plan incorporated the notion of lifelong education. This inclusion has facilitated a very significant reassessment of the programme: from the earlier sequential fragmented approach of basic literacy. The National Literacy Mission is developing a series of instruments/models to facilitate this process. However, still there are areas in the country educationally deprived and isolated where volunteers may not be available within the village for teaching because the overall levels of education within that village or area may be very low. These areas would be provided specially trained instructors from outside the community. The instructors will be specially chosen for their sensitivity to issues of gender and caste equality and their commitment to constitutional values of democracy and secularism. In India, a second chance would be provided to young adults and adolescents who lost the opportunity for formal schooling. It has been observed that wherever positive stimulation has been provided, adolescents have, undoubtedly, done us proud. The new approach in the Eleventh Plan Period ensured:

(i) That literacy is combined with skills for the enhancement of livelihood security and purchasing power provided for rural people under India's new legislation, the National Rural Employment Guarantee Act;

(ii) That literacy is synergised with the determinants of good health, namely, nutrition, sanitation, hygiene and safe drinking water under the National Rural Health Mission;

(iii) That literacy is incorporated with political empowerment, particularly of women elected to local self-governments;

(iv) That literacy reinforces and augments India's nation-wide campaign for Right to Information and that process leads to an informed citizenry, crucial to any democracy; and

(v) That literacy is intrinsically linked with universalisation of elementary education of equitable quality, so that the fresh flow of literacy is arrested.[36]

In India, the last census was conducted in the year 2011 and among other things, it showed a positive development in female literacy. More number of females have become literate compared to males in the decade 2001-2011. The largest increase in literacy rate was noticed in Dadra Nagar Haveli by 18.6 points- significant growth from 57.6 per cent in 2001 to 76.2 per cent in 2011 and Bihar by 14.8 points- from 47.0 per cent in last census in 2001 to 61.8 per cent in 2011. 'The gap between the literacy rate in urban and rural areas is steady declining in every census. In census 2011, the gap stands at 16.3 points. As per latest statistics, the literacy rate among urban population is 84.1 per cent while it is 67.8 for rural population.[37] Analysing the census data since 1961, the report suggested that the three-fourth of the population of age seven years and above is literate in the country. Four out of five males and two out of three females in the country are literate. The total population of literate females in the country was 224.2 million and in the past one decade it increased to 328 million showing a significant addition of 104.6 million literate females in the country. According to the census the total number of children is 164.5 millions about 660,000 more than the number recorded in 2001. The child sex ratio is an indicator of the further trends of sex ratio. The sex ratio in the age group 0-6 years attempts to bring out the recent changes in society in its attitude and outlook towards the girl child.[38] As a result of free education system in the villages, the literacy rate has gone up tremendously, especially among females. The following literacy rate in India from 1951 to 2011 is a full indicative of the analysis given above.

Table 1.1: Literacy Rates in India, 1951-2011

Census Year	*Persons*	*Male*	*Female*	*Male-Female gap in Literacy*
1951	18.33	27.16	8.86	18.3
1961	28.3	40.4	15.35	25.05
1971	34.45	45.96	21.97	23.98
1981	43.57	56.38	29.76	26.62
1991	52.21	64.13	39.29	24.84
2001	65.38	75.85	54.16	21.7
2011	74.4	82.14	65.46	16.68

Source: Census of India.

Literacy is an instrument of social change. It empowers individuals and communities, generates an awareness of one's own potentialities and inner strengths equipping people to combat oppression, exclusion and discrimination. Since independence literacy has been given due recognition for social and economic development. It is observed that during 1951-2011, female literacy rate has been increased by 6.3 times whereas in case of male, it is just two times. The improvement of the literacy rate among both male and female was quite considerable upto 1961 but this pace could not be maintained during 1961-1971. Still the female literacy rate is 65.46 per cent as against the male literacy rate of 82.14 and we can notice that the per cent of female literacy is 16.68 per cent less than that of male. Thus, in the context it is urgently required to take up a drastic step to bridge the gap between the two by making special arrangement to enhance the education level of female in India.

Much earlier to the present data the Government of India realised that the pace of improvement was not at the desired level and set up National Literacy Mission in 1978 to boost literacy among females and in backward areas. The Mission launched the literacy programme in all parts of the country during 1980s. Hence, results of census year 1991 showed efforts of the Mission in terms of improvement to marginal extent. The gender gap in literacy was narrowed down in 1971; it is increased in 1981 then narrowed down in 1991 to 24.84 points in 2001 to 21.59 points and to 16.68 points in 2011. Decadal difference in female literacy was constantly increasing upto 2001 followed by slight decline in 2011.

Table 1.2: Literacy Rate in India by Gender and Location

Year	*Rural and Urban*			*Rural*			*Urban*		
	Person	*Male*	*Female*	*Person*	*Male*	*Female*	*Person*	*Male*	*Female*
1951	18.33	27.16	8.86	12.10	19.02	4.87	34.59	45.06	22.33
1961	28.30	40.40	15.35	22.50	34.30	10.10	54.40	66.00	40.50
1971	34.45	45.96	21.97	27.90	48.60	15.50	60.20	69.80	48.80
1981	43.57	56.38	29.76	36.00	49.60	21.70	67.20	76.70	56.30
1991	52.21	64.13	39.29	44.69	57.87	30.62	73.10	81.09	64.05
2001	64.84	75.26	53.67	58.74	70.70	46.13	79.92	86.27	72.86
2011	72.99	80.89	64.64	67.77	77.15	57.93	84.11	88.76	79.11

Source: Census of India.

In 2011, the overall literacy rate in India is 74.04 per cent consisting of female and male literacy rate to be 65.46 per cent and 82.14 per cent respectively. Kerala being the highest literate state and Bihar the lowest. It is worth to be noted that the increase in female literacy rate has been higher than male literacy rate narrowing the gender gap particularly during the 1981 and 1991 census which can be explained through the expansion of education preferably due to the policies in favour of girls education by implementation of programmes like District Primary Education Programme (DPEP), National Literacy Mission, Adult Literacy Programme and others. Likewise the states of India have been classified into four levels of literacy development. States with a literacy rate of upto 40 per cent are said to be at a low level: those with 40.55 per cent are considered to be middle level; those having 55-70 per cent literacy are regarded as having a high level of literacy and those with 70 per cent and above are considered to be at a very high level. The literacy rates of States/Union Territories in the 1951 census were as follow:

Table 1.3: State-wise Literacy Rates-1951 Census (All India 18.33)

Sl. No.	*State/Union Territories*	*Literacy Rate in 1951*
1.	Jammu & Kashmir	-
2.	Himachal Pradesh	-
3.	Punjab	-
4.	Chandigarh	-
5.	Uttarakhand	18.93
6.	Haryana	-
7.	Delhi	Not Available
8.	Rajasthan	8.5
9.	Uttar Pradesh	12.02

(Contd...)

10.	Bihar	13.49
11.	Sikkim	-
12.	Arunachal Pradesh	NA
13.	Nagaland	10.52
14.	Manipur	12.57
15.	Mizoram	31.14
16.	Tripura	NA
17.	Meghalaya	NA
18.	Assam	18.53
19.	West Bengal	24.61
20.	Jharkhand	12.93
21.	Orissa	15.80
22.	Chhattisgarh	9.41
23.	Madhya Pradesh	13.16
24.	Gujarat	21.82
25.	Daman & Diu	-
26.	Dadra & Nagar Haveli	-
27.	Maharashtra	27.91
28.	Andhra Pradesh	-
29.	Karnataka	-
30.	Goa	23.48
31.	Lakshadweep	15.23
32.	Kerala	47.18
33.	Tamil Nadu	-
34.	Pondicherry	-
35.	Andaman & Nicobar Islands	30.30

Source: Census of India.

As a result of large scale efforts by government and non-governmental agencies especially in the last three to four decades the number of illiterates in every state has come down significantly, it however, has not achieved its target of total literacy. Like the first census of 1951, the last census held in the year 2011 also covered variations among states in sphere of literacy. In the 2011 Census, Kerala is the most literate State in India, with 93.91 per cent of literacy, followed by Lakshadweep at 92.28 per cent. Bihar is the least literate state in India, with a literacy of 63.82 per cent.[39] Every census since 1981 had indicated rising literacy in the country, but the population growth rate had been high enough that the absolute number of illiterates rose with every decade. The 2001-2011 decade is the second census period after 1991-2001 when the absolute number of Indian illiterates declined, indicating that the literacy growth rate is now outstripping the population growth rate.

Bihar is the only remain Indian state in the 2011 census where less than 65 per cent of the population was literate. It is also only one of two states where less than 75 per cent of the male population was literate and only one or two states where less than 55 per cent of the female population was literate. Six Indian States account for about 70 per cent of all illiterates in India: Uttar Pradesh, Bihar, Madhya Pradesh, Rajasthan, Andhra Pradesh and West Bengal. Slightly less than half of all Indian illiterates, 48.12 per cent are in the six Hindi-speaking states of Uttar Pradesh, Bihar, Madhya Pradesh, Rajasthan, Jharkhand and Chhattisgarh.[40] Thus, like the earlier censuses in the 2011 census there are few states at the top and bottom, most states are just above or below the national average.

Table 1.4: Rank List of States in Literacy, Census 2011[41]

Sl. No.	*State/UTs*	*Literacy*	*Male*	*Female*	*Overall increase in Per cent*
	All India	**74.4**	**82.14**	**65.46**	**8.66**
1.	Kerala	94.00	96.11	100.76	3.14
2.	Lakshadweep	91.85	95.56	82.69	5.19
3.	Mizoram	91.33	93.35	86.72	2.53
4.	Goa	88.70	92.65	82.16	6.69
5.	Tripura	87.22	91.53	78.98	14.03
6.	Daman & Diu	87.10	91.54	46.37	8.92
7.	Andaman and Nicobar Islands	86.63	90.27	71.08	5.33
8.	Delhi	86.21	90.94	68.85	4.54
9.	Chandigarh	86.05	89.99	64.81	4.11
10.	Pondicherry	85.85	91.26	84.05	4.61
11.	Himachal Pradesh	82.80	89.53	73.51	6.32
12.	Maharashtra	82.34	88.38	69.87	5.46
13.	Sikkim	81.42	86.55	66.39	12.61
14.	Tamil Nadu	80.09	86.77	73.14	6.64
15.	Nagaland	79.55	82.75	70.01	12.96
16.	Manipur	79.21	86.06	71.73	8.68
17.	Uttarakhand	78.82	87.40	67.06	7.2
18.	Gujarat	78.03	85.75	63.31	8.89
19.	West Bengal	76.26	81.69	66.57	7.62
20.	Dadra & Nagar Haveli	76.24	85.17	47.67	18.61
21.	Punjab	75.84	80.44	62.52	6.19
22.	Haryana	75.55	84.06	56.91	7.64
23.	Karnataka	75.36	82.47	66.01	8.72
24.	Meghalaya	74.43	75.95	71.88	11.87
25.	Odisha	72.87	81.59	62.46	9.79
26.	Assam	72.19	77.85	63.00	8.94
27.	Chhattisgarh	70.28	80.27	59.58	5.62
28.	Madhya Pradesh	69.32	78.73	59.49	5.58
29.	Uttar Pradesh	67.68	77.28	51.36	11.41
30.	Jammu & Kashmir	67.16	76.75	49.12	11.64

(Contd...)

31.	Andhra Pradesh	67.02	74.88	58.68	6.55
32.	Jharkhand	66.41	76.84	52.04	12.85
33.	Rajasthan	66.11	79.19	47.76	5.7
34.	Arunachal Pradesh	65.38	72.55	53.52	11.04
35.	Bihar	61.80	71.20	46.40	14.08

Source: Census of India.

India conducted in the year 2011, its 15th official census. When the British rule ended in India in the year 1947 the literacy rate was just 12 per cent. Over the years, India has changed socially, economically and globally. After the 2011 census literacy was found to be 74.04. Compared to the adult literacy rate, the youth literacy rate is about nine per cent higher. Though this seems like a very great accomplishment, it is still a matter of concern that till date so many people in India cannot even read and write. The number of children who do not get education specially in the rural areas are still high though the government has made a law that every child under the age of 14 should get free education, the problem of illiteracy is still enormous. The female literacy rate in India is also lower as many parents do not allow their female children to go to schools. Many families, especially in rural areas believe that having a male child is better than having a baby girl. Today, the female literacy levels according to the Literacy Rate 2011 census are 65.46 where the male literacy rate is over 80 per cent. The literacy rate in India has always been a matter of concern but many NGO initiatives and government advertisements, campaigns and programmes are being held to spread awareness amongst people about the importance of literacy. Also the government has made strict rules for female rights. India's literacy rate has shown significant rise in the past 10 years.

Current Status and Prospect

In the previous decades since independence in 1947 the proportion of literates among various age-groups of the population, with rural-urban and male-female classification, serve as key indicators of the socio-economic progress of the country. The survey estimates indicate that in 2007-08, less than two-thirds (64.5 per cent) of the population of all ages were literate. The overall disparity in literacy across the population is heightened by the presence of both rural-urban and male-female disparity. However, the survey results over the years also reveal the diminishing of disparities across the segments. The literacy rate for all ages among rural female, rural male, urban female and urban male populations was found to be 51 per cent, 68.4 per cent, 71.6 per cent and

82.2 per cent respectively. The corresponding rates two decades ago as estimated in NSS 42nd round (1986-87) were 24.8 per cent, 47.6 per cent, 59.1 per cent and 74.0 per cent respectively. Thus, there has been a quantum leap in the female literacy rates over the last two decades, with the rural female rate having more than doubled, although nearly half the female population of rural India still remains illiterate.

As per census, the adult literacy rate in India was 48.2 per cent in 1991 which increased to 61.0 per cent in 2001. The NSS estimates indicate that 66 per cent of the country's adult population was literate in 2007-08. Among rural females, rural males, urban females and urban males the adult literacy rates were 47.5 per cent, 71.8 per cent, 74.6 per cent and 88.7 per cent respectively. Comparison with past NSS rounds indicates that both the rural-urban and the male-female disparities have reduced over time but nevertheless remain significant.

According to the United Nations, Basic Literacy is the ability to read 40 words per minute, write 20 words per minute, and do 2-digit arithmetic. India has over 35 per cent of world's total illiterate population. India has also the largest number of illiterate people in the world. India faces major challenges, in terms of both the high number of illiterates and widespread disparities that exist between urban and rural areas. These pose as hindrances to national efforts to achieve education for all and eradicate poverty. About 80 per cent of the population lives in villages which has the largest concentration of illiterate people.[42] These areas have also maximum gender differentials. Some areas have specific differentials in attaining literacy rates, girls by and large suffered in their educational pursuits mainly due to ignorance on the parts of parents, poverty, geographical hazardous like North Eastern States of India and other hilly areas.

In this context the low literacy rate of women in India since independence has remained a matter of concern for all Indian governments. The development of any nation or region is indicated by the level of education and that too of both genders. That is why education for all is strongly recommended and focused on by our government. Although with all efforts in the sector literacy rate grew to 74.4 per cent in 2011 from meagre 12 per cent in 1947, the progress in this sphere is very slow. It has been estimated that at the current rate of progress, India will attain universal literacy only until 2060. In the census of 2011 there has been a substantial increase in the number of literate women and this gap is narrowing, it still persists. Females constitute about 50 per cent of country's human resource but lack of education snatches their chance to be a part of the progress and development of India. This means our pace of progress is less than the required pace. Even if females do not use education to work, total illiteracy has a huge negative impact on our society.

Low female literacy rate means an overall sluggish growth of India, as it impacts every arena of the development. India is struggling hard to stabilise its growing population through family planning programmes. But if females are illiterate, then this has a direct and negative impact on these initiatives. When a girl or a woman is not educated, it is not only she who suffers but the entire family has to bear the consequences of her illiteracy. It has been found that illiterate women face more hardships in life than literate ones. They have high level fertility as well as morality; they suffer from malnutrition and all other related health problems. In a survey it has been found out that infant mortality is inversely related to mother's educational level. In such a scenario not only women but their children also go through the same conditions.[43] She, who does not know the importance of education in life, does not emphasise the same for her kids. This hampers the family as well as nation's progress as a whole. Lack of education means lack of awareness. Illiterate women are not aware of their rights. They know nothing about initiatives taken by the government for their welfare. Illiterate women keep on struggling hard and bear harshness of life, family and even their husbands. The negative attitude of parents towards the girl child and her education is one of the major reasons of low female literacy rate in India.

In the circumstances the Government of India has taken several measures to improve the literacy rate in villages and towns of India. State Governments have been directed to ensure and improve literacy rate in districts and villages where people are very poor. Several states in India have executed successful programmes to boost literacy rates. Over time, a set of factors have emerged as being key to success: official will to succeed, deliberate steps to engage the community in administering the programme, adequate funding for infrastructure and teachers and provisioning additional services which are considered valuable by the community. September 8th of every year is observed as International Literacy Day. India has put its Literacy Mission high on agenda with the government initiating a number of measures including the adoption of the Right of Children to Free and Compulsory Education, to achieve higher literacy rate in the country. The measures also include the recasting of the National Literacy Mission to focus on literacy of women, reduction in the dropout rate of children at school levels and introduction of Public-Private Participation (PPP) in the school education. The Human Resource Development (HRD) Ministry has set a target of achieving 80 per cent literacy for women by the end of 11th Five Year Plan.[44] In addition, the Free and Compulsory Education for Children Bill, 2009, provides that every child in the age group of six to fourteen shall have the right to free and compulsory education in a neighbourhood school till completion of elementary education. This measure will lead to significant reform in the elementary education system besides ensuring universalisation of elementary education of satisfactory and equitable quality.

Even for the current Five Year Plan (2012-17) the Planning Commission has constituted a working group on Elementary Education and Literacy, under the Department of School Education and Literacy, Ministry of Human Resource Development. In terms of reference the working group will review the existing programmes under Elementary Education and Literacy in spheres of access, enrollment, retention, dropouts and with particular emphasis on outcomes on quality of education by gender, social and regional classifications.[45] The group was entrusted to suggest improvements in delivery mechanism for effective implementation of various schemes/programmes in the light of Right to Education (RTE) Act, passed earlier. It would also undertake an in-depth review of the implementation of MDMS, in terms of adequacy and effectiveness of the delivery systems and infrastructure and the impact of programmes on school attendance and on improvement in the nutritional status of children.[46] Among other things the terms of reference included that the working group would suggest measures for faster reduction in illiteracy in the country with emphasis on gender, regional and social dimensions and also incentivising states with higher literacy rates to achieve 100 per cent literacy during the 12th Plan Period.

Today, India is considered as one of the emerging economic superpower in the changing global scenario. But its achievements in human development indicators still lagging behind those countries against which the country's economic growth is competing, for instance, China. Also India's position in human development ranking falling behind some of the countries whose economic growth relatively poorer, for instance, Bangladesh. Besides, within the country there are huge variations with respect to economic and human development indicators across states and across regions\districts within the states. In fact, literacy and basic education are crucial for the human as well as economic development. India is one of the developing countries which are having historical trend of low levels literate rates in spite of the India's remarkable performance in terms of the child schooling especially since 1990's, its performance in literacy rate is relatively poor. It is because of the large stocks of illiterate population in the country particularly in the adult and older age groups who are ignored, so far, for the policy measures. The recent UNESCO's Education For All (EFA) Global Monitoring Report 2012 indicates that out of the total 775 million adult illiterates in the globe in 2010, 37 per cent of them are located in India; China's share is only seven per cent. Therefore, the policy concern is about the prospect of literacy and the policy intervention required for accelerating the progress in literacy rate in general and adult literacy rate in particular, in India.

Thus, the prospect of India in meeting the Education For All (EFA) goal with respect to improving literacy rates in the country would require policy attention and better initiative. Achieving the goal of 100 per cent literacy rate in the country depends on its policy intervention through adult literacy programmes, rigour in their implementation and their coverage. It is important because unless India improves its literacy levels remarkably, it will remain one of those poor performing countries at the global level in terms of Human Development Index (HDI).

3.3 Status of Indian Education System in Globalisation

Right from the well-planned and sound guru-shishya tradition days in which a student while living in his teacher's house as Brahmachari with simple living and high thinking education has never remained free from problems. The status of education and its system had been in the state of changing. Dimensions, one after the other, are necessary in this process. Today we live in an intensely interdependent world in which all the earth's peoples with their immense differences of culture and historical experience are compressed together in instant communication. The new phenomenon of globalisation has, no doubt, made education more accessible, but the biggest challenge in education is to make globalisation, work for the poor and integrate the nation's ethos without losing one's own identity.[47] Even the educational structures established in independent India are at stake and losing their content and spirit. As globalisation progresses, we will continue to see many changes in Indian educational system.

Historical Sketch

The different systems and structures remained in regular practice to impart education in ancient, medieval and modern India. It was not meant for personal welfare or individual exhalation of a chosen few but for the welfare of all, the whole world rather the whole universe and it provided educational bias for all aspects of life. It laid emphasis on firm philosophical, cultural and sociological traditions of the country which was wedded to the Indian concept of "Vasudhaiva Kutumbakam." Famous subjects taught in Vedic and later Vedic periods included grammar, mathematics, mineralogy, logic, morality-ethics, sciences in general and Brahmanvidya along with knowledge of Atman and self-realisation in particular. In the times of Mauryan Empire and Gupta the world-famous universities were established which attracted the students world over for learning various subjects of their interest. Further in the medieval period, under the Muslim rule in particular, emphasis on urban education could categorically be observed. In this phase along with promotion in urban education and establishment of several libraries and literacy organisations, foundation of primary schools for learning, reading, writing, particularly religious prayers and secondary schools for teaching advanced language skills, exegesis, prophetic traditions, law (religious) and related subjects could be seen.[48] Thus, the Indian system of education as prevailed in ancient and medieval periods was, apart from prescribed subjects, meant for moral and spiritual upliftment of the people.

In colonial India, under the British rule, education got another dimension. Thomas Babington Macaulay introduced English education in India through his famous minute of February 1835. The main purpose of this was to prepare a particular class of elite to strengthen the Rule. Further in 1844 through a Declaration knowledge of English was made compulsory for government employee. It made English medium schools very popular. Lord Macaulay clearly said that we must at present do our best to form a class, who may be interpreters between us and the millions whom we govern; a class of persons, Indians in blood and colour, but English in taste, in opinions, in morals and in intellect. At large the new education system had served a double purpose for the British rulers- they got the credit for the amelioration of the Indian society. But at the same time, through it, they devised a unique method of distribution of power, kept balance of power and prolonged their rule in India. Modern education did produce much needed man power for lower levels of administration, it however, also generated groups of visionary national leaders, intellectuals and reformers during second half of the twentieth century like Raja Ram Mohan Roy, Dadabhai Naoroji, Ferojshah Mehta, Gandhi, Jinnah, Ambedkar, Nehru and a host of others. The new intelligentsia class of India emphasised on education and science. They took upon themselves the responsibility to build a modern, open, plural, culturally rich, prosperous and powerful India out of a fragmented, poverty stricken, superstitious, weak, indifferent, backward and inward looking society.[49] Apart from all these the modern education system planned and implemented by the British had divided the whole of Indian society into many uncompromising groups. They adopted racial discrimination and many repressive policies in order to disintegrate Indian society.

Education in Independent India

With minor changes here and there, the education system basically remained the same after India's independence in 1947. Viewing the situation Karl Marx remarked that British, 'had a double mission in India, one destructive, the other regenerating; the annihilation of the old Asiatic Society and laying the material foundation of Western Society in Asia.'[50] British rulers made English language as a medium of learning and official language. There was modernisation in economic sphere. It led to political unification of the country and laid foundations for many democratic institutions. At the time the leaders of the national freedom movement were the products of formal educational institutions, usually of the Western variety. However, they made great and unprecedented efforts to make education process the basis of self-reliance in prevailing regional-national circumstances. As a result, many panels were formed to analyse the prevailing situation and requirements as per demand of time. Institutions were established for imparting education accordingly at primary, secondary and higher levels. In it besides self-sufficiency of man, stress was laid on making high moral values, humanity and universal unity the part of the process. Education acquired importance in the development process not only because it has been an important criteria for political elite recruitment and is regarded as the prime mover in economic growth but also because it is believed that without expansion in education India cannot enter into technological stage.[51] And through this all round development of personality was expected.

In this context it is necessary to note that only a sound education process can pave the way. For this a four-fold education process, which accords equal opportunity to one and all to acquire knowledge on the one hand and making them adept of bringing coordination at all levels- individual life to universal level on the other can be capable to achieve the purpose. The four-fold education process comprise :

(i) General education that is imparted at different levels according to prescribed syllabi and which ends with the earning of a degree - graduate, postgraduate, a doctoral or postdoctoral;

(ii) Physical education includes exercises to make the body and mind healthy and to fill them with agility, dynamism and constructiveness;

(iii) Moral education- to lead one to the righteousness and develop the sense of duty and responsibility on the one hand and to safeguard those values on the other, which ascertain the identity of a human being and are also essential for the proper conduction of the system- from individual life to the universal; and

(iv) Technical or practical education- to make one self-sufficient while being imparted along with the general education, which can, in fact, play a vital role in making education process meaningful and to lead one to achieve the real objective according to its meaning and also the spirit at its root.[52]

However, the educational system, implemented in India, following its independence failed to achieve the desired results. It developed a complex in the minds of many educated Indians about the primitiveness of Indian society and about efficiency of its value systems. Apathy towards their value systems had made a large number of intelligentsia alien in their own country. It had disassociated them from their own way of living, classical roots and traditional knowledge. In addition, it also erected a wide gulf between common man and educated people. Quality of education, especially in government or government-aided educational institutions has also deteriorated to a great extent. The costly nature of quality education especially in private institutions has further alienated uneducated masses from educated ones. On the other education is supposed to develop positive thinking in learners, so that they can channelise their efforts, make their thinking-base broader and flexible, increase openness to information and enhance spirit to work hard, sincerely in a responsible manner in order to attain desired goals. The education system introduced in post-1947 period miserably failed to inculcate these qualities in youth. In the circumstances based on the report and recommendations of Education Commission (1964-1966), the government under Indira Gandhi announced the first National Policy on Education in 1968 which called for a "radical restructuring" and equalise educational opportunities in order to achieve national integration and greater cultural and economic development.[53]

In line the government of Rajiv Gandhi in May 1986 introduced a new National Policy on Education and in the same year it was adopted by the Parliament. After the declaration of the new policy the Ministry of Human Resource Development, Government of India, announced the programme of Action for its implementation. It laid emphasis on vocationalisation of education as well as adult education.[54] The new policy called for special emphasis on the removal of disparities and to equalise educational opportunity, especially for Indian women, Scheduled Tribes and the Scheduled Castes communities. It called for a "child-centred approach" in primary education, and launched "Operation Blackboard" to improve primary schools nationwide. The central advisory board of education committee or Janardhana Reddy Committee reported in 1992, 'Every effort should be made to ensure that the constitutional obligation for providing free and compulsory education up to the age of 14 years becomes a reality before we enter the twenty-first century.'[55] By the time with the coming of globalisation the education system of India is undergoing constant changes. The phenomenon of globalisation is considered as the most widespread trend our country has ever witnessed. A globalised world is one in which political, economic, cultural, social and educational events become more and more multidirectional but yet interconnected.

Globalisation and Indian Educational System

The term "globalisation" means integration of economies and societies through cross-country flows of information, ideas, technologies, goods, services, capital, finance and people. Cross-border integration can have several dimensions- cultural, social, political and economic. In other words, the total education system of the world became under one roof. It requires the unification of teaching curriculum, methodology and upgradation of knowledge and system to remain in the context for efficiency and effectiveness by which transformation of knowledge in justified manner to attain the goods of life. Globalisation in historical context has a longer origin than most people are prepared to acknowledge. Two trends in the 1980s and 1990s influenced educational policies all over the world. In education the changes brought on by globalisation have been manifested through various channels and mechanisms as reforms of structure, modes of financial administration and curriculum. In several countries, they were expressed in the adoption of neo-liberal policies, they led to attempts to cut public expenditure and to maximise the economic benefits of educational spending by increasing its efficiency and directing its goals to economic rather than social or cultural ends. A positive step in this direction perhaps is the need to explore the use of innovative assessment procedures. The primary goals of authentic assessment which appear with the educational needs of contemporary globalised era are:

(i) To develop the learner's cognitive strategies for self-monitoring of progress.

(ii) To foster the learner's ability for higher-order thinking skills.

(iii) To measure the progress against learner's own development, not the norm, and

(iv) To provide more accurate evidence of a learner's abilities than traditional tests.

To the People of India in general and educated Indians in particular, globalisation seems to be rather mild and well meaning, more like an imperceptible breeze, which blows in silently, fills up the psychological atmosphere, creates a mental mood, inspires an intellectual attitude and finally settles down as a cultural climate-pervasive protein and ubiquitous.[56] Since its coming globalisation is exercising a profound influence on education and two significant developments may clearly be cited : the first is the advent of education as a business and profitable activity and secondly, the technological revolution has provided a new mode of delivering education. Especially the higher education system is increasingly becoming market-driven. Higher education has been a learning process and it enables us to become a good citizen of a civil society but this foundation of education is being seriously eroded by globalisation and the market demand is influencing what is taught and researched in universities.[57] As a result of privatisation the system of education has widely proliferated and become profit-oriented that is sharpening the gap between the rich and the poor in terms of access to quality education in our society. In India, students and their abilities are marred due to various situations like unavailability of multi-cultural and multi-disciplinary institutes, lack of research-based tutoring and high fee structure. The well-off strata choose amongst the top notch options and the middle level group is left with fewer institutes, which are screened on different criteria.

In response to the globalisation process the Government of India has viewed decentralisation as a way to increase efficiency by giving more responsibility to local level functionaries, which in turn, is expected to increase motivation and accountability. And as a part of liberalisation policy, it has been suggested that education should be progressively privatised and that access to it should be made subject to payment of appropriate prices. The government, therefore, encourages the establishment of a larger number of private institutions and even private universities are being encouraged. Simultaneously mechanism to cater to the needs of those who cannot afford payment of high fees is also being evolved. But despite this there is no end of the fear that the process of globalisation policy may apparently shape the perspective of educational reforms in favour of those who have already benefitted from the system as they are in a position to influence policy is haunting those who are not in a position to influence policy.

In sphere of higher education India is the third-largest higher education system, only behind the US and China producing almost 2.5 million graduates every year. Hence there are enormous opportunities for professionals trained in Indian universities and to pursue their career in teaching and research also, in addition to opportunities available in industries and business. At present there are 425 universities and university-level institutions in India apart from around 20,000 colleges including 1,800 women college. The total enrollment of students in universities and colleges is approximately 12 million while the number of teachers is 4.5 lakh.[58] Despite the large educational infrastructure, the efforts to privatise higher education in India by encouraging private agencies to set up institutions of higher learning have enjoyed limited success in general education. Also, the quality of higher education in India is poor and is facing enormous challenges in today's global world.

There is no doubt in the fact that globalisation has created unprecedented new opportunities for sustainable development and poverty reduction, simultaneously it has posed great threats to employment and livelihoods, to the environment and to human society in general. In particular, is the possibility of erosion of national values by imbibing alien culture. In India, during this period of globalisation, much of the contemporary thought has gone into the issues of programmed learning, multi-media teaching, macro-micro teaching, distance learning and other problems relating to curriculum. No subject has been so much neglected as the development of humanistic values, creativity, cultural, moral, emotional and spiritual dimensions of teaching-learning process. The threat is of the erosion of rich and old culture of human values. So, globalisation has transformed education and will continue to do so, leaving us with a future that is more unpredictable than ever.

In the era of globalisation to achieve peace and happiness, the interests of both the individual and the society should be taken into account. One cannot conceive of a society without individuals and the individual has no value without society. A truly composite cultural education will have to address simultaneously the requirements of global and national integration and the specific needs of particular culturally distinct communities, both in rural and urban settings. Globalisation and spirituality together can bring peace and integrity to our life.

References

1. V.R. Taneja, *Educational Thought and Practice* (Jallundhar: University Publishers, 1965), p. 308.
2. Ravindra Kumar, 'Education : Meaning, Purpose, Problems and Expectations,' *South Asia Politics*, Vol. II, No. 5, September 2012 (New Delhi: 2012), p. 39.
3. *Ibid.*, pp. 39-40.
4. *Harijan*, 19.1.1947, p. 494.
5. *Harijan*, 9.11.1947, p. 401.
6. Shant Bala, 'Gandhian Conception of Education-Its Relevance in Present Times,' *The Indian Journal of Political Science*, Vol. LXVI, No. 3, September 2005 (Meerut: 2005), p. 532.
7. *Educational Reconstruction* (2nd edition), Sevagram (Wardha).
8. Shant Bala, 'Gandhian Conception of Education-Its Relevance in Present Times,' pp. 535-41.
9. Harold Z. Hodgkinson, *Education in Social and Cultural Perspectives* (Prentice Hall, Englewood Criffs, 1962), p. 129.
10. Louis Malassis, 'Education and Agricultural Development,' *International Social Science Journal*, 21.2 (1969), p. 250.
11. Manish Didwania and Rajesh Sharma, 'The Role of Privatisation in Higher Education in India', *South Asia Politics*, Vol. 8, No. 10, February 2010 (New Delhi: 2010), p. 40.
12. Joseph Fischer, 'Indonesia' in James S. Coleman (ed.), *Education and Political Development* (Princeton: Princeton University Press, 1965), p. 37.

13. V.R. Taneja, *Educational Thoughts and Practice*, p. 37.
14. M.S.A. Rao, 'Education, Social Stratification and Mobility' *Sociology of Education in India* (New Delhi: NCERT).
15. Kapil Deo Singh, 'Education and Social Change' in Bishwanath Prasad, Sakendra Prasad Singh, (eds.), *Aspects of Education and Politics in India* (Patna: Swarna Prakashan), pp. 214-15.
16. David Barton, *Literacy: An Introduction to the Ecology of Written Language*, 2nd edition (Wiley Blackwell: 2006).
17. Paulo Freire, *Education for Critical Consciousness* (Sheed & Ward, 1974).
18. *United Nations Educational Scientific and Cultural Organisation* (UNESCO) *Conference* on adult education and literacy, held in Bangkok, 8-11 September 2003.
19. *UNESCO*, Literacy: Multiple Meaning and Dimensions, education sector position paper, pp. 2-3.
20. Pat Campbell (editor), *Measures of Success: Assessment and Accountability in Adult Basic Education* (Edmonton: Grass Roots Press, 2007), pp. 5-6.
21. *Canadian Council on Learning*, 'State of Learning in Canada: No Time for Complacency' (Ottawa: January 2007), p. 86.
22. Statistics Canada and Organisation for Economic Cooperation and Development (OECD), *Literacy Skills for the Knowledge Society: Further Results of the International Adult Literacy Survey* (Ottawa and Paris: 1997), p. 62.
23. Lars Osberg, 'Schooling, Literacy and Individual Earnings, [Ottawa: Statistics Canada and Human Resource Development Canada (HRDC)], June 2000, Catalogue no. 89-552-MIE, No. 7.
24. Daniel Boothby, 'International Adult Literacy Survey: Literacy Skills, Occupational Assignment and the Returns to Over and Under Education' [Ottawa: Statistics Canada and Human Resource Development Canada (HRDC)], January 2002, Catalogue no. 89-552-MPE, No. 9.
25. *Ibid.*, Statistics Canada and Organisation for Economic Cooperation and Development (OECD), 1997, p. 57.
26. *The Hindu*, 4 April 2011.
27. *Ibid.*
28. *Report of the Education Commission 1964-66*, p.108.
29. *Ibid.*
30. V.P. Matheswaran and R. Daphne, 'Policies Governing Adult and Continuing Education in Five Year Plans: An Overview,' *Indian Journal of Adult Education*, Special Issue, April-June 2011.
31. *Ibid.*
32. *Ibid.*
33. As estimated by *UNESCO Institute for Statistics*, July 2002, available at education@accu.or.jp

34. *Ibid.*
35. V.P. Matheswaran and R. Daphne, 'Policies Governing Adult and Continuing Education in Five Year Plans: An Overview'.
36. *Ibid.*
37. *The New Indian Express*, 1 May 2013.
38. *Ibid.*
39. Available at http://censusindia.gov.in/2011.
40. 'Literacy Rate on the Rise, 11th Plan Targets 80%.' *The India Post*, 4 September 2008.
41. Literacy rank of States in India, available at www.census2011.co.in/literacy.php
42. *The Vision*, 8 March 2014, available at www.drishtiias.com/upsc-current.affairs
43. *Ibid.*
44. 'India and Its Literacy Mission', *Ministry of Human Resource Development* 7 September 2009 (New Delhi: Press Information Bureau, Government of India, 2009).
45. For detail see *Planning Commission's Order*, dated 8 April 2011, p. 6.
46. *Ibid.*
47. Anisha Tamang, 'Globalisation and Indian Educational System', *South Asia Politics*, Vol.11, No. 6, October 2012 (New Delhi:2012), p. 43.
48. Rabindra Kumar, 'Education: Meaning, Purpose, Problems and Expectations,' in *Ibid*, Vol.11, No. 5, September 2012 (New Delhi:2012), pp. 40-41.
49. *Ibid.*, pp. 40-41.
50. P.R. Dutt, *India Today*, p. 476.
51. Braj Kishor Jha, 'Growth of Education and Political Development in India,' in Bishwanath Prasad, Sakendra Prasad Singh (eds.), *Aspects of Education and Politics in India.*
52. Rabindra Kumar, 'Education: Meaning, Purpose, Problems and Expectations,' p. 42.
53. *National Informatics Centre*, pp. 38-45.
54. Shant Bala, 'Gandhian Conception of Education-Its Relevance in Present Times'.
55. Extract from the *Report of Central Advisory Board of Education* or Janardhana Reddy Committee (1992), p. 398.
56. Anisha Tamang, 'Globalisation and Indian Educational System,' p. 44.
57. *The Times of India*, 25 February 2002.
58. Manish Didwania and Rajesh Sharma, 'The Role of Privatisation in Higher Education in India,' *South Asia Politics*, Vol. 8, No. 10, February 2010 (New Delhi: 2010), pp. 40-41.

Chapter - 4

Empowerment of Women: Scheme, Strategy and Status

4.1 Empowerment of Women in India

Respect for women is a necessary trait of a rising nation. It equally applies to the women in ancient India when they were not a meek, shy and weak creature but were bold, free and strong. In the pre-Aryan period, an average Indian women continued to lead a happy and contended life. In later years, Aryans changed from a pastoral people to agriculturists and they became conscious of preserving the purity of their race which made them the victim of growing social evils. The position of women in Indian society deteriorated further by the laws of Manu but improved a little as a result of the advent of Islam because it granted much stronger legal position. Europeans in general and Christians Missionaries in particular ushered India in an entirely new phase of women emancipation and gave birth to a powerful reformist movement led by Raja Ram Mohan Roy, justice Ranade and Swami Dayanand Saraswati and they all agreed that only women's education can solve the problems of Indian women.

Since Independence, there has been a dramatic change in the legal, political, educational and social status of women. Earlier the improvement of the position of women had been at the heart of the social reform movements from the first quarter of the nineteenth century. The Constitution of India ensures gender equality in its preamble as fundamental right with a view to remove black holes of ignorance and orthodoxy. It also undertook the task of modifying/enacting several laws regarding personal laws of Hindus the Special Marriage Act, Hindu Marriage Act, women labour family planning and educational opportunities for women.

In late eighties and early nineties, due to several constraints the phase of Liberalisation and Globalisation entered in economic affairs of which India became an integral part. In the changed situation the legal-judicial system of India became more responsive rather sensitive to women's needs especially in sphere of empowerment. Now the Government of India has drawn up a National Policy for the Empowerment of Women which outlined the legal, institutional and programmatic schemes. Lately, 2001 was observed as Women Empowerment Year to create large scale awareness with the active participation of women themselves. Apart from the constitutional guarantee, several schemes and programmes have been planned and executed from time to time to achieve the goal of empowerment and meet the challenges of twenty first century.

Position of Women

Empowerment of women in Indian context primarily means that they should be able to turn aspirations into policy and law. They should have control over their lives and livelihood decisions. They should also be able to pursue self-realisation and self-assertion, and live informed, rational, self-interested lives as those in the upper reaches of Indian society.[1] In today's world India occupies a strategic position in Asia being the largest in South Asian countries with a population of over one billion. Women constitute a population of 495.74 million, with 360.52 million in rural areas and 135.22 million in the urban areas. The human development status of women shows wide interstate and intrastate variations, there has been a systematic decline in women's status despite recent advances in their education and economic status. It is also in contrast with the position that women enjoyed in different phases of Indian history.

The worth of a civilisation can be judged from the position that it gives to women. A survey of Indian social history reveals the fact that women enjoyed a high dignity and freedom in society. She was adored by parents, cherished by husband and revered by children. In the Rigveda we read the existence of the son and the daughter side by side, the former taking to the profession of the father while the latter inheriting the glory and honour of her mother. The birth of a daughter was endorsed with acclamation in the period of the Upanisads for which certain rituals were prescribed to be performed by the man who wants a learned daughter to be born.[2] At that time Indian society was perhaps matriarchal and men and women enjoyed equal rights. Even in the initial phase of Aryan period the importance of women as mother or wife was recognised not as an auxiliary in the management of the household but the very centre of the domestic world and empress in her home. The husband identified her with his very home, his abiding hearth. A wife, says the great seer Visvamitra, "is home and dwelling. She is auspicious, the most auspicious who brings blessings and prosperity of her husband's household."[3] Thus, she enjoyed a high dignity and freedom in society especially in comparison to Spartan and Athenian position of women where they were treated merely as vegetables. Even in that period the social adjustment of the sex was so perfect that we find no complaint on the part of the women against the authority of the man.

However, at the close of the Rigvedic period various social restrictions were imposed on the freedom of women. This process started when Sakas, Abhiras, Hunas and others, who were also called the non-Aryans, raided the rich plains of India and were lost in the Aryan social fabric. The newcomers were enveloped in the Aryan folds and absorbed in the Indian social matrix. In that kind of situation the Aryans strove and struggled to devise means to keep their blood pure and then ran after an unreasonable mirage. They prescribed rules for early marriages and banned freedom of women in deed, speech and even thought. Further women's position in society was also weakened by the laws of Manu and its fundamental assumption that women are completely dependent on men. 'From the cradle to the grave, a woman is dependent on the male, in the childhood on her father, in youth on her husband, in old age on her son.' Manu advocated that married woman could own no property, "their wealth belongs to those whom they belonged."[4] His philosophy regarding women forced them to accept their lot with humility.

Around 1000 A.D. Muslims began invading India and temporary hopes were raised because Islam had granted much stronger legal position than that prevalent in India that time. But unfortunately all that the upper society borrowed from the Muslims was the system of Purdah in order to save Hinduism from the yoke of Islam. The social taboos were tightened and this further deteriorated the position of women. During the Muslim period of history women were deprived of their rights of equality with men. They were compelled to keep themselves within the four walls of their houses with a long veil on their faces. It was natural of the Muslim subjugation of India that woman was relegated to a plaything of man, an ornament to decorate the drawing room. The women members, such as Jodhabai, Nur Jahan and Mumtaz Mahal of the royal household who played an undeniable role in making the majesty can hardly be considered as representatives of the typical Indian women - Hindu or Muslim.[5] An important point in this regard is that this inferior position of women was largely confined to the North, particularly among the upper urban classes. In the South, society was more settled because it was not much influenced by the changes that took place in the North. At large both Muslim and Hindu women in this period remain restricted to the private domain and were expected to be in Purdah or behind a veil.

Emancipation of women in India witnessed a drastic change with the advent of Europeans, especially the Christian Missionaries, who undertook the work of social reforms as an essential part of their programme. Conversions made on behalf of these missionaries invited a criticism and reaction among the Hindus. Religious Hindus and social reformers sprang into leadership to take the initiative in such matters. In the Pre-British Indian society, except in the early periods of the Vedic times, woman was assigned a position subordinate to man. Law and religion did not recognise the equality and equal rights of man and woman. Society permitted man to have rights and freedoms from which woman was excluded. Emergence of the new economic environment, the establishment of the new political system and the spread of modern Western education found expression in the movements initiated in order to liberalise the women of India.[6]

In later years a powerful reformist movement led by Raja Ram Mohan Roy in Bengal, Justice Ranade in Bombay and Swami Dayanand Saraswati in Punjab sprang up. They denounced the disabilities that handicapped women's social advancement and tried to abolish practices such as Sati, early marriage etc, through legal means. With the help of Lord William Bentick in 1829 the system of Sati was abolished followed by the legalisation of the remarriage of widows in 1856. The thought that women's education was the only means to solve all the problems took a definite shape. This was championed and advocated by Swami Vivekanand and Ishwar Chandra Vidyasagar in Bengal that paved the way for the furtherance of women's education leading to the formation of Indian Federation of University Women and its seven branches in the state. Emancipation and empowerment of women in India was made a prime objective of the national movement which was being fought under the leadership of Mahatma Gandhi. The reformist and educationist movement continuing in India and as a result of the British influence on Indian culture and civilisation the position of women had, once again, undergone a change. They actively participated in the national movement and their warm patriotism and unabashed enthusiasm won for them the love and respect of their fellow countrymen who, after independence, became founding fathers of Indian constitution.

Women and Indian Constitution

As woman is the pivot of the family, programmes for women's welfare assume primary importance. Women in general can take advantage of different welfare schemes but there are certain categories which call for special care, women suffering from one disability or another, widows with or without children, women who had an unhappy domestic life, deserted, destitute or exploited women.[7] After Independence Dr B.R. Ambedkar has tried to remove the barriers in the way of advancement of women in India. The first natural attention in this regard was given to securing legal and constitutional rights. The Constitution of India was ahead of its time, not only by the standards of the developing nations but also of many developed countries, in removing every discrimination against women in the legal and public domain of the Republic. It provided complete equality to women and fulfilled the promise made many years ago by the national movement: women got the vote, along with men, without any qualification of education or property or income. A right for which women suffragettes fought long and hard in many western countries was won at one stroke by Indian women.

The principle of equality of women with men enshrined in the Indian Constitution in its Preamble, Fundamental Rights, Fundamental Duties and Directive Principles. Under the provisions the state is also allowed to adopt measures of positive discrimination in favour of women. For instance, Article 14 conferred equal rights and opportunities on men and women in the political, economic and social spheres, Article 15 prohibited discrimination against any citizen on the grounds of sex and Article 15 (3) empowered the State to make affirmative discrimination in favour of women and children. Likewise Article 39 enjoyed upon the State to provide equal means of livelihood and equal pay for equal work and Article 42 directed the State to make provisions for ensuring just and humane conditions of work and also for maternity relief. Article 51(e) imposed a fundamental duty on every citizen to renounce the practices derogatory to the dignity of women.

In the initial phase of independence, the most important step in the direction of women's development was the codification of Hindu personal laws. The government realised that any reform would be possible only by enacting laws. Earlier in 1941 a committee under the Chairmanship of B.N. Rau, the constitutional expert who prepared the first draft of the Constitution of India, had already gone into the matter and submitted a draft code in 1944. Another committee, chaired by B.R. Ambedkar, the law minister, after independence submitted a bill which raised the age of consent and marriage, upheld monogamy, gave women the right to divorce, maintenance and inheritance and treated dowry as stridhan, or women's property. It was because of the stiff opposition of the bill from conservative sections of society including President Rajendra Prasad, sections of the bill were passed as four separate acts: The Hindu Marriage Act, the Hindu Succession Act, the Hindu Minority and Guardianship Act and the Hindu Adoption and Maintenance Act. The enacting of legal rights to Hindu women was, although, not sufficient but it was a big step forward.[8] Thus, from the beginning the Government of India tried to give equal status and opportunities of life to women through laws.

The planning strategy of the Government of India regarding women has evolved from welfare to development to empowerment. The approach in the First Five Year Plan (1951-1956) was to provide adequate services to promote the welfare schemes of women so that they can play their legitimate role in the family and the community. In this Plan Period the Central Social Welfare Board (CSWB) was set up in 1953 to promote voluntary organisations at various levels, especially at the grassroots, to take up welfare related activities for women. The Second, Third, Fourth and Fifth Plans continued the same approach for the welfare of women. The end of the Fourth Plan witnessed the release of the monumental report of Committee on Status of Women in India entitled "Towards Equality." It revealed that the dynamics of development had adversely affected a large section of women and created new imbalances and disparities. In 1976, a Women's Welfare and Development Bureau was set up under the Ministry of Social Welfare to initiate necessary policies, programmes and measures for women.

The Sixth Plan (1980-85), for the first time, recognised women as participants of development and not merely as objects of welfare. It adopted a multi-disciplinary approach with a special thrust on the three core sectors of health, education and employment. In 1982, a Women's Employment Programme was introduced with assistance from

Norwegian Development Agency (NORDA). The theme of Sixth Plan continued in the Seventh Plan (1985-90) and stressed on generation of both skilled and unskilled employment of women through proper education and vocational training. In this plan period two new schemes - Support to Training and Employment (STEP) and Awareness Generation Programme for Rural and Poor Women (AGP) were introduced.[9] Apart from this several landmark reports namely, Sharam Shakti, the Report of the National Commission on Self-Employed Women and Women in Informal Sector, National Perspective Plan on Women (1988-2000) and SAARC guidebook on Women in Development were prepared. These all paved the way for empowerment of women in India, especially in this age of globalisation.

Globalisation and Indian Women

The concept of global village given by Marshall Mcluhan in the sixties is realising today. There are several things in it - an ideal, a destination to be reached and a conceptualisation of the ongoing transformation in the community. The earth in which we live is an integrated, interpenetrated and interconnected unit. The advances of communications and information technology have made the global village a virtual reality and this has paved the way for evolving frameworks of global governance.[10] In this context Globalisation, Liberalisation and Privatisation is gaining growing attention as a strategy for survival, competition and growth. The exploitation of resources to the detriment of common good has created many imbalances and there is growing awareness to the issues related to sustainable development. In addition to this a new horizon of peace and co-operation of global level opened with the end of cold war that resulted in international changes and diminished competition between the super- powers. Earlier excessive military expenditures, including global military expenditures and arms trade or trafficking and investments for arms production and acquisition have reduced the resources available for social development. In this phase, in many developing countries structural adjustment programmes have also been poorly designed and implemented. They have not been designed to minimise their negative effects on vulnerable and disadvantaged groups or on women, nor have they been designed to assure positive effects on those groups by preventing their marginalisation in economic and social activities.[11]

With a view to empower the marginalised groups of society and especially the women, in the early nineties the Government of India launched the liberalisation of its economy and expanded social structures to ensure the participation of women in national development. Immediately on assuming office in June 1991 the Government of Narasimha Rao began to unfold new policies in July whose major signpost are Stabilisation, Globalisation or linking up Indian economy with the economies of the world. According to government, it was necessary to generate confidence among the countries of the world in India's economic development and to restore its credit worthiness in the world.[12] The reform package covers a broad spectrum and includes fiscal correction, exchange rate adjustment, monetary targeting with inflation control, a high degree of economic liberalisation and financial sector reforms.[13] The rapid process of change and adjustments in all sectors has also led to increase unemployment and underemployment, with particular impact on women. Recent international economic developments have had in many cases a disproportionate impact on women and children, the majority of whom live in developing countries.

Women play a critical role in the family. The family is the basic unit of society and as such should be strengthened. The world public opinion alongwith the world body the UN have been active in this field and the exhaustive efforts started in 1975. Since then the knowledge of the status of women and men, respectively, has increased and is contributing to further actions aimed at promoting equality between women and men. The year was also proclaimed as the 'International Women's Year' by the United Nations General Assembly. The United Nations Decade for Women (1976-1985) was a world-wide effort to examine the status and rights of women and to bring women into decision-making at all levels. In 1985, a World Conference was held to review and appraise the achievements of the United Nations Decade for Women and Equality. Development and Peace was adopted at the Nairobi Forward-Looking Strategies for the Advancement of Women to be implemented by the year 2000.

In this circumstances the Government of India in the early nineties decided to bring a policy about the advancement, development and empowerment of women. It was aimed to create an environment through positive economic and social policies for full development of women to enable them to realise their full potential. As a positive development the National Commission for Women was set up by an Act of parliament in

1990 to safeguard the rights and legal entitlements of women. Recognising the role and contribution of women in development, the Eighth Plan (1990-95) adopted the strategy to ensure that benefits of development from different sectors do not bypass women and special programmes are implemented to complement the general development plans. Two new schemes for Women- Mahila Samridhi Yojana and Indira Mahila Yojana were introduced during this plan period and a National Commission for Women and National Credit and Fund for Women known as Rashtriya Mahila Kosh was set up.

However, the major breakthrough of the Plan Period was the passing of 73rd and 74th Constitutional Amendment Act which Guarantee that all local elected bodies reserve one-third of their seats for women. Passed in 1993 it laid a strong foundation for their participation in decision-making at the local levels. Since the creation of the quota system, the local women- the vast majority of them illiterate and poor- have come to occupy as much as 43 per cent of seats, spurring the election of increasing numbers of women at the district, provincial and national levels. Their mass participation through Panchayati Raj Institutions (PRI) have brought about significant changes in the lives of women who have become empowered, and have gained self-confidence, political awareness and affirmation of their own identity.

In continuation the Ninth Plan 1997-2002 made two significant changes in conceptual strategy for women. First, 'Empowerment of Women' became one of the nine primary objectives of the plan and the approach was to create an enabling environment where women can freely exercise their rights both within and outside home. Secondly, it attempted the convergence of existing services, resource, infrastructure and man-power available in both women-specific and women-related sectors. Likewise the Tenth Five Year Plan (2002-2007) constituted three working Groups: (a) Working Group on Empowerment of Women, (b) Working Group on Child Development and (c) Working Group of Improving Nutritional Status of Population with Special Focus on Vulnerable Groups. Secretaries of the respective departments would be Chairperson and Joint Secretaries would be Convenors of the Groups.[14] Under the Working Groups on Empowerment two sub-groups were constituted, on focusing on Social Empowerment of Women and the other on Economic Empowerment of Women.

Alike globalisation, empowerment of women is a multidimensional concept. The world opinion is active enough in this regard and the

Government of India, in cooperation with the state governments and different non-governmental organisations is doing its level best to empower the women in India.

4.2 Human Rights of Women and Globalisation

In larger context human rights refer to those inalienable rights that a person is entitled to enjoy irrespective of his/her nationality, caste, creed, sex, colour, religion, income or any other socio-economic divisive category. Human rights are those entitlements which an individual own just because of his/her existence as a human being. The theoretical roots of human rights can be traced back to the histories of ancient and medieval times in India as well as in the Western liberal and humanitarian philosophy. Both these roots have a considerable appeal of promoting human dignity. Human life is given a distinctive weight over other animals in most societies precisely because we are capable of cultivating the quality of our lives. Several strong arguments have been given in favour of protecting and promoting human dignity. They are not requisites for health but to those things needed for a life of dignity - a life that cannot be enjoyed without these rights.

The present status of women in society is a challenge for human rights. Women form nearly half of the human capital in the country but in terms of gender equality and gender equity, they remain the most deprived and long neglected segment of society, despite the constitutional guarantee for equal rights and privileges for men and women. In modern times all are given liberties and rights, freedom of expression as well as right to get education. Despite this women are fighting for crisis such as dowry, female infanticide, sex selective abortion, health, poverty, education, sexual harassment, domestic violence, etc.

In this era of globalisation the growing attention is considered as a strategy for survival, competition and growth. As a result of this a new economic environment has been created wherein only self-reliant and self-regulated economic enterprises, including women enterprises will survive. In the situation in many developing countries structural adjustment programmes have been poorly designed and implemented and they are unable to meet negative effects of globalisation. Empowerment of women is the theme of the time and the general trend is towards improvement, however the achievements have still fallen short of expectations, particularly in developing countries like India.

Theoretical Proposition and Conception

Today human rights are universally accepted as those conditions of social life which allow the full development of human personality. They refer to a wide continuum of values that are universal in character and in some sense equally claimed for all human beings. We claim for these rights all over the world simply by being human. The term 'human' is itself a vague since the life cycle of a human being ranges from conception to death and decay. Even before conception, sperm and eggs exist that contain human genetic material but decision is made easily on the issue because they are human cells and not human beings. In between the discussions and controversies various groups hold the view that there is some special quality of human life that provides a basis for possessing rights; when that quality is acquired, so are rights.[15] This approach is favoured by many since it allows for the distinction between humans and other animals. Human rights are rights particularly to human beings, thus the basis of the claim to rights should be something that differentiates humans from other animals.

The modern concept and interpretations human rights have its bases in ancient Indian times as well as in Western countries of early history when well-known human rights movements started with ancient religions and societies and showed the evolution of concepts and institutions of human rights across civilisations. In developing the basic notion of human right we cannot deny the role played by the influence of ancient Indian Dharma with its universalistic and humanistic approach. In general ancient Indian society was peaceful within the moral codes of conduct of the society provided by religion which in due course of time hegemo-nised all sections of the society within its rule of the game.[16] Ancient thinkers like Manu and Kautilya all have tried to protect the rights and dignity of individuals from the whims and tyranny of the rulers. This was done primarily by imposing some moral restrictions upon the activities of the rulers and thereby providing some kind of shield to the rights of the individuals.

Addition and enhancement of human rights aspects continued in mediaeval and British period. In medieval period the three basic elements of the ancient Indian tradition; universalism and humanism in its philosophical thought, the struggle against caste discrimination and religious tolerance received a fresh relevance and impetus from Islam. King Akbar's great regard for rights, justice and secularism could be cited as an example. Religious movements like Bhakti and Sufi made remarkable contributions towards eliminating the irreligious practices of the contemporary society. These movements tried to revive the ancient humanist tradition and preached the sacred principles of humanism and universalism.[17] With the coming of Britishers, English was introduced in education and some Indian leaders including Raja Ram Mohan Roy, being influenced, started a movement for Renaissance and Reformation. They demanded the abolition of Sati system, female infanticide, caste system and also initiated a movement for widow remarriage and female education. It resulted in the enactment of several humanitarian legislations in subsequent years.

Likewise the Western philosophical tradition manifests, from the ancient times, the stories of an inevitable conflict between the concept of individual rights and state authority. In the writings of great Greek individual's right to resistance against sponsored terror was highly glorified. In the later periods the theme of humanity was carried out in the classical philosophy of Plato and Aristotle who attempted to protect the citizens and non-citizens under a scheme of justice. Another Roman thinker Cicero first gave a philosophical foundation to the concept of rights and its association with the idea of natural law. The concept of natural right as a precondition for human development had received further staunch support in the works of Hobbes, Locke and Rousseau, who believed that the state as an institution is the most effective instrument for protecting the rights of the individual against the oppression of the rulers.[18] The concept of human rights found its further elaboration and promotion in the writings of Immanuel Kant (1724-1804), Thomas Paine (1737-1809), Jeremy Bentham (1748-1832) and Karl Mark (1818-1883), the revolutionary thinkers of the twentieth century.

However, in the evolution of modern human rights the ideas of liberal humanism and universalism played a significant role. For instance, John Rawls (1921-2002), who although did not assign the label of universalism to the concept of human rights, but attached a special status to it. 'These rights do not depend on any particular comprehensive moral doctrine or philosophical conception of human nature...but basic human rights express a minimum standard of well-ordered political institutions for all peoples who belong, as members of good standing, to just political society of peoples.[19] He also made the human rights distinct from the constitutional rights, or the rights of democratic citizenship, or from other kinds of rights that belong to certain kinds of political institutions, both individual and associations. Jurgen Habermas, another important contributor, called it a part of the post-modern agenda and believed that human rights and the principle of popular sovereignty constitute the sole idea that can justify modern laws.[20] In today's society, human rights have become the necessary condition of a regime's legitimacy and of the decency of its legal order.

In the phase of globalisation, privatisation and liberalisation, the concept of human rights has been defined and analysed by Amartya Sen, the philosopher-economist and Tony Evans, the noted theorist of international politics. Dr Sen has viewed rights usually in terms of political power and according to him the invoking of human rights tends to come mostly from those who are concerned with changing the world, rather than interpreting it. In the final analysis he concludes that human rights may or may not be reflected in a legal framework through specific human rights legislation, but there are also other ways of implementing human rights that includes, public recognition, agitation and monitoring.[21] While Tony Evans linked the concept of human rights and its universalisation aspect with the issue of power and hegemony.[22] For him, it is an instrument for empowering people in their fight against persecution and injustice. Evan's understanding of hegemony provides a new insight into the post-war politics of rights, particularly in the context of the emerging role of US as the leader of human rights.

The theoretical discussions held so far on the human rights, predominantly reflect that it is not citizens rights, but often a thinking about an abstract universal community and imposing political structures, conceptions of individual and peculiar relationships between individual and community that are not generally shared.[23] In the present there are three categorisation of right based on three major generations of the concept. The first generation of rights refers to the traditional or classical notion of rights denoting different political and civil rights. The second generation of rights mainly includes different types of socio-economic rights, while the third generation of rights emerges in course of the worldwide anti-imperial movement in different parts of the world and includes cultural rights, environmental rights, right to development, minority rights, etc. All these rights are essential not only because of our existence, as human being but these are needed also to make each one of us an ideal human being.

Context of Indian Women

The development of a society is measured not only in terms of its material resources, economic growth and wealth creation but also in terms of the opportunities and capabilities of its people to explore the material resources and to contribute equally in the growth of their society. Such a process becomes unjust and discriminatory if most women are excluded from its benefits.[24] Respect for women is a necessary trait of a rising nation. It equally applies to the women in ancient India when they were not a meek, shy and weak creature but were bold, free and strong. In the pre-Aryan period, an average Indian women continued to lead a happy and contended life. In later years, Aryans changed from a pastoral people to agriculturists and they became conscious of preserving the purity of their race which made them a victim of growing social evils.[25] The position of women in Indian society deteriorated further by the laws of Manu but improved a little as a result of the advent of Islam because it granted much stronger legal position. Europeans in general and Christians Missionaries in particular ushered India in an entirely new phase of women emancipation and gave birth to a powerful reforming movement.

The position of Indian women also deteriorated beyond imagination due to inequality inherent in gender. Gender is a basic organising principle of society that shapes how people have to think about ourselves. While gender concerns differ, it also involves hierarchy, because it affects the opportunities and constraints we face throughout our lives.[26] Females and males do differ biologically of course, but the physical activities of men and women are alike than we may think. In the social structure we can notice that men dominate in most of the categories of job and distribution of wealth. In any field, the greater the income and prestige associated with a job, more likely it is held by a man. But researches held so far show no overall differences in intelligence between males and females as Mahatma Gandhi once declared, 'Woman is the champion of man, gifted with equal mental capacities. She has a right to participate in every minute detail of the activities of man and she has an equal right of freedom and liberty as him. She is entitled to a supreme place in her own sphere of activity as man is in his.[27] There has been a dramatic change regarding the status of women in society and the earlier position has been totally transformed in the twentieth century where the female sex is in no way inferior to man.

The Constitution of independent India laid equal emphasis on human development and development of women, in particular. Generally there are three approaches used to measure the well being of the people as far as human development is concerned. The first one is, physical quality of life index which contains three indicators - adult literacy rate, infant mortality and life expectancy. The second approach is basic needs approach which argues that the basic needs of adequate nutrition, primary education, health, sanitation, water supply and housing available to the poorest to a reasonable extent. The third approach is human development index-most widely used index.[28] With a view to enshrine gender equality several provisions of the Constitution of India guaranteed equality before law and equal protection of law through Article 14. Articles 23, 42, 51A, 29 and 30 establish provisions for the development of women. On the other the Government of India has made concerted efforts towards removing various gender biases to ensure that women enjoy equal status with men in real sense. The major enactments passed by the government in this respect are Dowry Prohibition Act (1961), Medical Termination of Pregnancy Act (1971), Child Marriage Restraint Act (1976), Equal Remuneration Act (1976), and the 73rd and 74th amendments of the Constitution passed in 1992 and ratified in 1993.[29] The enactment which provided for 33 per cent reservation for women in local self-governing bodies is an important achievement in empowering women.

Thus, in the post-Independence period, the Indian women were given equal status with men by the Indian Constitution and various provisions have been made to protect the interests of the female population. Right from the days of First Five Year Plan (1951-56), adequate services were included to promote the welfare schemes of women so that they can play their legitimate role in the family and the community. The Second, Third, Fourth and Fifth plans continued the same approach for the welfare of women. In 1976, a Women's Welfare and Development Bureau was set up under the Ministry of Social Welfare to initiate necessary policies, programmes and measures for women. Indian Development Planning has always aimed at improving inequalities in the process of development recognising the fact that women lag behind due to several socio-economic-cultural-political impediments. But the Sixth Plan (1980-85), for the first time, recognised women as participants of development and not merely an object of welfare. In 1982, a Women's Employment Programme was introduced with assistance from Norwegian Development Agency (NORDA). In this plan period two new schemes- Support to Training and Employment (STEP) and Awareness Generation Programme for rural and poor women (AGP) were introduced.[30] In early 1992 (31 January) the National Commission for Women was constituted which works as a friend, a counsellor and educator for the Indian women who are now considered as agents for change in the era of globalisation liberalisation and privatisation.

Trends in Globalisation

Trends of globalisation reflected in India and abroad in the early years of 1990s which is defined as a process of stretching, deepening and speeding up of global interconnectedness, i.e., the multiplicity of networks, flows, transactions and relations which transcend the states and societies which constitute the contemporary global system.[31] In the present pattern of globalisation, politics of rights is no longer a prerogative of the state authorities, diplomats and theorists. It involves plurality of agencies; governmental, non-governmental and inter-governmental together. In the new world order dominated by the neo-liberals following the collapse of socialism and the emergence of cyber age not only the idea of human rights but the position of women worldwide faces certain paradoxes with positive and negative effects in sphere of women's development at large. Earlier, the United Nations Decade for Women (1976-85) was a global effort to examine the status and rights of women and to bring women into decision-making at all levels.

As a result, the Government of India in the early nineties decided to bring a policy about the advancement, development and empowerment of women. Recognising the role and contribution of women in development, the Eighth Plan (1990-95) adopted the strategy to ensure that benefits of development from different sectors do not bypass women and special programmes are implemented to complement the general development plans. In continuation the Ninth Plan (1997-2002) made two significant changes in conceptual strategy for women. First 'Empowerment of Women became one of the nine primary objectives of the plan and secondly, it attempted the convergence of existing services, resource, infrastructure and manpower available both in women-specific and women-related sectors. Likewise, the Tenth Five Year Plan (2002-2007) constituted three working groups: (i) Working Group on Empowerment of Women, (ii) Working Group on Child Development and (iii) Working Group of Improving Nutritional Status of Population with Special Focus on Vulnerable Groups.[32] Thus, the Five Year Plans have been paying special attention to women's welfare emphasising female education, access to resources and their political empowerment.

However, working of globalisation has not only widened the gap between the developing and developed countries but has also increased the difficulty of poor/developing nations and they are unable to cope with the challenges of this new trend. It has generated social crises arising from the increasing fear of marginalisation of some sections of society caused by the indiscriminate spread of capitalism and the free economy. Despair caused by social marginalisation, economic deprivation, and political defeat is another consequence of this modern phenomenon.[33] As a positive effect globalisation has enabled additional and various opportunities for women because employers within global, export-oriented sectors employ women and thus provide women opportunities to acquire new skills and knowledge. But on the other hand, due to gender discriminatory forces within the labour market and women's care responsibilities, women tend to earn lower wages and work fewer days than men.[34]

Today, Indian women are emerging as equal partners of men in all fields of human endeavour. But the feminist revolution is far from being won, and the exploitation of women continues in many ways. In this situation, women themselves should be seen as agents to transform the existing power relations in society. External agents can only help them with material support and information but they can not bestow empowerment on them. Empowerment should lead to a situation where each one can become a whole being regardless of gender, and use their fullest potential to construct a more humane society for all.

4.3 Gender Equality: Post-modern Prospects and Challenges

Gender equality holds the key-position in the world-wide development. In every society people as male and as female are expected to make some exclusive role performance. This role internalisation is done through the process of gender socialisation. Irrespective of gender, people have equal access to the resources and services necessary to achieve their individual potential and fulfil their obligations to household, community and more broadly, society. Traditionally, the expected role performance of the female places them in a secondary position in the -social structure and in the minds of men and women alike. All institutions-social, economic, political, religious and ideological have been dominated by men. Despite legislative steps prejudices, traditional attitudes and practices continue to perpetrate discrimination against women and actually no country in the world can claim to have fully achieved gender equality. Significantly enough national efforts and international movement got momentum in previous decades and agencies have started adopting measures for integrating women into the development process. The present position is a step forward but far from satisfactory or set goals in this sphere.

Fact-File of the Problem

The term 'Gender' arose as an analytical tool for analysing the inequalities between the sexes due to the patriarchal institutional structures. It started with assessing gender role and gender analysis, gender needs, gender interests and perspectives. At present the entire world community and the developing nations like India in particular, is focussing its attention as matters relating to gender discrimination which led to societal imbalances. The realisation of the necessity of bringing to the limelight the issues of gender, gender equality, gender inequality has been primarily due to the fact that women constitute one of the crucial segments of the human population and it is widely accepted that without the active participation of women all developmental programmes remain fruitless. Women's special status and women's debilitated status stem from a common ideology, from a belief in an essentialist, biological and psychological incapacity which spans not only assessment of physical capability but also mental capacity.[35] Be they philosophers, religious preachers, political leaders, social reformers or scientists, they all justified inferior status of women in society. The natural differentiation between man and woman does not imply inequalities. Yet, natural and social differentiations have been manipulated through creation of systems of stratification and pattern of inequality.

The notion of society in this regard needs to be understood in terms of social conditions which specified the women to particular types of works and assigns that provided them lower status than that of men. Her lower status in comparison to men is generally irrationally legitimatised on the basis of her child-bearing capacity, distinct physical attributes and a built which is shorter in height than man and in certain sense her vulnerability. In fact, the social structure was itself so arranged and patterned that its consequences led to inequality between genders. In a patriarchal society, the institutional patterns of residence, inheritance and lineage, patrilocal, patrilineal and patriarchal family structure, all represent and justify inequality between genders.[36] There is a direct relationship between marital residence and male dominance. Researches reveal that non-male based residence gives women more freedom of choice in mate selection, more protection from a potentially abusive husband and more freedom to end an unsatisfactory marriage. Altogether economic, legal, social and cultural beliefs generated a social definition and self-image of women in a society.

Apart from these, religion as an institution, has been one of the most pervasive and persistent factor in defining women's role and her status. Ruether identifies religion as 'Undoubtedly, the single most important shaper and enforcer of the image and role of women in society. The transcendental source- which is omnipotent and sacred- acquires extremely powerful instrumentality of legitimacy for various pronouncements affecting the status of women directly and indirectly. In behavioural and institutional forms, it governs the entire life cycle and every day life of women in most of the societies.'[37] Likewise, in monotheistic religions, a woman can never have her full sexual identity affirmed as being in the image and likeness of God, whereas this experience is freely available to every man in the existing culture. The overall milieu of values creates conditions in which women work, behave and live in a particular way and it also creates a psyche and self-image which leads to development of self-perceived as inferior to men. Further it leads to formation of belief systems regarding women and also assigns them specific roles and defines the code of their behaviour pattern both within family and outside.

Basically, the gender inequality itself existed in the structure of division of work into public and private domains which leads to: (i) Non-recognition of the work related to women in family-child-rearing and other domestic functioning. (ii) Certain economic activities undertaken by her in fields, economic activities related to handicraft etc; are not recognised as her economic contribution both by the society and for a long time by planners and officials. (iii) Creation of such values and institutions which make her work within family and deprive her of all such activities which are outside home and socially recognised. Commonly there are two distinct features of gender role of women. First, her role as a woman and second her status as a woman and unfortunately women suffer from dual deprivations: one that of being a woman and the other, of being a woman of a lower caste or class. Thus, women are never viewed as persons on their own rights. Moreover, women don't view themselves as autonomous being due to their cultural socialisation. Because of their marginalisation in society women hardly exist as a public phenomenon.

The issue of gender equality is closely related to law, equality and justice and its denial has led discrimination of women in almost all fields of human activity. Social equality and social justice is one of the most prized ideals of contemporary society but social inequality and injustice has been a feature of every known society - past and present. Different forms of atrocities are linked to one another and are manifestations of gender ideology. 'The world which has always belonged to the men is still in their hands, the institutions and the values of the patriarchal civilisation still survive in larger part.[38] In this circumstances, the status and role of women and related issues, have attracted the attention of the academicians, political thinkers and social scientists both in developing as well as developed countries, because of the widely accepted truth that a society built on the inequality of men and women involves wastage of human resources which no country can afford. It is unanimously accepted fact that gender equality could be realised only by making women economically, socially and politically empowered. Women's empowerment has become the goal or ultimate objective of many development policies and programmes which also demanded for indicators of empowerment, both to reveal the extent to which women are already empowered and to evaluate if such policies and programmes have been effective towards their stated aims.

Global Response

The process of the first phase of development in relation to the human societies commenced in post-World War II period and the goal was rapid economic growth through rapid industrialisation in order to foster fast economic growth which would eventually hoped to benefit the entire population. After de-colonialisation during the 1950s and 1960s only the economic role of women in reproduction as home-makers, bearers and rearers of children and housewives was perceived by the development organisations, which was reflected in the inclusion of family planning, population, mother and child care policies in development planning in several developing countries like India. The initial development plans and their implementation were based on the separation of the public and the private spaces. The public space was designed on the model of the worker without any caring responsibilities and was the sphere of the breadwinner who was obviously the male. It placed women in the private space which gave her the care giving and domestic role. The concept of development in a broader sense is related to improvement in quality of life based on equality and social justice through such programme and activities which consequently could alter the structure and culture and create self-generating continuous processes.[39] However, gradually new openings came which were instrumental in breaking the traditional shackles not only for women but some other deprived sections also.

Meanwhile, the old role-models and concepts began to change globally. In the 1950s and 1960s the women activists who took active part in freedom movements of the newly independent states took keen interest in raising the development questions in the UN and challenged the legalistic perspective of the Commission on the Status of Women (CSW) which was formed by the world body in 1947 to monitor UN activities on behalf of women. The said commission observed, 'Women who contribute half of the world's population by virtue of an accident of birth, perform two-thirds of the world's work, receive one-tenth of its income and own less than one hundredth of its property.[40] Soon it was realised at world level that because women comprise more than half of the human resources and are central to the economic as well as the social well-being of societies, development goals cannot be fully reached without their participation. The changing dimension of development and the international movement for the development of women have created a policy perspective for gender equality which recognises both women's and men's needs and, most importantly, their healthy interactions. Against this backdrop of situation, Dreze and Sen viewed that gender equality and social justice are the urgent need not merely because of the fact that it is an 'issue' of the day. Rather, 'the emancipation of women is an integral part of social progress, not just a women's issue'.[41] The movement started earlier has called upon worldwide countries and international development agencies to adopt measures for integrating women into the development process which received a major breakthrough in 1970s.

The new policy perspective was promoted further by the publication of Easter Boserup's book, *Women's Role in Economic Development* in 1970 which demonstrated that development processes have been strongly male-biased and bypassed women led the international aid community to attempt to integrate women into the production system so that the economy could grow more vigorously. The book not only ignited a worldwide discussion on the need of women's participation but also seriously challenged the argument that benefits from development projects would automatically 'trickle down' to women and other disadvantaged groups in Third World nations. By the time, perhaps, being influenced from the new concept a new approach 'Women in Development' (WID) was coined which was based on the philosophy that women are lagging behind in society and the gap between men and women can be bridged by remedial measures within the existing structure.[42] In 1975, the First World Conference on Women held in Mexico brought about the issue in the forefront. As a result, the United Nations declared in the mid-seventies the 'United Nations Decade for Women (1976-85). It followed in 1977 the introduction of its first guidelines on WID. In 1986, the Women in Development issue became one of the four priority issues of UNDP and thereby, the Division of Women in Development (DWID) had been created in the next year (1987).[43] In 1992, the DWID has been renamed as the 'Gender in Development Programme' (GIDP). In the 1990s, the UNDP's new development discourse and its focus on 'equity' and empowerment created a new dimension in terms of women's development approach.

Gradually the world opinion and institutions as well responded in favour of gender equality and, in line in the late 1980s the concept of Women in Development was shifted to Gender and Development Approach (GAD). The new approach is based on two perspectives: Firstly, it argues that women's status in society is deeply affected by their material conditions of life and by their position in the national, regional, and global economies; Secondly, it recognises the fact that women are deeply affected by the nature of patriarchal power in their societies at the national, community and household levels. It advocates for basic intervention with the analysis of men's and women's roles and needs, in an effort to empower women, to improve their position in relative to men in ways which will benefit and transform society as a whole. In the GAD two policy approaches - the Practical Gender Needs (PGN) and the Strategic Gender Needs (SGN). Practical gender needs relate to women's daily needs in caring for themselves and their children, whereas strategic gender interests relate to the task of changing gender relations and challenging women's subordinate position.[44] This new approach, GAD focuses on the interconnection of gender, class and race and the social construction of their defining characteristics. It recognises the differential impact of development policies and practices on women and men and sees women as agents, not simply as recipient, of development.

Within this context, meaning and perspective, the UNDP in the decade 1990s, introduced agenda for fruitfully incorporating the various development approaches. Its new development discourse and focus on 'equity' and 'empowerment' created a fresh dimension in terms of women's development approach. The earlier paper prepared by the GIDP named "Gender and Sustainable Human Development: Policy Perspectives (1995); now 'gender equality and equity' is put forward as the essence of the programme and the operation of UNDP."[45] The contents of the paper also justifies women in terms of the goals of equality and empowerment. Women's empowerment is central to human development. Human development, as a process of enlarging people's choices, cannot occur when the choices of half of humanity are restricted. Targeted actions aimed at empowering women and righting gender inequalities in the social and economic sphere, as well as in terms of civil and political rights, must be taken alongside efforts to engender the development process.

Thus, the perspectives of global policy have enabled the developing countries to identify the underlying causes of gender inequality. And, these have helped to develop a more desirable strategic approach, which has made it clear that 'Gender Equality' and 'Sustainable Human Development' are intertwined. Also, it has recovered a new sense of reality that girls and women should have opportunities for personal growth, security, realisation of rights, control of fertility and health, literacy and opportunities to participate in political and economic system.[46] In tune with this international movement, there has been a profound change in the status of women. The gender gap is narrowing down and women are entering in the production system, thus breaking the barriers of social moulds.

Other developing countries alike, India, perhaps the most complex democracies in the world, has a history of commitment, since the beginning of 1970s, to women's welfare and empowerment through constitutional provisions, legislations, policy and plans even while at deep levels structural gender biases persist within families, communities, economies and politics. Women still don't occupy a space as equal members and citizens in India and in other liberal democratic countries. The Government of India's II and III periodic Report on the Convention on the Elimination of All Forms of Discriminations against Women (CEDAW) 1997-2005 stated that the underlying causes of gender inequality are related to social and economic structures that are based on the social norms and practices. In India, where patriarchy from time immemorial has maintained a strong grip, the realisation of gender equality would not be a fruitful one unless some sort of positive discriminations for women like special social protection is not given.

Present Status

Gender discrimination acts as slow poison for the society and it is a growing recognition that countries cannot reach their full potential as long as women's potential to participate fully in their society is denied. Women's participation has become a key factor for success of all developmental programmes. In Third World countries the concept of development has come to identified with government programmes to be managed by government with or without involvement of community. Institutions like panchayat have been associated and involved in execution of these plans. The social structure and cultural values determine consciousness. Consciousness raising shall help in greater participation in the women empowerment programmes. The term women empowerment has come to connote the processes by which the efforts of the women themselves are united with those of governmental authorities to improve the economic, social and cultural conditions of women and to integrate these women into the life of the nation and to enable them to contribute fully to national progress. Thus, women with respect to development-have to be viewed as both the participants and beneficiaries.

In general we see two contrasting trends: first, the growing poverty and misery of women accompanied by multifarious efforts of deprivation and secondly, despite the long wait for the change of women's position in society, the present global scenario gives some evidences to reaffirm that 'gender equality for the millions of people is not attainable'. Rather, today women are getting to the top more than ever before and their knowledge and insights are being treated significant, and the misconceptions about women are being dispelled.[47] Further, there is a need for development for women as a specific category and their full integration in the total development process. N. Yavari-d' Hellencourt, the coordinator for the United Nations Development Fund for Women (UNDFW) viewed in this regard, 'If we do not empower women, there will be no peace and no way out of poverty'[48] because, women have more potentiality than men and they can play the role of silent developer in a family. Because, 'a women gives first priority to her children; her second priority is the household. A man has different priorities; he does not give family the top position.[49] Thus, women, at large, hold key position in all round development of a nation - both developed and developing.

It is a time to rethink, regroup and move forward on the issue of gender equality. An essential step forward has been made in general discussion of the role of women in society. Mechanism for change such as women's forums, citizens' forums and issue-specific organisations and other supportive groups should mobilise establish goals and develop a plan of action. In fact, it is evident that the gender development policies are formulated without understanding the ground realities of the situation faced by the women. The value-base of the society restricts women's role and status and the government programmes regulates women's rights to access and control self and resources. Any sensitive issue occurring in the society affects women since they have limited control, power and choices over resources. It is not enough to have right laws and the institution of justice, but also a change in values is necessary for the right implementation of justice to women out of patriarchal biases. It would be a significant contribution on women empowerment and justice in all societies in order to address the gender gaps and find a gender equality with sustainable human development.

References

1. Verghese Koithara, *Society State and Security - The Indian Experience* (New Delhi : Sage Publications, 1999), p. 268.
2. B.S. Upadhyaya, *Women in Rigveda*, (New Delhi : S. Chand and Co., 1974), p. 42.
3. *Ibid.*, p. 136.
4. Mala Singh, 'Women of India, the Old Order Changeth-But only for a Few', *The Illustrated Weekly of India*, August 9, 1970, p. 8.
5. Sugata Bose and Ayesha Jalal, *Modern South Asia, History, Culture, Political Economy* (New Delhi : Oxford University Press, 2004), pp. 35-36.
6. A.R. Desai, *Social Background of Indian Nationalism* (Bombay : Popular Prakashan, 1948), pp. 273-76.
7. *Plan and Prospects of Social Welfare in India, 1951-61*, p. 14.
8. Bipin Chandra, Mridula Mukherjee and Aditya Mukherjee, *India After Independence 1947-2000* (New Delhi : Penguin Books, 2002), pp. 451-52.
9. Dr Priyanka Tomar, *Indian Women* (New Delhi : Shree Publishers, 2006), pp. 216-18.
10. B. Ramesh Babu, 'The Liberal Capitalist West as the New Global State', Bansidhar Pradhan, ed., *International Studies*, Journal of the School of International Studies, Jawaharlal Nehru University, Vol. 43, No. 3, July-September 2006 (New Delhi: Sage Publications, 2006). p. 291.

11. Gurkirat Kaur, *Women and Law* (New Delhi : Shree Publishers, 2005), pp. 227-30.
12. Vijaya Nambiar, *Liberalisation and Development - Agenda for Economic Reforms* (New Delhi : Commonwealth Publishers, 2003), pp. 101-02.
13. G.S. Batra and R.C. Dangwal, *Liberalisation, Globalisation and International Business* (New Delhi : Deep and Deep Publications, 2006), pp. 97-98.
14. Dr Prianka Tomar, *Indian Women*, pp. 219-22.
15. Prakash Talwar, *Human Rights* (Delhi : Isha Books, 2006), pp. 1-2.
16. Suresh Kumar, 'Human Rights Protection in India - An Institutional Framework', *South Asia Politics*, Vol. 7, No. 3, August 2008 (New Delhi : 2008), pp. 36-37.
17. *Ibid.*
18. Sarbani Guha Ghosal, 'Human Rights : Concept and Contestation', *IJPS*, Vol. LXXI, No. 4, October-December 2010 (Meerut : 2010), pp. 1103-7.
19. John Rawls, 'The Law of People', in Belgrade Circle (ed.) and Obrad Savic introduced, *The Politics of Human Rights* (London and New York : Verso, 2002), pp. 31-33.
20. Jurgen Habermas, 'Private and Public Autonomy', in *Ibid.*, pp. 60-64.
21. Amartya Sen, 'Elements of a Theory of Human Rights', *Philosophy and Public Affairs*, Vol. 32 (4), October 2004.
22. Tony Evans, 'Introduction : Power, Hegemony and the Universalisation of Human Rights', in Evans (ed.), *Human Rights Fifty Years On - A Reappraisal* (UK : Manchester University Press, 1998), pp. 1-7.
23. Michael Freeden, *Rights* (New Delhi : World View, 1998), p. 40.
24. *Human Development Report*, Government of Punjab (2004), p. 112.
25. Rajkumar Singh, *Contemporary India with Controversial Neighbours* (New Delhi : Gyan Publishing House, 2011), p. 61.
26. Myra Marx Ferrie and Elaine J. Hall, 'Rethinking Stratification from a Feminist Perspective : Gender, Race and Class in Mainstream Textbooks', *American Sociological Review*, Vol. 61, No. 6, December 1996, pp. 929-50.
27. Reddy Narayan, Kumar Vijay, Nalani S., *Women and Development Challenges and Achievements* (Delhi : Serial Publications, 2005), p. 1.
28. K. Muthalagu and Dr K. Vijayarani, 'Perspectives on Human Development in India', *Third Concept*, Vol. 20, No. 235, September 2006 (New Delhi : 2006), p. 38.
29. S.S. Sree Kumar, 'Representation of Women in Legislature : A Sociological Perspective in the Indian Context', *IJPS*, Vol. IXVII, No. 3, July-September 2006 (Meerut : 2006), p. 620.

30. Dr Priyanka Tomar, *Indian Women*, pp. 216-18.
31. Anthony G. McGrew, 'Human Rights in a Global Age : Coming in Terms with Globalisation', in Tony Evans (ed.), *Human Rights Fifty Years On - A Reappraisal*, p. 189.
32. Dr Priyanka Tomar, *Indian Women*, pp. 219-22.
33. Sheikh Saleem Ahmed, 'Dimensions of Terrorism and Religious Extremism: Two Sides of the Same Coin', in Mahavir Singh (ed.), *International Terrorism and Religious Extremism - Challenges to Central and South Asia* (New Delhi : Anamika Publishers, 2004), p. 38.
34. C. Sheela Reddy, 'Globalisation - A Human Rights Perspective', *South Asia Politics*, Vol. 5, No. 11, March 2007 (New Delhi : 2007), p. 39.
35. Susan Edwards (ed.), *Gender, Sex and the Law* (New Hampshire, USA: Croom Helm, 1985), p. 1.
36. Mridula Bhatnagar, 'Gender Politics: In the Context of Social Structure and Development', *IJPS*, Vol. LXX, No. 4, October-December 2009 (Meerut: 2009), pp. 1035-38.
37. Ruether R. (ed.), *Religion and Sexism-Images of Women in the Swedish and Christian Traditions* (Simon and Schuster, 1974), p. 9.
38. Antrobuo Peggy and Bizot Judith, 'Women's Perspective: Towards an Ethical, Equitable, Just and Sustainable Development', *Women and Development, ISIS*, International Issue 4/92 and 1/93, p. 30.
39. Mridula Bhatnagar, 'Gender Politics: In the Context of Social Structure and Development', p. 1039.
40. As quoted in K.G. Karmakar, *Rural Credit and Self-Help Groups-Micro - Finance Needs and Concepts in India* (New Delhi: Sage Publications, 1999), p. 168.
41. Jean Dreze and Amartya Sen, *India-Economic Development and Social Opportunity*, pp. 140, 167 and 178.
42. Dolly Phukon, 'Gender Development Approach and Social Protection: Understanding the Case of Assam', *IJPS*, Vol. LXIX, No. 4, October-December 2008 (Meerut : 2008), pp. 771-74.
43. Khaiber Ali Mia, Mohammad Yasin and Yasmin, 'Gender Equality-Rhetoric or a Panacea ? : A Review of the Present Concerns', *Ibid.*, Vol. LXVIII, No. 4, October-December 2007 (Meerut: 2007), p. 742.
44. Dolly Phukon, 'Gender Development Approach and Social Protection: Understanding the Case of Assam', pp. 775-76.
45. Shahra Razavi and Carol Miller, *Gender Mainstreaming-A Study of Efforts by the UNDP, the World Bank and the ILO to Internationalise Gender Issues*, Occasional Paper 4, August 1995, UNRISD (Geneva: 1995), pp. 22-23.
46. *UNDP Human Development Report*, June 1997, p. 9.

47. Khaiber Ali Mia, Mohammad Yasin and Yasmin, 'Gender Equality-Rhetoric or a Panacea ? : A Review of the Present Concerns', pp. 744.
48. Clive Shirley, 'The Banker From Jamaat Karasu's in Choices', *The Human Development Magazine*, March 2002, p. 17.
49. Yunus Muhammad, 'The Grameen Bank Story: Rural Credit in Bangladesh' in Anirudh Krishna, Norman Uphoff and Milton Esman (eds.), *Reasons for Hope - Instructive Experience in Rural Development* (New Delhi: Vistaar Publications, 1997), p. 16.

Chapter 5

Changing Face of Indian Judiciary : An Overview

5.1 Indian Judiciary and Social Requirement

Judicial system in any part of the globe does not operate in a vacuum. It involves the process of deciding what is just in a controversy between two or more contending parties. The administration of justice has a social function and the judicial process is only a part of the larger social process. Though the Indian Judiciary has been honest and independent in the performance of its duties as regard to the executive control and influence in ancient, medieval and modern times, under the changing socio-economic-politico situations in the country people have higher expectations from the judiciary. In the event of poverty and illiteracy, its challenging task is to ensure justice to all. The entire system of governance is based on the principle of equal justice for all. Under the present Constitution the position of judiciary has been made doubly secure so that it can become in reality the most impartial arbiter of the conflicts and controversies which fall within its jurisdiction. The Constitution of India is supreme legal document of the country. There are various levels of judiciary in India - different types of courts, each with varying powers depending on the tier and jurisdiction bestowed upon them. Thus, in the Constitutional scheme, the judicial system works as an active catalyst to secure justice for every citizen. It acts as the engine of social welfare to secure justice in the various spheres of life.

Inheritance of Judiciary in India

India has the oldest judiciary in the world and we find a true and correct picture of legal system of ancient India in the original/religious texts of the time. On the basis of texts, it has been discovered that Indian jurisprudence was founded on the rule of law, that the King himself was the subject to the law; that arbitrary power was unknown to Indian political theory and jurisprudence and the king's right to govern was subject to the fulfilment of duties the breach of which resulted in forfeiture of kingship; that the judges were independent and subject only to the law. The disputes were decided essentially in accordance with the same principles of natural justice which govern the judicial process in the modern State today. Even at that time in criminal cases the accused could not be punished unless his guilt was proved according to law while in civil cases the trial consisted of four stages like any modern trial - plaint, reply, hearing and decree. The decrees of all courts except the king were subject to appeal or review according to fixed principles; the fundamental duty of the court was to justice without favour or fear. For instance, the legendary book Mahabharata, mentions, 'A King who after having sworn that he shall protect his subjects fails to protect them should be executed like a mad dog'. Likewise in a further description, it is said, 'the people should execute a king who does not protect them, but deprives them of their property and assets and who takes no advice or guidance from any one. Such a king is not a king but misfortune.'[1] These provisions indicate that sovereignty was based on an implied social contract if the king violated the traditional pact, he forfeited his kingship.

There was no relaxation but a complete system of judiciary we witness in the times of Mauryan Empire and Kautilya describes the duties of a king in the *Arthshastra*, 'In the happiness of his subjects lies the king's happiness, in their welfare, his welfare; whatever pleases him he shall not consider as good but whatever pleases his people he shall consider to good. According to the *Arthshastra* the realm was divided into administrative units called Sthaniya, Dronamukha, Khrvatika and Sangrahana, equivalents to the modern concept of districts, tehsils and parganas. *Sthaniya* was a fortress established in the centre of eight hundred villages, a *dronamukha* in the midst of 400 villages, a kharvatika in the midst of 200 villages and a *sangrahana* in the centre of ten villages. Law courts were established in each sangrahana and also at the meeting places of districts. The court consisted of three jurists (*dharmastha*) and three ministers (*amatya*). The ancient list of jurists included the names of Manu, Yajnvalkya, Katyayana, Brihaspati and others. According to *Brihaspati Smiriti*, there was a hierarchy of courts in ancient India beginning with the family courts and ending with the king. The lowest was the family arbitrator. The next higher court was that of the judge; the next of the Chief Justice who was called Praadivivaka or adhyaksha; and at the top was King's court. The jurisdiction of each was determined by the importance of the dispute, the minor disputes being decided by the lowest court and the most important by the king. The decision of each higher court superseded that of the court below.[2] It was almost similar to today's judicial system of India which consists of a hierarchy of courts organised on the same principle- the village courts, the Munsif, the Civil Judge, the District Judge, the High Court, and finally the Supreme Court which takes the place of King's Court.

In course of time, a full-fledged judicial hierarchy was created which relieved the king of much of the judicial work, but leaving untouched his powers as the highest court of appeal. But despite this there was no compromise on the integrity and quality of justice. The concept of integrity was given a very wide meaning and the judicial code of integrity was very strict as Brihaspati says, 'A judge should decide cases without any consideration of personal gain or any kind of personal bias'; and his decision should be in accordance with the procedure prescribed by texts. In the procedure a trial had to be in open court and judges were forbidden to talk to the parties privately while the suit was pending because it was recognised that a private hearing may lead to partiality. According to *Sukranitisara* there are five causes - attachment, greed, fear, enmity and hearing a party in private which destroy impartiality and lead to judges taking sides in disputes. Another safeguard of judicial integrity as realised by our ancients was that when two minds confer, there is less chance of corruption or error and they provided that the King must sit with his counsellors when deciding cases, and judges must sit in benches of uneven numbers. Kautilya was also of the view that suits should be heard by three judges. Even our present judicial system created by the British, does not follow this excellent safeguard. Today, every suit is heard by a single Munsif or Civil Judge or District Judge for reasons of economy. In view of the vital part played by custom in society, the state was required to maintain an authenticated record of the customs observed in the various parts of the country. By gearing law to changing customs Indian jurisprudence gave the concept of law a secular content. It developed the evolutionary concept of law and rejected the concept of an absolute, eternal, never-changing law.

In the medieval India after the disintegration of Harsha empire and before the coming of Mughals in which the country was divided once more into small kingdoms, the political instability did not result in any change in the judicial system that has taken roots during the preceding thousands of years. The standards and ideas of justice were maintained in each kingdom in spite of political divisions, the unity of civilisation was preserved, and the fundamental principles of law and procedure were applied throughout the country. However, the establishment of the Muslim rule in India opened a new chapter in our judicial history. The Muslim conquerors brought with them a new religion, a new civilisation and a new social system. The ideal of justice under Islam was one of the highest in the middle ages. The Prophet himself set the standards and said in the Quran, 'Justice is the balance of God upon earth in which things when weighed are not by a practice less or more. And he appointed the balance that he should not transgress in respect to the balance; wherefore observe a just weight and diminish not the balance.'[3] This high tradition reached its zenith under the first four Caliphs. The first Qadi was appointed by the Caliph Umar who enunciated the principle that the law was supreme and that the judge must never be subservient to the ruler. The Muslim kings in India bought with them these high ideals, and individual Sultans had very high ideals of justice. But unfortunately the administration of justice under the Sultans worked fitfully. The reason was that the outstanding feature of the entire Sultanate period was confusion and chaos. No Sultan felt secure for a long time. One dynasty was replaced by another within a comparatively short period and the manner of replacement was violent. Consequently the quality of justice depended very much on the personality of the sovereign. Thus, during the Sultanate, Islamic standards of justice did not take root in India as an established tradition unlike the judicial traditions of ancient India which had struck deep-roots in the course of several thousand years and could not be uprooted by political divisions.

Under the Mughal Empire the country had an efficient system of government with the result that the system of justice took shape. In this period the unit of judicial administration was under Qazi- an office which was borrowed from the Caliphate. Every provincial capital had its Qazi and at the head of judicial administration was the Supreme Qazi of the empire. In addition, every town and every village large enough to be classed as Qasba had its own Qazi. In theory, a Qazi had to be 'a Muslim Scholar of blameless life, thoroughly conversant with the prescriptions of the sacred law.[4] On the appointment of a Qazi, he was charged by the Imperial Diwan in the words like, 'Be just' be honest, be impartial. Hold trials in the presence of the parties and at the court house and the seat of government. Do not accept presents from the people of the place where you serve, not attend entertainments given by anybody and everybody. Write your decrees, sale deeds, mortgage bonds and other legal documents very carefully, so that learned men may not pick holes in them and bring you to shame. Know poverty to be your glory'. But due to lack of supervision and absence of good tradition, these noble ideals were not observed. In spite of this there is overwhelming evidence that all the Emperors from Akbar to Aurangzeb took their judicial function seriously and discharged their duties. Jahangir made a great show of it and his Golden Chain has become famous in history.

Unlike the British the Mughals failed to make a long-term impact on the existing judicial system of India. No Indian Emperors or Qazi's decisions was ever considered authoritative to lay down a legal principle to elucidate any obscurity in the Quran or supplement the Quranic law by following the line of its obvious intention in respect of cases not explicitly provided for by it. Hence, it became necessary for Indian Qazis to have at their slow a digest of Islamic law and precedent compiled from the accepted Arabic writer. Muslim law in India was, therefore, incapable of growth and change, except so far as it reflected changes of juristic thought in Arabia or Egypt. However, the Mughal judicial system has left its imprint on the present system and a good part of our legal terminology is borrowed from it. Our civil courts of first instance and called Munsifs, the plaintiff and the defendants are termed Muddai had Muddaliya and scores of other legal terms remind us of the days. After the conquest of Bengal by the British the process of replacement of the Mughal system of justice by the British began but it took a long time to be established.

The present judicial system of India is at large a part of the inheritance India received from the British after more than 200 years of their colonial rule and the same is obvious from the many similarities the Indian legal system shares with the English legal system. Earlier Muslims came to India when they conquered Sindh in 712 A.D. The Delhi Sultanate came into existence in 1206, when Qutubuddin Aibak of the Slave dynasty became the first independent Sultan of Delhi. From 1206 to 1526 five different dynasties- the Slaves, the Khaljis, the Thughluqs, the Sayyids and the Lodhis ruled India. The Mughal dynasty was established in 1526 and continued till 1857, it was in decay since the death of Aurangzeb Alamghir in 1707. The foundations of the British Empire in India was laid down by East India Company which was organised to further British interest in overseas countries. The representative of the Company arrived in India in 1604 and by the 1661 the Company had factories in Surat, Madras and Bombay.[5] The Company delivered justice arbitrarily which could be called as 'trader's justice' because the Company's officials were all traders and had no knowledge of law. However, after its coming the East India Company slowly and gradually started interfering in the local justice system by acquiring revenue collection of 38 villages in 1717 near Calcutta. Soon the Company also acquired the administration of justice in the areas under its control and the role of Muslim qazis and judges was over. Company's officials became judges without any formal training and at the time the Privy Council was born as the highest court of appeal.

Since the establishment of East India Company was made to promote British interests in India, the expansion of Company's judicial jurisdiction and enactment of different judicial acts took place simultaneously. Further after the battle of Plassey, the Company installed Mir Zafar as the Nawab of Calcutta who ceded the Zamindari of the 24 Parganas to the Company which now controlled 800 square miles of area called 'moffussil'. The Company provided the adalat system for the administration of justice in the moffussil. The 1772 plan provided for a moffussil Diwani Adalat in each district with collector as judge to decide civil cases. For Muslims the court was to apply the Quran while for Hindus it was applying Shaster. The Regulations of 1793 referred to Hindu law and Mohammedan laws instead of Quran and Shaster. In case of Muslim cases the collector was to be advised by the Qazi while in case of Hindus, by a Pandit. In an important decision on December 3, 1790 the Criminal justice system was taken from the Muslim Qazis, Muftis and Maulvis and was given in the hands of the Company's English servants. The Regulation Act of 1773 authorised the Supreme Court in Calcutta to enrol English, Irish and Scottish attorney at law.[6] Likewise in 1793, Cornwallis created a regular profession authorising the Sadar Diwani Adalat to enrol pleaders or *vakeels*, both Hindus and Muslims for all Company's courts. The 1857 war of independence changed the fate of India. The Bill of 1858 gave all territories in the possession or under the government of the East India Company to the Crown. However, before the take-over by the Crown the East India Company done the ground work for the colonisation of the subcontinent. The British rulers changed the whole administration of country especially the law and justice. The British East India Company established a system of courts in each of the three Presidencies. The types of courts and their jurisdiction varied from Presidency to Presidency, until the Crown replaced the Company's administration and greater uniformity in the entire judicial structure became possible. In a nutshell, the judicial conditions during the prolonged period of seventeenth and eighteenth century in British India was taken up as a solemn effort, paving the way for future law developments.

The system of administration of justice and laws as we have today is the product of well thought out efforts of the British Government. No less than four law commissions and other committees were appointed during the years 1834 to 1947 to give shape to the system. Administration of justice is one of the most essential functions of the state.[7] If men were gods and angels, no law courts would perhaps be necessary though even then the skeptics might refer to quarrels among gods, particularly in the context of goddesses. As it is we find that though man may be a little lower than the angels, he has not shed off the brute. Not far beneath within the man, there lurks the brute and the brute is apt to break loose on occasions. To curb and control that brute and prevent degeneration of society into a state of tooth and claw, we need the rule of law. We also need the rule of law for punishing all deviations and lapses from the code of conduct and standard of behaviour which the community speaking through its representatives has prescribed as the law of the land. Being human disputes are bound to arise amongst us. For the settlement of these disputes, we need guidelines in the form of laws and forums to redress the wrongs in the form of courts. Laws and courts have always gone together. There is a close nexus between them: neither court can exist without the laws or laws without the courts. The judicial system deals with the administration of the laws through the agency of the courts.

The British rule in India introduced a more or less unified legal system in the continent, which may be considered a major step in the globalisation of laws. The quarter of a century following the takeover by the Crown the governing of India from East India Company in 1858 was the major period of codification of law and consolication of the court system in India. During this period a series of Codes based on English law were enacted which were applicable throughout British India. By 1882, there was virtually complete codification of all fields of commercial, criminal and procedural law, except some aspects of personal law. In the context initially, the British Administration of Hindu law elevated Brahminical textual law over the customary law that was practiced by

Indians. To prevail over the written law in British courts a custom must be proved to be immemorial or ancient, uniform, invariable, continuous, certain, notorious, reasonable, peaceful obligatory and it must not be immoral to an express enactment or to public policy.[8] On the basis of the above criterias and with the help of local leaders like Veereshalingam Kandukuri of Andhra and Raja Rammohan Roy of Bengal encouraged social reform and established firmly British-Indian law much against the local law. As a result, the new British-Indian law, in contrast to the earlier allowed divorce and remarriage, prohibited child marriages and banned the practice of Sati. But slowly the Brahminical law was completely ignored and dependence on the judicial precedent and legislation took over the legal system.

From the earliest India has a wide system of caste, kinship, religion, economic activity or land tenure, but now there is an all-India legal system which handles local disputes in accordance with uniform Indian standards based mainly on common law. The new legal system provides machinery and the ideology for legislation to be enforced throughout the continent. In opposite, today the government usually does not make any laws to reform Muslim Personal Law for the fear of hurting the sentiments of Muslims, thereby hurting the political future of the government. Even the judiciary's intervention into affairs of Muslims is considered violation of minority rights. This pampering of minorities by politicians for votes has its impact on modernisation of Islamic personal law.[9] But the British system of law made possible unprecedented consolidation and standardisation of the Indian societies in general and provided a unifying element in India in a way that neither Brahminical nor Muslim law ever did. Likewise, in the matter of succession and other allied matters, the parties were left to be governed by the personal. Although the impact of the English common law was perceptible in the codified law of India departure from the common law was also made whenever, it was considered, necessary, to local needs.

At this juncture, in answer to the criticism that the present judicial system is unsuited to the Indian conditions and something alien transplanted on the Indian soil, it may be observed, as stated by the Law Commission, that though some of the changes in the early period of British rule in India were influenced by the system prevailing in England in those days, the changes did not have the effect of ousting the personal law. No judicial system in any country is wholly immune from, and unaffected by, outside influences, nor can such outside influence be always looked upon as a bane. The laws of a country do not reside in a sealed book; they grow and develop. The winds of change, and the free flow of ideas, do not pass the law idly by. Even in procedural law, which was codified by the foreign rulers in this country, the basic principles of a fair and impartial trial, which were well known to their predecessors were adhered to. In the matter of substantive law as well, the British did not wholly bring in the Western concepts. The personal law of the various communities living in this country remained the determining factor in questions like succession, inheritance, marriage, caste, religious institutions, etc. New laws were enacted to provide for matters which were either not fully covered by the indigenous law, or where such laws were not clearly defined and ascertainable, or were otherwise not acceptable to the modern way of thinking. Such outside influences are, however, an integral part of the historical process of development of thought and institutions all over the world, and once the new concepts get assimilated, they cease to be alien in character.[10] The people have become fully accustomed to this system to more than a hundred years of its existence. The procedures and even the technical terms used by the lawyers and the judges are widely understood by the large majority of litigants.

The judicial system in essence pertains to the courts and the judges, their hierarchy and mode of functioning. By its very nature, it is inextricably connected with the rule of law. It deals with the administration of the laws through the agency of the courts. The system provides the machinery for the resolving of the disputes on account of which the aggrieved party approaches the courts. Nothing rankles in human heart more than a brooding sense of injustice. No society can allow a situation to grow where the impression prevails of their being no redress for grievances. Particularly after the Crown Government of India adopted the Indian Panel Code (1860) and the Indian Code of Criminal Procedure 1861, amended in 1872, 1882, 1898, the criminal jury was obligatory only in the High Courts of the Presidency Towns; elsewhere, it was optional and rarely used.[11] Of all the branches of the government about judiciary it is said that it is the weakest of the three organs. It has neither the power of the purse nor the power of the sword, neither money nor patronage, not even the physical force to enforce its decisions. Despite that, the courts have by and large enjoyed high prestige amongst and commanded respect of the people. This is so because of the moral authority of the courts and the confidence the people have in the role of the courts to do justice between the rich and the poor, the mighty and the weak, the state and the citizen, without fear or favour.

Judiciary and Indian Constitution

The judicial or legal system of a country is part of its social system and reflects the social, political, economic and cultural characteristics of the society. It is therefore, difficult to understand the legal system outside the socio-cultural milieu in which it operates. In the case of India the legal system is still alien to the majority of the Indian's whose legal culture is more indigenous and whose contact with the formal legal system is marginal if not altogether non-existent. The language, technicality and procedure of the inherited legal system are indeed factors, which limit access to justify for the illiterate, impoverished masses of our country. Nevertheless, the rights and benefits conferred by the laws and constitution offer opportunity for those very people to enjoy the fruits of a welfare democracy which the people of India have given into themselves on the 26th January, 1950. The framers of the Constitution were aware that democratic freedoms were meaningless in the absence of an independent machinery to safeguard them. No subordinate or agent of the government could be trusted to be just and impartial in judging the merits of a conflict in which the government itself was a party. Similarly, a judiciary subordinate either to the Centre or States could not be trusted as an impartial arbiter of conflicts and controversies between the Centre and the States.[12] These were the compelling reasons for the creation of an independent judiciary as an integral part of the Constitution and for the adoption of judicial independence as a basic principle of the Constitution. Fortunately at the dawn of India's independence this task of keeping judiciary independent and impartial was done by the keen legal mind of B.R. Ambedkar, M.K. Gandhi and Jawaharlal Nehru.[13] Perhaps it is the consequent understanding of law and its relation to society that prompted the founding fathers to devote the energy required to form a Constitution of unprecedented magnitude, in both scope and length. The judiciary in India, even under the British, was noted for its integrity and independence but after independence it was made doubly secure so that it can become in reality the most impartial arbiter of the conflicts and controversies which fall within its jurisdiction.

India adopted the path of Parliamentary democracy. The British Parliamentary system left a big impression on Indian Constitution. The freedom of judiciary was taken from the United States of America. In USA, there is considerable power given to judiciary rather than Parliament and there is a clear and distinct line that separates the three major organs, the executive, legislative and the judiciary. To make the constitution supreme in the country, India made the biggest written constitution in the world.[14] In the Preamble of Indian Constitution the importance is given to justice at the highest level. The people go to the judiciary in the quest of justice. The constitution lays down the structure and defines the limits and demarcates the role and functions of Parliament and judiciary and establishes the norms for checks and balances. Independence of the judiciary is essential for upholding the rule of law.[15] Thus, the Constitution of India is the guiding light in all matters of executive legislative and judiciary. It is extensive and aims to be sensitive. The constitution turned the direction of system originally introduced for perpetuation of colonial and imperial interests in India, firmly in the direction of social welfare. The Constitution explicitly and through judicial interpretation seeks to empower the weakest members of the society.

In this context the world famous constitutional expert Granville Austin says, 'Indian Constitution is first and foremost a social document. Its founding fathers and mothers established in the Constitution both the nation's ideals and the institutions and processes for achieving them. The ideals were national unity and integrity and a democratic and equitable society.'[16] The new society was to be achieved through a socio-economic revolution pursued with a democratic spirit using constitutional, democratic institution. This observation aptly describes the Indian State, as contemplated by the framers of the Constitution, which is based on the objective resolution of Jawaharlal Nehru,[17] asserts that 'We the people of India' through this Constitution, aim at establishing a Sovereign, Socialist, Secular, Democratic, Republic of India and to secure to all its citizens, justice, social, economic and political.

The Constitution of India which came into being on 26 January 1950 adopted a federal system but it has not provided the country a double system of courts as in the United States. Under our constitution there is a single integrated system of Courts for the union as well as the states which administer both Union and State laws, and at the head of the entire system stands the Supreme Court of India. Below the Supreme Court stand the High Courts of the different States and under each High Court there is a hierarchy of other courts which are referred to in the constitution as 'subordinate courts'.[18] The organisation of subordinate judiciary varies slightly from State to State. Below the High Courts are a hierarchy of subordinate courts such as the civil courts, family courts, criminal courts and various other district courts. The District Courts of India are established by the State governments in India for every district or for one or more districts together taking into account the number of cases, population distribution in the district. They administer justice in India at a district level. These courts are under administrative control of the High Court of the State to which the district concerned belongs.[19] The decisions of District Court are subject to the appellate jurisdiction of the concerned High Court.

Recently under the Gram Nyayalayas Act 2008, Gram Nyayalayas having the power of Judicial Magistrate of the first class are being established at Panchayat levels. There is also a provision of village courts, called Lok Adalat (People's Court) or Nyaya Panchayat (justice of the villages) that compose a system of alternative dispute resolution.[20] The present system of justice at the village level was known even in colonial India and first it was recognised through the 1888 Madras Village Act and developed, especially after 1935 in various provinces which India followed after independence. The model from the Gujarat, with a judge and two assessors was used from the 1970s onwards. In 1984, the Law Commission recommended to create Nyaya Panchayats in rural areas. The 2008, Gram Nyayalayas Act have foreseen 5,000 mobile courts in the country for judging petty civil (property cases) and criminal upto two years of prison cases. However, the Act has not been enforced properly and till May 2012 only 151 functional Gram Nyayalayas have been established against the target of 5000 such courts.[21] The major reasons behind the non-enforcement includes financial constraints, reluctance of lawyers, police and other government officials.

On 26 January 1950, the day India's constitution came into being, the Supreme Court of India was formed in Delhi. The inauguration of the apex court took place two days later on 28 January in Princes Chamber in the Parliament building complex where the Federal Court of India had sat for 12 years between 1937 and 1950. It got its own building in 1958[22] and in 1979 two new wings- East wing and West wing were added to the complex. The original constitution of 1950 envisaged a Supreme Court with a Chief Justice and seven puisne judges- leaving it to Parliament to increase this number. In addition, Parliament has the power to make laws regulating the constitution, organisation, jurisdiction and powers of the Supreme Court. In the early years, all the judges of the Supreme Court sat together to hear the cases presented before them. But as the work of the court increased and arrears of cases began to accumulate, Parliament increased the number of judges from 8 in 1950 to 11 in 1956, 14 in 1960, 18 in 1978 and 26 in 1986. Presently, the Supreme Court of

India comprises the Chief Justice and 30 other judges. As the number of the judges has increased they sit in smaller Benches of two and three, coming together in larger Benches of five and more only when required to do so or to settle a difference of opinion or controversy.

The Supreme Court of India is the highest court of land as established by Part V, Chapter IV of the Constitution of India. According to the Constitution of India, the role of the Supreme Court is that of a federal court, guardian of the constitution and the highest court of appeal. Articles 124 to 147 of the Constitution of India lay down the composition and jurisdiction of the Supreme Court of India. Primarily, it is an appellate court which takes up appeals against judgements of the High Court of the States and territories. However, it also takes writ petition filed under Article 32 which is the right to constitutional remedies or if a case involves a serious issue that needs immediate resolution.

In line there are 24 High Courts at the State level. Article 141 of the Constitution of India mandates that they are bound by the judgements and orders of the Supreme Court of India by precedence. These courts have jurisdiction over a state, a union territory or a group of states and union territories. High Courts are instituted as constitutional courts under Part VI Chapter V and Article 214 of the Indian Constitution. The High Courts are the principal civil courts of original jurisdiction in the state along with District Courts which are subordinate to the High Courts. However, High Courts exercise their original civil and criminal jurisdiction only if the courts subordinate to the High Court in the state are not competent or not authorised by law to try such matters for lack of pecuniary, territorial jurisdiction. The primary work of most of High Courts consists of Appeals from lower courts and writ petitions in terms of Article 226 of the Constitution of India. Writ jurisdiction is also original jurisdiction of High Court.

Established by the State governments, the District Courts of India are presided over by one District Judge appointed by the State Government. In addition to the district judge there may be number of Additional District Judges and Assistant District Judges depending on the workload. The Additional District Judge and the court presided have equivalent jurisdiction as the District Judge and his district court.[23] The district judge is also called "Metropolitan Session Judge" when he is presiding over a district court in a city which is designated "Metropolitan area" by the state government.[24] The district court has appellate jurisdiction over all subordinate courts situated in the district on both civil and criminal matters. Subordinate courts, on the civil side are, Junior Civil Judge Court, Principal Junior Civil Judge Court. Senior Civil Judge Court also called sub-court. Subordinate courts, on the criminal side are Second Class Judicial Magistrate Court, First Class Judicial Magistrate Court and Chief Judicial Magistrate Court. Thus, the Indian Judiciary is organised in a hierarchical form. At the bottom there are numerous Nyaya Panchayats and at the apex there is the Supreme Court.

In the context, it is rightly said that modern democracies are inconceivable without judiciary. This organ is not only guardian of the constitution but also protector of fundamental rights of the citizens. As Lord Bryce observed, 'There is no better test of the excellence of a government than the efficiency of judicial system, for nothing more nearly touches the welfare and security of the average citizen than his knowledge that he can rely on the certain and prompt administration of justice'.[25] Similarly Garner put it, 'A society without legislative organ is conceivable and indeed, fully developed legislative organ did not make their appearance in the life of the State until modern times, but a civilised state without judicial organ is hardly conceivable.[26] The importance of judiciary is more for the citizens than for the States. And in Indian political system, the judiciary has carved out a very significant space for itself. In fact, the transition from a feudal to a democratic order and from colonial bondage to a free society needed an institution to protect individual's life, liberty and property.

The framers of the Indian Constitution at the time of framing of our constitution were concerned about the kind of judiciary our country should have. In course of the discussion on Indian judiciary Dr B.R. Ambedkar responded properly in the Constituent Assembly and asserted, 'There can be no difference of option in the House that our judiciary must be both independent of the executive and must also be competent in itself. And the question is how these two objects can be secured'. The answer to this question lies in the very basic understanding that so as to secure the stability and prosperity of the society, the framers at that time understood that such a society could be created only by guaranteeing the fundamental rights and the independence of the judiciary to guard and enforce those fundamental rights. Also in a country like India, the independence of the judiciary is of utmost importance in upholding the pillars of the democratic system hence ensuring a free society.[27] On the enforcement of the constitution in January 1950, this system was expected to adapt itself to facilitate the transformation of Indian society into a nation and to become an effective instrument for carrying out the mandate of Article 38. Judiciary being an important instrumentality for exercise of state judicial power, it had to shoulder the burden along with other wings to set up a welfare state in which justice - social, economic and political - shall inform all the institutions of national life. It must also shoulder the primary responsibility of eliminating inequalities in status, facilities and opportunities not only amongst group of people residing in different areas engaged in different vocations.[28] After independence all the organs of the government, including judiciary, attempted to bring harmony and justice.

Post-Independence Judicial Scripts

The framers of the Constitution of India provided the country an independent and impartial judicial system which in coming years has been functioning as one of the foremost institutions of India's republican democracy as an instrument of rule of law. The benefits of a good judicial system are many covering economic, political and social spheres. The importance of the judiciary lies in checking abuses of government power, enforcing property rights, enabling exchanges between private parties and maintaining public order. A balanced, swift, affordable and fair justice delivery system - besides promoting law and order - aids in the development of markets, investment and affects economic growth positively. Good economic policies need strong and accountable institutions to support and implement them. Strong justice institutions thus form the basis of lasting social order.[29] Similar view was also expressed when Alladi Krishnaswami Ayyar, a leading member of the Constitution Drafting Committee predicted, 'the future evolution of the Indian Constitution will depend to a large extent upon the Supreme Court and the direction given to it by the Court. While its function may be one of interpreting the Constitution, it cannot... ignore the social, economic and political tendencies of the times... On certain occasions it may appear to strengthen the union at the expense of the units and at another time it may appear to champion the cause of provincial autonomy and regionalism. On one occasion it may appear to favour individual liberty as against social or state control and another time, it may appear to favour social or state control. It is the great tribunal which has to draw the line between liberty and social control.[30] Till date in performing the difficult and complex tasks with considerable erudition, understanding and wisdom, the judicial system as a whole and the summit court, in particular, has made an important and enduring contribution to nation building.

The Constitution of India in post-1947 period started its operation in happy harmony with the instrumentalities of the Executive, Legislature and Judiciary. Among the three pillars of the democratic set-up the three wings have their own rights, duties and bounds within the framework of the Constitution. The legislature is to legislate the subordinate norms for the good governance of the country, in all walks of national life which require a well established and regulated path to proceed on. The Executive is to implement the legal policies of the legislature and the likewise tasks. And on the other judiciary is to watch the validity and conformity of all the legislative enactments and the application thereof the Executive in the manner intended by the legislature and prescribed by the Constitution with the philosophy of the Rule of Law. Clearly it was based on the principle of separation of power which meant that the three organs of the State, the legislature, the executive and the judiciary must respect each other and must not ordinarily encroach into each other's domain, otherwise the system cannot function properly.[31] Since Independence the high judiciary, especially the Supreme Court, has fully utilised its rights and obligation to enforce and interpret the Constitution. It has set up high standards of independence from the executive and legislative arms of the government. It has also been in the forefront of the defence of fundamental rights. According to Article 32, the Supreme Court has original jurisdiction in case of appeals or writs relating to enforcement of Fundamental Rights, that is, a person can straightway appeal to the Supreme Court without going through the normal layers of the judicial hierarchy. The Supreme Court has also original jurisdiction in all disputes between the Union and States as well as between states.

The Supreme Court has played a major role in interpreting the Constitution especially with regard to the changing relationship between Fundamental Rights and Directive Principles. While it is limited in its powers in comparison to the US Supreme Court when it comes to declaring any law unconstitutional, since it does not have the clause of 'due process of law' or standards of natural justice, it has made up by evolving the doctrine of 'Basic Features' on the basis of which even an amendment to the Constitution can be declared invalid if it is destructive of the Basic Features of the Constitution. It has not only inherited the mantle of the Judicial Committee of the Privy Council as the final court of appeal in all matters but has also been made the ultimate interpreter of the laws and the Constitution, the arbiter of federal disputes and the constitutional protector of the fundamental rights of individuals and of minority groups.[32] In sheer amplitude of judicial powers and the variety and range of jurisdictions, the Supreme Court of India is without a rival in any other system in the world. The nature of controversies which our Supreme Court has called upon to resolve inevitably makes its role vital and vulnerable. In a sense and to a certain extent, the Constitution is what the Supreme Court says it is.[33] All authorities, civil and judicial are obliged to act in aid of the Supreme Court.

Initially for years the Indian judicial system represented a conservative and status quoist character and remained insensitive to social issues and movements and resulted in its standing in the way of radical socio-economic legislation in the name of defence of individual rights. For instance, at the beginning the Supreme Court interpreted the right of property to negate land reforms, nationalisation of banks, etc. It also tended to ignore the Directive Principles of State Policy laid down in the Constitution.[34] It was the period when Indian judiciary was maintaining the British legal system but the new system of India combined the principles of liberal democracy with socialist aspirations of general equality and welfare. In fact, the Supreme Court performs judicial functions but it has also to deal with many issues and controversies which have partisan origins and political consequences. A constitutional court, howsoever moderate and self-restrained, cannot evade or avoid pronouncements on matters of public concern. It cannot turn a deaf ear to complaints against arbitrariness. It cannot turn a blind eye to unreasonable invasion on fundamental rights. In several judgements relating to the rights of prisoners, the court has done substantial justice by holding that a prisoner does not totally lose his fundamental right to liberty once he enters the prison.

Since its inception, the peculiarity of the Supreme Court is that it exercises not only a legislative function but also a constituent one for it can make and unmake constitutional amendments. In the context judicial review is a substantive and cherished right of the judiciary to declare a statute invalid; if it comes in conflict with the constitution. Article 372(1) mentions that all the pre-constitutional laws would remain in force 'subject to the provisions of constitution' if those laws are not inconsistent with the cherished rights of the citizens enshrined in Part III of the Constitution. Likewise Article 245(1) vests legislative powers in the Parliament and make it 'subject to the provisions of the constitution'. Whether a law pre or post is in accordance with the provisions of the Constitution or not is a question comes under the purview of the concept of Judicial Review.[35] Besides, Article 13 also gives powers of Judicial Review in the sense that a law should not be in detrogation to Part III, dealing with Fundamental Rights.

In addition, there has been the practice of judiciary to invalid the law made under Article 368 on the ground of breach of "Basic Structure." The power of judiciary to review and determine the validity of a law or an order may be described as the power of "Judicial Review." It means that the Constitution is the Supreme Law of the land and any inconsistent therewith is void. The term refers to "the power of a court to inquire whether a law, executive order or the other official action conflicts with the written constitution and if the court concludes that it does, to declare it unconstitutional and void". In brief, the term judicial review has two prime functions: (i) Legitimising government action; and (ii) to protect the Constitution against any undue encroachment by the government." The Constitution of India, in this respect, is more akin to the US Constitution than the British. In Britain the doctrine of Parliamentary supremacy still holds goods. No court of law there can declare a parliamentary enactment invalid. In India, the power of judicial review of legislation is given to the judiciary both by the political theory and text of the constitution. Along with the Supreme Court the High Courts are also made protector and guarantor of Fundamental Rights under Articles 32 and 226. Articles 251 and 254 say that in case of inconsistent between union and state laws, the state law shall be void.

On the issue of invalidating the laws/executive orders, the Supreme Court of India, in the historic case of Golaknath vs. The State of Punjab (1967) in which the validity of three constitutional amendments (1st, 4th and 17th) was challenged, reversed its earlier judgements made in 1951, 1955 and 1964 by a majority of six to five and held that Parliament under Article 368 has no power to take away or abridge the Fundamental Rights contained in Chapter II of the Constitution. In this judgement the Supreme Court had opined that the decision in Shankri Prasad case contained the seeds of destruction of the cherished rights of the people. In this very case an iron wall before the implied powers of the Parliament to amend the Constitution under Article 368, was built by the Supreme Court.[36] In Golaknath's case, the Supreme Court experimented two doctrines, viz., Ultravires and "Prospective Overruling." By applying the doctrine of prospective overruling the laws prior to the date of decision were declared valid and by applying the doctrine of "ultra vires" the Parliament was restrained to amend particularly the provisions of Part III with effect from 27 February 1967. The decision of Golaknath's case which was decided by a "paper thin" majority of 6:5, was made crystal clear: (i) that the Parliament can amend any part of the constitution; and (ii) provided by the "Basic Structure" of the constitution cannot be amended by the Parliament. Thus, in initial years the Indian judiciary laid stress on personal, inalienable rights and protected the traditional social structure. In general, old laws protecting privileges were actively enforced whereas reforms in favour of the oppressed, meant to foster social change were inadequately implemented.

Viewed particularly the judicial judgements from the premiership of Jawaharlal Nehru to his daughter Indira Gandhi's first term in office, the Indian Supreme Court was not seen as an ally of the poor and oppressed. Rather, it was considered to be a conservative protector of the economically better off. Nehru was in favour of land reform. But the Supreme Court insisted on full financial compensation of former landlords reducing the Indian Republic's redistribution options. Nehru repeatedly criticised specific rulings, but being a trained lawyer himself, he never put the judicial processes or institutions in doubt. In opposite to her father Indira Gandhi intended to nationalise the Indian banking sector and abolish the privy purses and other privileges of the nobility that had formally ruled Indian princely states in colonial days. The Supreme Court overruled her decrees as not being in line with the constitution. As a next step, Indira Gandhi portrayed the government as being obliged to pursue socialist policies by Part IV of the constitution, the Directive Principles of State Policy. She accused the Supreme Court of not being committed to these goals and also claimed that the directive principles were superior to the fundamental rights. An important consequence of this analysis is that in the process of constitutional adjudication, intentionally or unintentionally, the court is invariably drawn into the politics of the establishment or the politics of the opposition. In the context of the Indian state, which is dominated by one party or coalition of parties, the implication of this is that opposition groups come to the court for protection from the tyranny of the dominant party. They also challenge the pursuit of policies or values of the ruling party through the process of constitutional adjudication, and in such cases the court cannot just give a neutral result.[37] A theory of the state is therefore, a necessary precondition to the understanding of the role of the judiciary. 'Invalidating status is not only an act of judicial wisdom but also an act of political will.[38] It is in this role that the court has time and again tried to influence the "agenda for political action" and in the sense the legal process is a speces of the political processes.

Especially after the breaking down of emergency rule, the Supreme Court of India has reasserted its position and sought to refurbish its image with a new activism which championed the rights of those who are prevented from the claiming the privileges of full citizenship because of social and economic disability. The success of the Supreme Court's attempt to open its doors to new constituencies, and its efforts to curb the lawlessness of government and enhance public accountability, greatly depend on the strength of social action movements which have produced a new consciousness about problems and struggle for survival of the poor. This move and Public Interest Litigation (PIL) of Supreme Court was also interpreted by some analysts as an expression of the ongoing conflict between Parliament and the Supreme Court. However, it has now become more sensitive to social issues, from the rights of women, workers and minorities to ecology, human rights, social justice and equality and social discrimination. With the practice of Public Interest Litigation (PIL) and its widening the poor and the disadvantaged have actually acquired an easy access to justice. It has opened a window that was completely shut earlier. Over the years since its inception, the Court has advanced, rationalised and consolidated the law in its myriad applications in our vast sub-continent. Its integrating and unifying impact on the life of the nation has been substantially conducive to our national coherence, stability and a sense of fraternity.

5.2 Analysis of Judicial Activism : Modern and Post-modern

The Constitution of India has embodied a faith in the words of Abraham Lincon 'that the Government of the people, for the people and by the people shall not perish upon this earth'. In consideration, the founding fathers who wrote the constitution, created three arms-Parliament, Executive and the Judiciary. In the Constitutional scheme parliament is not supreme. It is subject to a major limitation-that legislation does not violate any fundamental rights or constitutional values. In the context, the judiciary can strike down any law that is beyond Parliament's legislative competence or is violative of the Constitution. In line, Article 142 of the Constitution hands a unique extraordinary power to our Supreme Court to do complete justice in any matter before it. As the umpire of the constitutional system and the legal process, the Supreme Court has to strive to relieve the tensions of a developing nation, to resolve the conflicts of a diverse and open society and to accommodate adjudicate antagonistic demands for justice. In performing those difficult and complex tasks with considerable erudition, understanding and wisdom, the judicial system as a whole and the summit courts, in particular, has made an important and enduring contribution to nation-building.[39] In the light of these the judiciary has shed its pro-status-quo approach and taken upon itself the duty to enforce the basic rights of the poor and vulnerable sections of society, by progressive interpretation and positive action. Judicial activism refers to the interference of the judiciary in the legislative and executive fields. It mainly occurs due to the non-activity of the other organs of the government and relates closely to constitutional interpretation, statutory construction and separation of powers.

Constitutional Basis

In a democratic polity, good government is indispensable for any state and the three organs of the government - Legislative, Executive and Judiciary constitute three pillars of good and effective governance. The Constitution of India has provided an independent judiciary because the founding fathers of the Constitution were well aware that only independent and fearless judiciary free from the legislative and executive control can play an active role. Various constitutional provisions regarding the independence of judiciary have strengthened the argument that the Indian Constitution has always assigned a very active role to the judiciary as guardian of the Constitution, as final interpreter of the Constitution, as an arbitrator to settle the disputes between the Union and the States on the one hand and amongst the States on the other. Being an interpreter of the Constitution, the judiciary has to interpret its own role according to the changing socio-economic conditions of the society.[40] In the event of poverty and illiteracy, its challenging task is to ensure social justice to all. In the Constitutional scheme, the judicial system works as an active catalyst to secure social justice for every citizens.

The universal demand for social justice to all citizens of the country was not sudden and during the framing of the Indian constitution in the 1940s, the engrafting of Directive Principles of State Policy was inspired from the Irish example. To ensure the objectives of Constitution the Indian judiciary has been constitutionally vested with the power of review to keep the Executive and Legislature within constitutional boundaries.

Articles 13, 21, 32, 226 and 227 encompass this power in which judiciary can strike down any law that is beyond Parliament's legislative competence or is violative of the Constitution. Similarly, it can strike down any Executive action, if there is any patent illegality or arbitrariness to it. The inclusion of explicit provisions for judicial review were necessary in order to give effect to the individual and group rights guaranteed in the text of the Constitution. Dr B.R. Ambedkar, who chaired the drafting committee of our Constituent Assembly, had described the provision as the heart of the Constitution. Article 13 (2) of the Constitution of India prescribes clearly that the Union or the States shall not make any law that takes away or abridges any of the fundamental rights or any law made in contravention of the aforementioned mandate shall, to the extent of the contravention, be void.[41] However, in most cases, the power of judicial review is exercised to protect and enforce the fundamental rights guaranteed in Part III of the Constitution. For decades the scope of judicial review has three dimensions - firstly, to ensure fairness in administrative action, secondly to protect the constitutionally guaranteed fundamental rights of citizens and thirdly to rule on questions of legislative competence between the centre and the states. At large the doctrine of 'judicial review' helps in binding a polity to its core constitutional principles.

Especially in post-World War II era, the memory of devastating conflicts and oppressive colonialism ensured that these principles were initially centered on the protection of basic civil-political rights such as free speech, assembly association and movements as well as guarantees against abusive practices by state agencies such as arbitrary arrest, detention, torture and extra-judicial killings. Depending on the social profile of a country's population, the safeguards against authoritative atrocities may be in the nature of a proactive measures designed for the advancement of historically disadvantaged communities and poorer sections of society. Such initial safeguards which are meant to tackle social differences based on factors such as religion, caste, gender, class and region among others have also clear socio-economic dimensions. Therefore, the role of the Courts in protecting Constitutional values goes beyond the enforcement of clearly defined civil-political rights that can be litigated by individual citizens and incorporates a continuously evolving understanding of 'group rights' which necessarily have socio-economic dimensions as well.[42]

In a country like India the social, economic and political justice can be achieved if every instrumentality under the Constitution functions as per the mandate of the Constitution.[43] The inactivity, incompetence, disregard of law and constitution, by the legislature and callousness, negligence, corruption, greed for power, and money, indiscipline in the executive had created the vacuum as a result of which both the organs of the government failed to fulfil the constitutional obligations and compelled the judiciary to play an active role,[44] in order to fill the vacuum created by the executive and the legislature and to check the unconstitutional behaviour of the executive and the legislators. Thus, judicial activism refers to the interference of the judiciary in the legislative and executive fields. It mainly occurs due to the non-activity of the other organs of the government. It is the adoption of pro-active approach by the judiciary and reflects the situation when the judiciary comes out of its sphere of traditional role and becomes active in its working while laying down the policies and programmes to ensure the protection of rights and liberties of the people which otherwise is within the discretion of the executive and legislature.

Implementation and Interpretation

In the early years of the Indian constitutional experience, civil liberties and the protection against deprivation of life and liberty were understood mainly as imposing duties of restraint on governmental agencies as well as private citizens. At the same time, in contrast to these justiciable negative rights the directive principles of state policy allude to several socio-economic objectives which had a positive dimension. The Indian courts have responded to these negative and positive rights by trying to collapse the distinction. While the fundamental rights of citizens enumerated in Part III of the constitution are justiciable before the higher judiciary, Part IV deals with the Directive Principles of State Policy that largely enumerate objectives pertaining to socio-economic entitlements. The Directive Principles aim at creating an egalitarian society whose citizens are free from fulfilling their best selves. They are the creative part of the Constitution, and fundamental to the governance of the country. Even at the time of drafting the Constitution, some of the provisions which are presently part of the Directive Principles were part of the declaration of fundamental rights adopted by the Congress party. K.M. Munshi, a noted lawyer and a member of the Constituent Assembly had included in his draft list of rights, the 'rights of workers' and 'social rights' which included provisions protecting women and children and guaranteeing the right to work, a decent wage and a decent standard of living.[45] Dr B.R. Ambedkar, Chairman of the Drafting Committee was also in favour of its importance when insisted on the use of the word 'strive' in the language of Article 38 which mentions the governmental objective of an equitable distribution of material resources. Participating in Constituent Assembly Debates on 19th November 1948 he clarified, We have used it because it is our intention that even when there are circumstances which prevent the government or which stand in the way of the government giving effect to these directive principles, they shall, even under hard and unpropitious circumstances, always strive in the fulfilment of these directives.....Otherwise it would be open for any government to say that the circumstances are so bad, that the finances are so inadequate that we cannot even make an effort in the direction in which the Constitution asks us to go.[46] Gradually, the themes relating to fundamental rights and directive principles have been expanded and include several socio-economic entitlements for citizens which place positive obligations on the state. Now judges refer directly to the language of provisions contained in the part dealing with directive principles and it has transformed the substantive character of the protection of life and property. Even the Supreme Court of India has interpreted the protection of life and personal liberty as one which contemplates socio-economic entitlements.

The implementation of new dynamic approach as adopted by the judicial system pertaining to socio-economic environment of the country has widely expanded its nature and scope as well. Every fundamental right is not spelt out comprehensively in the Constitution, but the right to shelter, right to privacy, right to go abroad and right to education have all been deduced through creative interpretation of judges. Likewise, the Supreme Court has deduced the freedom of the press from the guarantee of free speech and thus press freedom has been given a constitutional status by creative judicial interpretations. Judicial interpretations are based on the realities of the situation. Every country has to work out its Constitution according to its problems, needs and demands. Once Justice Krishna Ayer said rightly, 'Every new decision, on every new situation, is a development of law. Law does not stand still. It moves continually. Once this is recognised, then the task of the judge is put on higher plane.' The courts cannot remain mute spectators when laws are not enforced and consequently, fundamental rights are violated. If the judiciary does not intervene, it would be an inactive judiciary. Especially after the Constitution Twenty Fifth Amendment Act, 1971, primacy was given to

Directive Principles of State Policy by making them enforceable. In the situation decades ago the judiciary has shed its pro-status-quo approach and taken upon itself the duty to enforce the basic rights of the poor and vulnerable sections of society, by progressive interpretation and positive action.

The decade 1970s was a turning point in the judicial history of India when several judgements delivered by the Supreme Court relating to Amendments, Judicial Review, Fundamental Rights, Directive Principles of State Policy and the significance of Social Action Litigation (SAL) affected the different spheres of polity and society. In the changed circumstances the primary functions of the judiciary are not restricted to the settlement of disputes and punish the defiance of law, but to safeguard individual liberty and social cohesion against undue institutional encroachment.[47] In the famous Kesavananda Bharti case delivered in 1973, the Supreme Court of India held that basic features of the Constitution of India such as democracy, rule of law, federal system, secularism and independence of judiciary can not be amended. If it is amended, then the Supreme Court will declare such law as unconstitutional. Beginning with the first few instances in the late-1970s, the category of Public Interest Litigation (PIL) has come to be associated with its own 'people friendly procedures'. The foremost change came in the form of the dilution of the requirement of 'locus standi' or initiating proceedings. Since the intent was to improve access to justice for those who were otherwise too poor to move the courts or were unaware of their legal entitlements, the court allowed actions to be brought on their behalf by social activists and lawyers.[48] In most public interest-related litigation, the judges began to take on a far more active role in the literal sense as well as by posing questions to the parties as well as exploring solutions. In other words, the growth of constitutionalism has been synonymous with that of liberal values which seek to safeguard an individual dignity as well as collective welfare at the same time. Thus, from 1979, the judiciary led by the Supreme Court in India became relevant to the nation in a manner not contemplated by the makers of the Constitution and became an active participant in the dispenser of social justice.

However, the Public Interest Litigation began halting with little idea of its potential when the Supreme Court, in 1979, entertained complaints by social activists drawing the attention of the Court to the conditions of certain sections of society or institutions which were deprived of their basic rights. In the same year Supreme Court advocate Kapila Hingorani drew the court's attention to a series of articles in a newspaper exposing the plight of Bihar undertrial prisoners, most of whom had served pretrial detention more than the period they could have been imprisoned if convicted. Further in 1980, two professors of law wrote a letter to the editor of a newspaper describing the barbaric conditions of detention in the Agra Protective House for Women which was made the basis of a writ petition in the Supreme Court. In dealing with such cases, the Court evolved a new regime of rights of citizens and obligations of the State and devised new methods for its accountability. In 1982, Justice P.N. Bhagwati, corrected and stated the purpose of PIL as it originated. He emphasised it as 'a strategic arm of the legal aid movement which is intended to bring justice within the reach of the poor masses, who constitute the low visibility area of humanity, is a totally different kind of litigation from the ordinary traditional litigation'.[49] Over the years this original, beneficial and unexceptionable character of the Court's activism in PIL has been largely converted into a general supervisory jurisdiction to correct actions and policies of government, public bodies and authorities. With Public Interest Litigation, the common man, the disadvantaged and marginalised sections of society had also easy access to the Court with the help of social activists. It has provided an opportunity to citizens, social groups, consumer rights activists etc, easier access to law and introduced a public interest perspective. Justices P. N. Bhagwati and V.R. Krishna Ayer have played a key role in promoting this avenue of approaching the apex court of the country, seeking legal remedies in areas where public interests are at stake. In this context it is needed to clarify that judicial activism is not the performance of the function of settling the disputes in accordance with Constitution or law of the land. A judge who selects a bold course of action is generally understood as representing judicial activism.[50] No doubt, it has improved the quality of governance in India.

Judicial activism means an activism by taking recourses to judicial process, which means judicial pronouncement on different intricate issues whereby new legal philosophy can be created.[51] Black's Law Dictionary defines judicial activism as a philosophy of judicial decision-making whereby judges allow their personal views about public policy, among other factors, to guide their decisions. Another scholar and Professor of Political Science Bradley Canon has posited six dimensions along which judge courts may be perceived as activist:[52] majoritarianism, interpretive stability, interpretive fidelity, substance/democratic process, specificity of policy and availability of an alternate policy-maker. While Justice P.N. Bhagwati and Justice A.S. Anand observed that judicial activism is a central feature of every political system that vests adjudicatory power in a free and independent judiciary. 'The term judicial activism is not the term of fashion or popularism but a term signifying an important source of judicial power, which judges should use for the realisation of willed result.[53] And, in line, Justice Anand holds, 'the judicial activism reinforces the strength of democracy and reaffirms the faith in the rule of law. It would not be in the interest of the democratic society, if the judiciary shuts its door to the citizen who finds that the legislature is not responding and the executive is indifferent. It must be seen that the authorities come out of the slumber and perform their role.'[54] In a nutshell, it means different persons.

Prospects and Caution

Judicial activism is gaining prominence in the present day and mainly in the form of Public Interest Litigation (PIL) citizens are getting access to justice. During the past decade, many instances of judicial activism have gained significance. The areas in which judiciary has become active are health, child labour, political corruption, environment, education, etc. Through various cases the judiciary has shown its firm commitment to participatory justice, just standards of procedures, immediate access to justice, and preventing arbitrary action. After the PIL judgements in relation to poor and marginalised sections of society the Courts have assumed an active role in shaping the society. The approach and working of the judiciary has undergone an incredible change because the erosion of values in public life since seventies have brought into focus the Supreme Court of India. It has adopted a proactive approach having regard for the peculiar socio-economic conditions prevailing in the country.

Meanwhile a look at major High Court and Supreme Court decisions in recent years shows that they have clearly transcended the limits and undertaken functions that fall within the domain of either the Legislature or the Executive. A court is not equipped with the skills and competence to discharge the functions that essentially belong to the other organs of the State. Judges are neither trained to deal with macro-economic policy issues nor do they have the required skills or administrative infrastructure to handle them. Consequently, many are critical of judicial activism as an exercise of judicial power which displaces existing law or creates more legal uncertainty than is necessary, where or not the ruling has some constitutional, historical or other basis. This, it is argued, violates the doctrine of separation of powers. An accusation of judicial activism implies that the judge is not performing his or her duty as an interpreter of the law, but is instead ruling on the basis of personal political convictions or emotions. Critics say that this can violate a judge's sworn allegiance to uphold the constitution, because, in effect, it encourages judges to write their own constitutions.

In fact, by interfering in the jurisdiction of the Legislature and the Executive as given by the Constitution of India, the practice of judicial activism somewhere disregarded the separation of powers under the Constitution. The philosophy behind the doctrine of judicial restraint is that there is broad separation of powers under the constitution, and the three organs of the State must respect each other, and must not ordinarily encroach into each other's domain, otherwise the system cannot function properly. The Judiciary must realise that the legislature is a democratically elected body, which expresses the will of the people and in a democracy this will is not to be lightly frustrated or thwarted.[55] In several decisions this theme of Indian Constitution have been recognised by the apex court very clearly. In Asif Hameed vs. The State of Jammu and Kashmir, AIR 1989, (paragraph 17 to 19), the Indian Supreme Court observed, 'Although the doctrine of separation of powers has not been recognised under the Constitution in its absolute rigidity, the Constitution-makers have meticulously defined the functions of various organs of the State. The legislature, executive, and judiciary have to function within their own spheres demarcated in the constitution. No organ can usurp the function of another. In another recent judgement delivered in 2006 in Divisional Manager, Aravali Golf Course vs. Chander Haas the Supreme Court of India upheld, 'judges must know their limits and not try to run the government. They must have modesty and humility and not behave like Emperors. There is broad separation of powers under the Constitution, and each of the organs of the state must have respect for the others and must not encroach into each other's domain.[56] In a democracy, the remedy for a malfunctioning legislature and executive must come from the people, not the judiciary.

However, despite the clear theory and practice of separation of powers under the Indian Constitution and acceptance of judicial activism, in its true sense, which is sought for enforcing the rights of the disadvantaged or poor sections of society, the apex court began to dilute the dimension of PIL. In this type of litigation, the court's intervention is sought simply for correcting the actions or omissions of the executive or public officials, or departments of government or public bodies. For example, in the interest of preventing pollution, the Supreme Court ordered control over automobile emissions, air and noise and traffic pollution, gave orders for parking charges, wearing of helmets in cities, cleanliness in housing colonies, disposal of garbage, control of traffic in New Delhi etc. Even very recently the Supreme Court has directed the most complex engineering of interlinking rivers in India and on its own, the Court has taken notice of Baba Ramdev being forcibly evicted from the Ramlila grounds by the Delhi Administration. All these managerial exercises by the Court are hung on the dubious jurisdictional peg of enforcing fundamental rights under Article 32 of the Constitution. The Court is only moved for better governance and administration, which does not involve the exercise of any proper judicial function.[57] A review of case laws proves that judicial activism may work towards the benefit of the society but that is not always the case. Some judgements have been delivered with great insight and vision but some others are based only on self-conviction and belief, that such a judgement would help the parties, without taking into consideration the repercussions on the law or on the society at large. There has been an increase in the number of frivolous cases being filed and as a result genuine cases got receded to the back-ground and privately motivated interests started gaining predominance in Public Interest Litigation cases. In view of this, the Supreme Court has framed certain guidelines in this regard.

To conclude, the analysis leads us to the fact that judicial activism has given some very good case laws and even led to revolutionary changes in society. At the same time judges should be careful not to make judicial activism judicial adventurism. It is essential for the progress of the country that all the three wings should function in complete coordination. The judicial activism and judicial restraint should go side by side so that all the three wings of the State can continue harmoniously.

5.3 Judging Judicial Corruption in India

In a country like India the working of democracy under rule of law is dependent much on the health of its courts. The Constitution of India enjoins the State to separate the judiciary from the executive with the intent to immunise the judiciary from any form of executive control or interference. In the context independence of judiciary and rule of law are the basic features of the Constitution. Independence of judiciary in a narrow sense deals with independence and impartiality of individual judges in relation to the appointment, tenure, payment of salary etc, while in a broader sense the concept is about institutional independence of the judiciary. Of course, the judiciary cannot operate in isolation from the other arms of the government. An independent and impartial judiciary has important consequences for trade, investment and financial markets. On the other corruption in judiciary diminishes trade, economic growth and human development; and most importantly, it denies citizens impartial settlement of disputes with neighbours or the authorities. Corrupt judiciaries fracture and divide communities by keeping alive the sense of injury created by unjust treatment and mediation. Judicial system debased by bribery undermines confidence in governance by facilitating corruption across all sectors of government, starting at the helm of power. In so doing they send a blunt message to the people: in this country corruption is tolerated.

Concept and Kinds of Corruption

Corruption in judiciary is defined as 'the abuse of entrusted power for private gains'. This means both financial or material gain, such as the furtherance of political or professional ambitions. It includes any in appropriate influence on the impartiality of the judicial process by any actor within the court system. For instance, a judge may allow or exclude evidence with the aim of justifying the acquittal of a guilty defendant of high political or social status. Judges or court staff may manipulate court dates to favour one party or another. Other parts of the judicial system may influence judicial corruption. Criminal cases can be corrupted before they reach the courts if police tamper with evidence that supports a criminal indictment, or prosecutors fail to apply uniform criteria to evidence generated by the police. Thus, judicial corruption extends from pre-trial activities through the trial proceedings and settlement to the ultimate enforcement of decisions by court. In addition, the appeals process, ostensibly an important avenue for redress in cases of faulty verdicts, presents further opportunities for judicial corruption. In general, distinction exists between judicial systems that are relatively free of corruption and those that suffer from systemic manipulation.

Other countries alike there are two types of corruption in India that most affect judiciaries: political interference in judicial process by either the executive or legislative branches of government, and bribery. Despite several decades of reform efforts to protect judicial independence, judges and court personnel around the world continue to face pressure to rule in favour of powerful political or economic entities, rather than according to the law. Not only in India but in other nations too, political interference comes about by threat, intimidation and simple bribery of judges. Judicial independence is founded on public confidence. The perceived integrity of the institution is of particular importance, since it underpins trust in the institution. In developing countries judicial and political corruption are mutually reinforcing. Where the justice system is corrupt sanction on people who use bribes and threats to suborn politicians are unlikely to be enforced. The ramifications of this dynamic are deep as they deter more honest and unfettered candidates from entering or succeeding in politics or public service.

Bribery, the second kind of judicial corruption can occur at every point of interaction in the judicial system: court officials may extort money for work they should do anyway: lawyers may charge additional fees to expedite or delay cases, or to direct clients to judges known to take bribes for favourable decisions. For their part, judges may accept bribes to delay or accelerate cases, accept or deny appeals, influence other judges or simply decide a case in a certain way. In the situation when defendants or litigants already have a low opinion of the honesty of judges and the judicial process, they are far more likely to resort to bribing court officials, lawyers and judges to achieve their ends. It is also to mention here that in the developing world the formal judicial system handle only a fraction of disputes; while traditional legal systems or state-run administrative justice processes account for an estimated 90 per cent of non-legal cases in many parts of the globe.

Judicial corruption in any form affects the stages of impartial decision making in: (i) ascertaining the facts, (ii) finding laws, (iii) interpreting the legal materials selected and (iv) applying the resulting legal percept to the cause. At each of these stages of judicial decision-making, impartiality is essential and at every stage, the possibility exists that the judge's experience and values may influence the outcome. The common form of corruption in judiciary comes from greed, or which is driven by ambition. Judges have an obligation to avoid corruption of those, or similar kind. They also have an obligation to avoid less obvious forms of partiality, or even the appearance of it. There is a need, here, to balance the rights of judges as individuals, to pursue causes in which they believe, on the one hand, with the need for public confidence on the other.

Possible Remedies

In a democracy the cornerstones of judicial integrity are independence, transparency and accountability. But the real strength of the judiciary is the trust and confidence of the people in it and that such trust and confidence will continue only when judiciary is seen as a noble, virtuous, incorruptible institution; and if there is wide publicity about corruption in the judiciary, people will loose their faith in the system thereby further eroding the strength of the judiciary. Till date, much money has been spent training judges without addressing expectations and incentives for judges to act with integrity. Money has also been spent automating the courts or otherwise trying to reduce court workloads and streamline case management which, if unaccompanied by increased accountability, risks making corrupt courts more efficiently corrupt.

Of the three integral cornerstones, especially independence of judiciary has been universally acknowledged as the hallmarks of Indian democracy. By independence of judiciary we mean, 'the capacity of courts to perform their constitutional function free from actual or apparent interference by, and to the extent that it is constitutionally possible, free from actual or apparent dependence upon, any person or institutions, including in particular, the executive arm of government, over which they do not exercise direct control'. Independence of judiciary and rule of law are the basic features of the Constitution. It cannot be abrogated even by constitutional amendments. Likewise, transparency in judicial system is essential for impartial and responsible justice as it would minimise the scope for judicial corruption. In particular, transparency requires in spheres of organisation, work culture, prosecution service, disclosure of assets, due process of rights, freedom of expressions and civil society engagement etc. Maximum transparency in judiciary will provide the public with reliable information about its governance.

For decades and especially in recent past there have been repeated calls for judges to be more accountable. In the context, judges are regularly accused of making law rather than of applying it. These accusations are often made in circumstances in which the judges have done no more than develop the common law in accordance with accepted principles, in order to keep pace with changing social conditions, in much the same way as they have done over hundreds of years. In fact, the scope of accountability or responsibility can range from a rigid subject of one person to the control of another, to a degree of responsiveness on the part of one person to the interests or wishes of another. But in spite of recent calls to make judges more accountable in respect of their efficiency and as regards their spending of public money, the objective of accountability to promote good decision-making is becoming relevant day by day.

The other measures to combat the judicial corruption include the system of Performance Indicator, Performance Review and Judicial Education and Training. Under the first proposal the court should collect and report performance indicators and then engage in benchmarking. Benchmarking involves developing performance standards which can then be used to compare the organisation and efficiency of a court with the benchmarked standard. The purpose of benchmarks is to permit comparison between different courts, the comparison being an objective one. In a system of performance reviews the arrangement for performance appraisal is to be made by members of the legal profession and there is wide talk and discussion on the issue in Australia and England. There is no doubt in it that performance reviews could aid in the improvement of judicial standards, any formal system of evaluation raises concerns for individual independence. The aim of judicial education and training is to prepare judges for the task of social justice adjudication. It is pertinently relevant in a developing country like India which is inhabited by over a billion people professing different religions, speaking different languages and living at present in extreme levels of poverty and affluence.

However, there is no magic set of structures and practices that will reduce corruption in all situations. No single mechanism for maintaining an independent judiciary can be transplanted elsewhere without amendment and have the same effectiveness. Even though the problems of India's justice delivery system are many and varied but these are not insurmountable. Similar problems plague the judiciaries of other countries also. The only difference is that we lag behind in implementing solutions. Differing situations may require measures that would not be helpful elsewhere, but the recommendations/suggestions of different communities can serve as a guide for reform efforts to promote judicial independence and accountability, and encourage more effective, efficient and fair enforcement. In the situation multi-faceted holistic reform of the judiciary is a crucial step toward enhancing justice and curbing the corruption that degrades legal systems and ruins lives the world over. Reforms should be an ongoing agenda forever.

References

1. Translated from the Sanskrit Sloks of Mahabharata as quoted in Justice S.S. Dhavan's article, 'The Indian Judicial System: A Historical Survey', p.1, also available on www.allahabadhighcourt.in.
2. *Ibid.*, p. 2.
3. D. Ross (ed.), Fakhr-ud-din Mubarak Shah, p.12.
4. *Encyclopaedia of Islam*, Vol. II, p. 606.
5. Junaid Iqbal Awan, 'Judicial System of East India Company', also available on www.academia.edu/.../judicial-system-o.
6. *Ibid.*, p.11.
7. S.D. Sharma, *Administration of Justice in Ancient India* (New Delhi: Harman Publishing House, 1988), p.170.
8. Mark Galanter, *Law and Society in Modern India* (New York: Oxford University Press, 1994), pp. 15-99.
9. Robert W. Stern, *Changing India* (New York : Cambridge University Press), p.15.
10. R.C. Majumdar, *The History and Culture of the Indian People: The Mughal Empire* , Vol. Vll (Bombay : Bharatiya Vidya Bhavan, 1974), p. 553.
11. Jean- Louis Halperin, 'Lay Justice in India', 25 March 2011.
12. M.V. Pylee, *India's Constitution* (Bombay: Asia Publishing House, 1979), p. 29.
13. Minattur Joseph, 'Indian Legal System', *Indian Law Institute* (2006), pp. 22-23.
14. Fali S.Nariman, 'Constitution Under Threat', *The Tribune*, 15 August 2007.
15. K.G. Balakrishnan, 'Executive to Blame for Delayed Justice', *in Ibid.*, 10 April 2007.
16. Austin Granville, *Indian Constitution: The Cornerstone of the Nation* (New Delhi: Oxford University Press, 2007), p. IX.
17. *Constituent Assembly Debates*, Vol.1 (New Delhi: Parliament Secretariat), p. 57. Also see, Shiva B. Rao (ed.), *The Framing of the India's Constitution, Select Documents*, 2 (Delhi: Universal Law Publishing, 2006), pp. 3-4.
18. Durga Das Basu, *Introduction to the Constitution of India*, Tenth Edition (New Delhi: Printice Hall of India, 1983), p. 253.
19. Court Judgements, Government of India's website.
20. Jean-Louis, 'Lay Justice in India'.

21. Dhananjay Mahapatra, 'Fund Crunch Lukewarm Response Mar Gram Nyayalayas' *The Times of India*, 22 May 2012.
22. *The Supreme Court of India's website* on 15 July 2012.
23. *District Courts of India's official website*, 16 March 2012.
24. See, Section 8 in *The Code of Criminal Procedure, Central Government Act*, 1973; available on http:// indiakanoon. org.
25. Dr Surya Narayan Misra, 'Constitutional Democracy, Judiciary and Social Justice in India', *Odisha Review*, January 2013, p. 2.
26. *Ibid.*
27. Atin Kumar Das, 'Independence of Judiciary in India: A Critical Analysis', available at mulnivasiorganiser. bamcef.org.
28. *The 117th Report of the Law Commission* (1986) as quoted in Dr K.N. Chandrasekharan Pillai, 'The Mission and Vision of Indian Judiciary', available at www.nja.nic.in
29. 'Judicial Impact Assessment: An Approach Paper', *Study Report, India Development Foundation*, May 2008, p.1.
30. As quoted in Bipin Chandra, Mridula Mukherjee and Aditya Mukherjee, *India After Independence 1947-2000* (New Delhi: Penguin Books, 2002), pp. 62-63.
31. Markandey Katju, 'Lessons in Judicial Restraint', *The Hindu*, 20 July 2012.
32. Dr L.M. Singhvi, 'Supreme Court's 30 Fruitful Years', *The Times of India*, 30 January 1979.
33. *Ibid.*
34. Bipin Chandra, Mridula Mukherjee and Aditya Mukherjee, *India After Independence 1947-2000*, p. 475.
35. Ram Babu Soni, 'Indian Judiciary-Today and Tomorrow', *Career Digest*, November 1976, p.1099.
36. *Ibid.*, p.1100.
37. Indira Jaising, 'Two Faces of Judiciary', *The Times of India*, 6 September, 1979.
38. Upendra Baxi, *The Indian Supreme Court and Politics* (Eastern Book), as quoted in *Ibid.*
39. Dr L.M. Singhvi, 'Supreme Court's 30 Fruitful Years', *The Times of India*, 28 January 1979.
40. M.M. Semwal, Sunil Khosla, 'Judicial Activism', *The Indian Journal of Political Science'*, Vol. LXIX, No. 1, January-March 2008 (Meerut:2008), p.118.
41. From the text of address by K.G. Balakrishnan, Chief Justice of India, on Judicial Activism under the Indian Constitution, at Trinity College, Dublin, Ireland, October 14, 2009, p. 2.

42. *Ibid*, pp. 9-10.
43. R.K. Bag, 'Judicial Activism vis-à-vis Public Administration', *The Administrator*, Vol. XLII, April-June 1997, p.167.
44. *Ibid*.
45. K.G. Balakrishnan, 'Judicial Activism Under the Indian Constitution', pp. 11-12.
46. *Constituent Assembly Debates* 19-11-1948.
47. Susanta Chatterji, 'For Public Administration : Is Judicial Activism Really Deterrent to Legislative Anarchy and Executive Tyranny,' *The Administrator* Vol. 42 (2), April-June 1997, p. 9.
48. Susan D. Susman, 'Distant Voices in the Courts of India : Transformation of Standing in Public Interest Litigation', 13 *Wisconsin International Law Journal* 57, 1994.
49. T.R. Andhyarujina, 'Disturbing Trends in Judicial Activism', *The Hindu*, 6 August 2012.
50. P.M. Bakshi, ' Judicial Activism, Some Reflections', *The Administrator*, Vol. XLII (2), April-June 1997, p. 5.
51. M.M. Semwal, Sunil Khosla, ' Judicial Activism', p. 115.
52. Bradley C. Canon, 'Defining the Dimensions of Judicial Activism,' Judicature, 66.6, 1983.
53. A Lakshminath, ' Jurisprudence of Judicial Activism', *The Administrator*, Vol. 42 (2), April-June 1997, p. 109.
54. C.M. Jariwala, 'Poorman's Access to Judicial Justice : A Reality or Myth', *Indian Journal of Public Administration*, Vol. XLV, No. 3, July-September 1999, p. 336.
55. Markandey Katju, 'Lessons in Judicial Restraint', *The Hindu*, 20 July 2012.
56. *Ibid*.
57. T.R. Andhyarujina, 'Disturbing Trends in Judicial Activism'.

Chapter - 6

Crucial Challenges of Indian Polity

6.1 Genesis of Political Corruption in India

In India and abroad the issue of corruption drew the attention of analysts and public as well from the time of the emergence of civil societies in ancient times to the complex politics of the present day. Corruption is a fact of life. It is as old as the human society itself. It exists in one form or another in every society as said by Ralph Braibaniti, 'Governmental corruption is found in all bureaucracy and in all periods of political development. But its degree is not uniform at all times or under all conditions. It is also obviously more common in some societies than in others and more common at some times in the evolution of a society than at other times.[1] In recent times corruption has assumed the shape of a "hot issue" and its tentacles have become not only widespread but also far more serious. The phenomenon has become very serious both in developed and developing countries. Even the international organisations are busy in arranging scholarly debates on the causes and consequences of corruption because corruption is not only a human issue but developmental as well as social and economic issue.

Corruption Defined and Analysed

Rampant corruption is something which does not need any emphasis. Everyone of us knows it, everyone of us sees it, every moment of our life, wherever we go, it is present in some form or the other. The challenge begins with how to define it. Most people know corruption when they see it. The problem is that different people see it differently.[2] The word is often used loosely in a very narrow sense and often used with a wide connotation, but somewhat confined to morals or public offences.

The etymology of the word can be traced back to a Latin word meaning "to break", which means that something is broken, such as, moral or social code of conduct and more importantly the violation of any law or administrative rule. Apart from outright graft or bribery, the use, abuse and non-use of power, legal or political, for personal or private gain to oneself or others not rightfully entitled to it, does cover the various hues and nuances of corruption.[3] Thus, the term includes all improper or selfish exercise of power and influence attached to a public office or to a special position one occupies in public life.

At large there is no internationally accepted definition of corruption. It depends upon the state of awareness, education, customs and contention, ethics, culture, state of economic development and legal framework over the interest of the society. High level of corruption is the result of wide divergence between the attitudes, aims and the methods of the government of a country and those of the society in which they operate, in particular, of the procedures and aims of the government which put particular groups of the population at a special disadvantage. In political context the word corruption has two aspects - social and political. Social aspect includes social behaviour, moral and religious while political aspect implies political and administrative or politico-administrative. Social corruption includes breach of social customs, habits, creeds affecting people; sexual harassment, creation of social evils etc. The politico-administrative corruption generally defiles the entire structure of society much more than social aspect.[4] The path of corruption has become clear and smooth when democratically elected people have come to constitute the administrative machinery and overtly or covertly indulge in corrupt practices.

India is rated as one of the most corrupt countries in the world. The global corruption perception Index of India is 87th out of 178 countries, slipping from 84th in 2009.[5] As a social phenomenon corruption has become so widespread that it has started eating into the vitals of our economy, our polity and our society. From top to bottom, prime minister to a peon, cutting across every office or organisation of all governments, Central State or local, the vast majority of public officials in this country have become corrupt. From the practical viewpoint, corruption as defined by the 19th Conference of European Ministers of Justice, held in Malta in 1994, seems to serve the overall purpose, 'Bribery and other behaviour in relation to persons entrusted with responsibilities in public or private sector which violates their duties that follow from their status as a public official, private employee, independent agent or other relationship of that kind and is aimed at obtaining undue advantages of any kind for themselves or others.[6] However, the overall composition of phenomenon of corruption in case of India and other developing countries may be summarised as follow :

Driving force	:	Individual need and greed
Supportive environment	:	Political interference
Restrictive environment	:	Transparency and accountability
Opportunity	:	Secrecy and complex regulation
Corrective measures	:	Certainty of punishment

There is also an attempt by some to explain corruption as a process by which members of society can manipulate a political system which is unable to cope with the demands made upon it. They explain corruption within the framework of the 'leading' and lagging classes existing within any society undergoing rapid social change, and very much divided its values and allegiances.[7] In the situation who gets what from corruption depends in large part on the nature of both the political system and the political elite. Corruption takes place where there is a meeting of opportunity and inclination. Three forms of corruption - parochial, market and systematic are dominant in government organisations. Parochial corruption represents a situation where only ties of kinship, affection, caste and so forth determines access to the favour of power holders while the market corruption signifies a virtually impersonal process in which influence is accorded to those who can pay the most regardless of who they are. But systematic corruption is primarily a political phenomenon and those in power use the government to transfer illicit benefits to themselves or to the clients... that the governing elite will seek to expand the flow of illicit benefits through official channels.[8] The presence of corruption is an important hindrance to economic growth and progressive social change.

Antecedents of Corruption

The problem is all the more important in developing countries because high political corruption would impede the establishment of a political order and the stability of political institutions and the legitimacy of the political class. In pre-democratic societies, where power rested on lineage and birth, corruption was not a salient issue because the actions of the rulers are perceived to be legitimate. But when politics emanate from the collective activity of the public and where the power of the politicians is based on public consent, corruption takes a newer dimension. Corruption, as agreed by all, is pervasive in all societies, though in different degrees and forms. Corruption inheres in all social systems, feudalism, capitalism, socialism, and communism. It affects all classes of society; all state organisations, monarchies and Republics; all situations in war and peace; in all age groups; both sexes and all times; ancient, medieval and modern.[9] To say that all was pure and idyllic in the early period of history will be travesty of truth.

Political issues - related corruption remained prevalent during the ancient and mediaeval period in Egyptian, Babylonian and Hebrew societies where judges did not hesitate to receive bribes. In Greece, the growth of corruption was attributed to the increase of economic activity and political apathy.[10] In ancient Rome corrupt practices prevailed and bribery was a regular source of income for those who were in charge of issuing contracts of public works, however, the prevalence of wide-scale corruption seems to have been the consequence of an unwieldy electoral system which derived from history.[11] During the mediaeval times corruption manifested itself in Rome in the form of extortion of revenue by the local and central officials and the perversion of justice. Those who were in the service of the kings and feudal barons became instrumental in the collection of illegal money.[12] Even in the period of exploration and colonisation, corruption took the same form as under the Roman Republic.

Other countries alike, the period of ancient and mediaeval India was not free from corruption but the extent of evil was certainly far less than what is at present. A. L. Basham, the famous historian, while writing on the administration of justice in India observed, 'Though judicial corruption is often referred to, the standard set for judges and magistrates is very high, they are to be learned, religious, devoid of anger, and as impartial as is humanly possible to prevent bribery. Kautilya in his *Arthasastra* has written a chapter entitled 'Detection of what is embezzled by government servants out of state revenue[13] and mentioned about forty types of embezzlement."[14] In the medieval period under the Khilji Rule, Tughlaq Dynasty and in the Mughal Empire, the problem of corruption was rampant at various levels of administration. Wrote Sir Thomas Roe at the end of the sixteenth century, 'the people of India live as fishes do in the sea and the great ones eat up the little. For first, the farmer robs the peasants, the gentleman robs the farmer, the greater robs the lesser, and the king robs all.'[15]

However, in the colonial days of British rule in India there was a systematic corruption which involved almost all officials starting from the Governor down to the lowest revenue official. From the days of Lord Clive and Warren Hastings down to a comparatively recent period bribery and corruption were prevalent even among the highest and were literally winked at by the Government.[16] Further under the British rule in the nineteenth and twentieth centuries, corruption and nepotism wove a strange pattern. About the British period it is commonly said that from the Governor down to the meanest factor people came to India not for the "good but for the 'goods' of the country."

A certain degree of dishonesty and corruption had existed althrough human history, in Independent India the issue has become rampant and all pervasive. Unlike earlier, today whosoever is indulged in immoral and corrupt practices is not socially discarded but are considered talented due to faulty implementation of systems, the political in particular. As a result, many well-meaning people, both in the rural areas and cities, seem to have become reconciled to the evil of corruption and even compromised by referring to their experience and inventing ways and means as to how to circumvent them. Politicians' cupboards are overflowing with skeletons and what is more, they appear to be out of the reach of the rule of law. The country is here because the political system is self-perpetrating and no party is accountable to anyone except a coterie of people that dominates all decisions. More worrisome than individual corruption is the wide-spread dishonesty at party levels. The aim of present day anti-corruption movements is also to strike at the root cause which is responsible for the omnipresence of corruption in all walks of life.

Birth of Real Danger

In the sphere of political corruption real danger started with the dawn of India's independence in August 1947. The situation has completely changed as in the past the scope for corruption as well as temptation was limited. The British evolved an impersonal law and enforce it by and large impersonally. Indian on the other hand have traditionally, accepted corruption and nepotism with a certain amount of tolerance. Resentment is felt and expressed only. When there is high-handedness or corruption is excessive in the Indian set of common values, it is generally assumed that those who exercise authority or happen to be close to those who do so must be entitled to privileged position and that, upto a point, their indiscretion must be overlooked.[17] Under British the economy was primitive, and only a segment of the population came in contact with public authorities. Official corruption therefore, touched their lives but rarely and briefly. In the period even the Indian National Congress which was almost the only effective political organisation, at the time of India's independence, had been something much more and much less than a political party. It was called by some writers an 'umbrella organisation, with men and women of diverse belief, outlook and background. Being in politics before independence also meant being in national mainstream and people in those days joined politics or supported the Party for reasons of high idealism, prestige and spirit of service in the cause of the country. They were not motivated by lust for public office or lure for political power or for getting rich quick through easy money.'[18] However, everything changed with the assumption of power by the mainstream party. It ceased to be the all-embracing and unifying national movement but became a political party and the government of the country.

The broad fact of independent India is that it inherited two legacies from its past. The Raj gave to independent India, by and large, a clean public administration. The other with which India started its career as an independent country, was the heritage of clean politics led by Mahatma Gandhi. Gandhiji spiritualised politics, and for him the purity of means was of paramount importance. A politician was thus expected to observe always and without exception a high standard of purity, simplicity, nobility and selflessness. Clean politics and a strong and dedicated public administration were India's most valuable in 1947.

India following its independence made a constitution which came into force in 1950 and with its coming the mode of recruitment became election. Hitherto, anyone could join politics provided he had an urge as well as the willingness to defy the colonial rule and all that it signified and, if necessary, to go to jail at the call of national leadership. What politics promised was a self-chosen career of sacrifice and suffering.[19] Election, the new method of choosing of political leaders is expensive and costs money. Elections began to be bought at a very high pitch, costing many times more than the legally prescribed ceiling. As a result, politicians of the Gandhian era steadily bowed out of the electoral arena and the space so vacated was filled by the new politician, who had little resemblance to the first generation of politicians. The new politician was the product of electoral processes. He was one who had spent a lot of money in contesting the election and who necessarily had to collect funds to be ready for the next election.

In post-independence India, the laws and rules which are seemingly for the benefit of the people, are mostly theoretical exercises. These are not, actually, operational with respect to a citizen's problems. In reality, a different way of functioning prevails, to the advantage of those who wield power, namely, people in politics and in the government and people outside who are their friends and associates. They run what has been called a parallel government, treating the people and the nation's resources as their private property. The politicians in power and the bureaucrats can act in disregard not only of laws and rules but of national interests and of rationality and morality. The decisive factor in each case is the advantage, monetary, political or other, to the politicians or bureaucrats in question or their friends and associates.[20] With the assumption of power by the dominant organisation at the Union and State levels, personal ambitions, fight for loves and fishes, in group rivalry, caste, communal, regional, and linguistic pulls within the Party began to grow much faster than any actual differences of ideology.

Wider Scope in Indian Context

In addition, with the advent of independence and the beginning of economic planning, the corruption front opened up for large-scale escalation. Because of its very nature, we have no systematic information of the shape or size of the monster of corruption and graft, but by all accounts they are truly formidable. The Central and State governments publish, from time to time, reports of the number of officers of various ranks arrested, prosecuted, convicted, fined, the figures published are themselves substantial.[21] Concern for political corruption was occasionally voiced in as early as the mid-forties; the responsible ministers coming to power were dogged by the talk of corruption and groupism.[22] In this background, in the years following independence of the country there emerged a general feeling that corruption in India spread to every part of the governmental machinery, and had a more rapid growth among politicians of many political parties.

In the whole atmosphere of political corruption, the Second Five Year Plan (1957-1962) with its industry orientation, acted as a catalyst. As a result, the businessman, either potential or actual, the politician, and the civil servant were drawn closer to each other, the new link being in exchange of money or favour. The businessman wanted a license; the minister was the granting authority; and the civil servant had to process the papers and make out a case in favour of the former. These developments speeded up the already existed political corruption and in the late 1960s or so, it has assumed an alarming proportion in public mind. The situation changed radically in the second and third decades of our Independence. Politics emerged as a well-entrenched profession. Politicians in power or close to power and authority realised that politics could prove the gateway to pelf and power.[23] A feeling began to grow that those in political power or with proximity to it could get away, although corruption may be legally a crime as well as social evil. And gradually even social or moral disapprobation ceased to have any value or effect.

In a nutshell, the corruption of leaders tends to affect the trust, loyalty and personal integrity of their followers. The famous political thinker Machiavelli put it, 'Corruption of leaders is dangerous because leaders are the paradigms of the body politic. The leaders are usually those individuals charged with rooting out corruption.[24] And the Latin proverb goes 'Corruption of the best is worst.' Many Western writers, while taking the problem of corruption in developing countries like India, have two different stands. One group thinks that corruption is intrinsic and unavoidable in developing countries due to traditional values, social practices and community connections, extended family relationships, etc. This means the lack of modernisation and its people are bound to live with corruption and, at best, some efforts at containing the evil can be hopefully made.

The other school of thought opines that in a slow-moving, insensitive, inefficient developing country, corruption acts as a lubricant to make the wheels of governmental machinery move, ensuring economic growth and hence need not be looked as an unmitigated nuisance.[25] In case of India's corruption and the frequency of scandals bear testimony to both the facts of life. Foreign observers like Dr Gunnar Myrdal and Myron Weiner commented on political corruption in India in late sixties and held the view that, 'Corruption was not only rampant but that it was growing particularly among higher officials and politicians, including legislators and ministers and they further argue that known offenders can continue their corrupt practices with little risk of punishment, are apt to re-inforce the conviction that this type of cynical asocial behaviour is widely practised in the Indian context.[26] In the 1960s, the atmosphere was thick with rumours about corruption and the government was forced to appoint the K. Santhanam Committee for Prevention of Corruption (1962) and S. R. Das Inquiry Commission (1963). The reports of both the committee confirmed the existence of widespread corruption in India.

From the mid-1960s onwards the whole structure and the political party system in India ushered in a new era in which members, legislatures were openly bought and sold like cattle and the prevailing prices were freely quoted. A trend began in which politics ceased to be for any purpose of public service. It became more and more an exclusive and lucrative profession and a specialised craft in the perennial pursuit of power for its own sake, with all those in the business of politics trying to get to power and once there to somehow retain it and augment it. Politics began to appeal to many as a gateway to better career, high status in public eye and not unoften considerable material gain.[27] The pressure of vested interests on the politicians grew stronger, and with it, corruption became profitable. Politics became a gainful calling with high social status and opportunities to wield power and avenue to privileges and patronage.

There was a contextual statement on corruption in the late 1960s that, 'It was a worldwide phenomenon', heralded the dawn of the first stage of indulgence. It coincided with the enormous growth of black money and the emergence of money politics as a major factor in public life. Since 1970s the anti-social elements began to openly enter in the political arena, first at lower levels. All political parties of the land began more or less mobilising such anti-social elements to win the election. Such elements have their own motivations to cover them with legitimacy and gain immunity from police action under the law.[28] The nexus between crime and politics, thus, began to develop which had the effect of impaling public agencies responsible for law enforcement. Many of the elected members are directly involved in cases of extortion and murder. The countryside is brimming with gun carrying criminals, trotting as politicians. Crime is their sources of livelihood but politics provides them the necessary cover of protection from law.[29] Vohra Committee's report revealed the nefarious nexus among the criminals, officials of law enforcing authorities and politicians.

In coming years there was a clear degradation and erosion of the democratic process. Earlier, the criminals preferred acting as the back-room boys; they themselves remained in the background and were content to support the politicians. This support was part of the larger protection deal, which they needed and in practice even got. The muscleman is made to carry out multiple tasks in Indian politics. The muscle power is used to intimidate the voter, to capture pooling booths and eventually to win the election. In several States, fighting elections is said to have become impracticable without the candidates having their own private armies or goonda gangs. In large cities, slums are big business both for the politicians and the criminals. The new business of kidnappings and abductions is known to be prospering with the active connivance of the politicians and even the Ministers and Chief Ministers involved in settling the deals. In this context the Shah Commission (1977-79) and Vohra Committee report have certified that there is a growing nexus between the politicians, criminals, bureaucrats, and politics.[30] They are virtually running a parallel government, pushing the state apparatus into irrelevance.

Clearly Supportive Environment

The forms and manifestations of corruption are continually changing. Although the incidence of corruption in public life is a worldwide phenomenon, in recent years it has assumed frightening proportions. It has not only spread to every part of the government machinery, but also has had a more rapid growth among professional politicians, party men at all levels and even in the highest echelons of political leadership both at the State and Central levels. The record of no political party in India is better than that of another on that score. The people's acceptance of corruption in public life and the feeling that those indicted with political corruption invariably go scot-free and in the process amass more power, status and wealth have led to a situation, where even the most determined efforts to fight the evil have failed miserably.[31] The government seems to be aware of the existence of the evil all around, and is also aware of the possible ways to check its monstrous growth, but seems to be lacking in will to enforce such measures effectively.

Further a number of scams took place such as the recently 2G scam and allocation of coal blocks etc. In fact, since independence India has lost many of its noble values and goals. Political corruption has been increasing enormously in India. Politicians' cupboards are overflowing with skeletons and what is more, they appear to be out of the reach of the rule of law. Now the people have become greedy with huge amounts of unaccounted black money indulge in extravagance and vulgar display of wealth. These filthy rich by their spending spree have been influencing the decision-making authorities and subverting and corrupting the social and political system. The democratic system that has emerged is not strong enough in fighting the sinister interest, which accumulate and multiply the ill-gotten money surreptitiously.[32] The major cause for the perpetuation of such sordid practices is due to the general apathy, passivity and totally indifferent attitude towards the corrupt and corruption.

Over the years as one study concludes that, 'it is likely that elective institutions have amplified the pressure towards corruption and made it more systematic, because spiraling cost of fighting elections and nursing a constituency between elections[33] and also pointed out that the essential business of a State Minister is not to make policy. It is to modify the application of rules and regulations on a particularistic basis in return for money and loyalty. According to newspaper editorial corruption in India has passed through three different stages: "gaining legitimacy widespread indulgence and shameless defence."[34] Decades ago scholars, Dwivedy and Bhargava observed, 'It is not uncommon for a political branded corrupt to continue to be a national leader.[35] Hence, a fairly large section of society seems to have lost faith in the fairness and impartiality of the entire system of governance.

In this context two things have to be borne in mind. One, it is essential to devalue the importance of politicians in nation's daily life. While there are some very good men and women in our public life, the general run politicians today are social parasites and enemies of nation-building. The political parties are no better than politician-criminal combines sharing power and loot. They have no relationship with democracy and no concern for political good. Two, the people have lost faith in the ability of the system as a whole to provide protection, security, growth or conflict resolution. Only political party or electoral reforms alone would not succeed in stemming the rot. What is needed is a full-scale review of our politico-constitutional edifice and fundamental structural-functional changes. Mere patch work or piecemeal tinkering here and there will serve no purpose.

One of the best anti-dote to minimise corruption is to change the perception of corruption as low-risk high profit to high risk low profit understanding, since corruption is usually not a simple matter of enforcement, for the casualties often include the integrity system itself. As such, the national integrity system is to be designed to prevent corruption from occurring in the first place. In addition, the phenomenon of corruption can be combated by increasing judicial activism, restricting our supportive environment, increasing our destructive environment, minimising the opportunities and controlling our needs with the help of existing control mechanism as well as by adopting new methodology in this era of Liberalisation, Privatisation and Globalisation.

6.2 Naxalism: Origin, Orientation and Overview

Naxalism, like communalism, fundamentalism and sectarianism has become one of the severe threats and internal security challenge ever faced by our country. Started from a village named 'Naxalbari' in West Bengal in May 1967 soon it became a revolutionary peasant uprising with the motto to free the oppressed classes living in the countryside from the clutches of the landlords and feudal elements. Its founder leaders-Charu Mazumdar, Kanu Sanyal and Jangal Santhal organised peasants' conference and gave a call for ending landlords' monopoly on land and land distribution. Although the initial armed struggle of naxalism was crushed within months, the ideology gained rapid momentum in many parts of India. Naxalism, in decades of its journey, witnessed several ups and downs, but its ideological underpinnings have not changed and in a major breakthrough the two prominent naxalite outfits - Peoples War Group (PWG) and the Maoist Communist Centre of India (MCCI) merged in October 2004. The formation of new entity has given the ongoing movement a sharpened tooth and impelled the Central and State governments to address the problem of growing left extremism with sound policy and greater attention.

Ideological Motivation

Naxalism, which is the most powerful armed struggle in the history of independent India, is heavily based on Marxism-Leninism and strategic alliance of Maoism as practised by him in Chinese context. The two basic philosophers - George Hegel (1770-1831) and Karl Marx enunciated that 'idea' and 'matter' are the essence of the universe and were the force behind all historical development. Although they both depended on the old Greek concept of dialectics in order to substantiate their philosophies, they remained essentially differ about the absolute truth. In contrast to Hegal, Marx proclaimed that the philosophy of Dialectical Materialism formed the empirical basis and held the view that social, political, and intellectual relations prevailing at any epoch of historical development is directly proportional to the economic conditions in that period. The integral part of historical materialism is class conflict or class struggle:

the constant struggle between the dominant and the dependent classes. Marx and Engels had full faith in the Proletariat. They believed that it would topple capitalism and establish an egalitarian communist society. At the same time they also made a distinction between base and super structure. The base is the economic foundation of the society whereas the superstructure comprises of the institutions, organisations, literature, art etc. The political ideas of Mao Zedong in China did not grow from vacuum and he picked up from the point where Karl Marx had left.

Mao Zedong who practised and experienced Marxism in China stated that the class struggle does not vanish with the establishment of a communist state, rather takes on new forms. His understanding of the socio-political and economic condition of the Chinese peasantry was so supreme that it aided him to devise pragmatic strategies keeping in mind the Chinese scenario. He proclaimed the famous slogan, 'Political power grows out of the barrel of a gun', and he was successful, both in his judgement as well as in his implementation with the establishment of a communist regime in China in October 1949. The success of Chinese revolution created a wave of joy amongst the oppressed countries in South Asia. It served as the required fuel to ignite the hidden passions of freedom for many a third world countries.[36] In a primarily agrarian society like India, Maoism finds strong grounds, quite similar to the Chinese scenario. And in line in the period 1948-51 the undivided Communist Party of India characterised the newly independent Nehru government as a legacy of Anglo-American imperialism and that independence that India has got was a sham. It believed that masses of India were prepared to support an armed revolution to overthrow the Nehru government and in pursuit of that formulation prepared the party for armed rebellion after the second Congress of the Communist Party in Calcutta when B. T. Rana Dive was elected the new Secretary of the Party. As a result the Communists in Bengal, Kerala and Andhra and Telengana took to arms and mounted attacks on police stations. The communists armed actions or battles, were most extensive and intense in the Telengana region of Andhra Pradesh. The well-armed communist waged war, just like the Maoists of today against the government.[37] Sardar Patel, the then Home Minister and the Government of India saw this war in its true colour, that is, a communist armed rebellion against the state of India. The Government of India used the armed forces to engage and destroy and decimate the communist armed gangs. As a step further the Naxalism of 1960s gathered fresh strength in India basing on the epicentre of Marxism and in afterwards they both agreed to work in unison. In order to bring change one needs to fight in whatever form one wishes to. It can be a non-violent non-cooperation Satyagraha on the lines of Gandhi or it can be an armed struggle to the finish like the Chinese or the Vietnamese or the Cubian revolutions.

The term 'Naxalism' typify a particular kind of militant and violent armed struggle by the peasants, tribals, and dalits led by leadership drawing doctrinal support from Marxism-Leninism and strategic inspiration from Mao Zedong. It began with the 'land to tiller' slogan and inspired similar revolts in other parts of the India.[38] A section of the Communist Party of India (Marxist) particularly consisting of cadres who opposed the participation of the party in the election and government formation under Charu Mazumdar, organised the peasant resistance to landlords over land to the tiller issue in Naxalbari - a small village in the then Siliguri Subdivision of Darjeeling district in West Bengal. It started on March 2, 1967, when a tribal youth, who had a judicial order to plough his land, was attacked by goons of local landlords. Tribal peasants started retaliating by attacking the local landlords and started forcefully capturing back their lands. The incident echoed throughout India and Naxalism was born. The ideology of naxalism soon assumed larger dimension and various sections of the state units of Communist Party of India (Marxist) throughout the country joined the struggle. The birth and growth of naxalism is closely linked to the Sino-Soviet split in the Communist movement in India. In the context of structural realities of India the Communists were divided in pro-Chinese and anti-Soviet Union postures. The Naxalbari uprising was fully supported and praised by the organ of the Communist Party of China (CPC) as the movement advanced the revolutionary line adopted by Chinese leader Mao Zedong.[39] In succeeding years naxalism unleashed a flow of events that brought about far-reaching changes in India's socio-culture scene.

However, solid grounds were prepared for the Naxalbari uprising of May 25, 1967, from the early fifties following the Communist success in China in the year 1949. In Naxalbari area of Darjeeling district in North Bengal, Communists had been organising sharecroppers and tea state labour, mostly belonging to the Santhal, Oraon and Rajbanshi tribal communities. The sharecroppers worked for Jotedars or landlords under the 'adhiar' system in which the jotedars provided the ploughs, bullocks and seeds and got a share of the crops. Dispute over shares followed with the coming of the United Front (UF) government because of the fear that sharecroppers would be given the land. Charu Mazumdar, a prominent leader of the area was working on the issue and it became clear since 1965, that his ideas about agrarian revolution and armed struggle, apparently based on Mao Zedong's thoughts.[40] After coming of the UF government, Charu, alongwith other leaders organised around 15,000 to 20,000 peasants and formed peasants' Committee in villages who became the nuclei of armed guards, who occupied land, burnt land records, declared debts cancelled, delivered death sentences on hated landowners, and set up a parallel administration. They denied any agreement and, anticipating repression, the leaders began to incite the peasants against the police and the things took their predictable and inexorable course with a vicious circle of attacks on police, police reprisals and further clashes as we face today even after four decades of Naxalbari event.

Expansion and Support Base

Within months the Naxalbari uprising was crushed by the police forcefully, it however, expanded soon in other parts of the country with the same ideology and methods. The writings of Charu Mazumdar - the most famous being the 'Historic Eight Documents' formed the basis of Naxalite ideology. In the same year (1967) the Naxalites organised the All India Coordination Committee of Communist Revolutionaries (AICCCR) and it followed the birth of the most notable Naxalite organisation, the Communist Party of India (Marxist-Leninist) in 1969 which defined the objective of the party as, 'seizure of power through an agrarian revolution'. The strategy was the elimination of feudal order in the Indian countryside to free the poor from the clutches of the oppressive landlords and replace the world order with an alternative one that would implement land reforms. The tactics to achieve it was through guerilla warfare by the peasants. Gradually, they would set up a "liberated zone" in different parts of the country that would eventually coalesce into a territorial unit under Naxalite hegemony.[41] By the early 1970s, the Naxalite movement had spread from farflung areas like Andhra Pradesh and Kerala in the south, to Bihar in the east, and Uttar Pradesh and Punjab in the north. But in Andhra Pradesh and in West Bengal, the Naxalites found their main support among the aboriginal tribal communities, who had been the most oppressed and marginalised in Indian society - the Girijans in Andhra Pradesh and the Santhals in West Bengal.[42] Its continuity can be explained by the persistence and exacerbation of the basic causes that gave it birth - feudal exploitation and oppression over the rural poor.

The Maoists draw their sustenance from existing inequalities. Due to the existence of problems relating to land, in the absence of land reforms the small farmers, landless labourers and the tribals continue to suffer. The Naxalism, its ideology and means to achieve the object expanded rapidly in all parts of the country only because the fundamental factors behind the alienation persist: poverty, inequality, illiteracy, economic exploitation, uncertainty of the farm sector, unresolved issues of land relations and land acquisition, a large army of unorganised labour in the farm sector, exclusion and exploitation of Dalits and Adivasis, failure to rehabilitate those displayed by development and so on. Although the Naxal movement underwent much churning in the succeeding decades, organisationally and politically, yet the emphasis on agrarian revolution remained at the core.

In post-1967, Naxalbari movement the works and objectives of Naxalism were fulfilled by its two groups - the Maoist Communist Centre of India (MCCI), originally formed in the early 1970s and CPI (ML) People's War Group founded in 1980. Both groups are referred to as Naxalites, and prior to their consolidation in 2004 the MCCI ran a virtual parallel government in remote areas, where it collected a 'tax' from the villages and, in turn, provided infrastructure improvements such as building hospitals, schools, and irrigation projects. It ran a parallel court system wherein allegedly corrupt block development officials and landlords - frequent MCCI targets - had been punished by amputation and even death.[43] While People's War Group conducted a low-intensity insurgency that included attempted political assassination, theft of weapons from police stations, kidnapping police officers, assaulting civilians extorting money from construction firms, and vandalising the property of multinational corporations.

In addition, the newly formed Marxist group-The Communist Party of India (Maoist) is conducting people's war', a strategic line developed by Mao Zedong aims to establish a Compact Revolutionary Zone from which to advance the people's 'New Democracy Revolution'. Like the CPI (ML) People's War, it rejected Parliamentary democracy and capturing political power through protracted armed struggle based on guerilla warfare. It believed to be enlarging the scope of its influence and operates in the Indian states of Andhra Pradesh, Odisha, Jharkhand, Bihar, Chhattisgarh, and parts of West Bengal. It has also a presence in

Bihar-Nepal border. The Maoist outfit has also been making attempts to establish and expand its presence in several other states such as Gujarat, Haryana, Punjab, Rajasthan and Himachal Pradesh. While the MCC's areas of influence extend over Bihar and Jharkhand, with some sway in Uttar Pradesh, the PWG's areas of dominance include Andhra Pradesh, Odisha, Chhattisgarh, Karnataka, Maharashtra and Tamil Nadu. Thus, the various groups of Maoists, be they called Naxalite or People's War Groups or otherwise adjectived, all have declared very clearly that they have no faith in the Constitution of India, in the multi-party democracy and elections.

For the expansion of support base of Naxalism and other forms of Maoists the process of globalisation is heavily responsible as it has polarised the world today than even before. Following the adoption of globalisation the society, at large, stood divided in two classes or categories - a small section that has enjoyed the benefits of globalisation and the second - a major category that is poor and devoid of facilities.[44] For instance, between 1970 and 2000 the level of poverty rose from 20 per cent to 70-85 per cent. Six out of eight children died before their first birthday, while eight die before eighth birthday. In year 2000, 2.8 billion people all over the world over, earned less than 2 $ per day while 1-2 billion earned less than 1 $. It appeared that globalisation does not about human development, which is restricted to small elite only. This inequality, not only creates disintegration, but also causes the emergence of social and national divisive forces. Globalisation also goes against the process of nation-building so far as the case of developing country, like India, is concerned and the concept itself has become irrelevant.[45] Violence, intoxication, terrorism, civil war, ecological degradation, economic disparity and terrorism have been globalised. Neither democracy nor civil society is meaningful for globalisation. Peasants, instead of producers are being turned into consumers. This kind of development is creating the feeling of loneliness in which the individual is getting cut off from his society and non-material sources of his life.[46] It has paved the way for the rise of cultural colonisation. Drug, violence, sex and artists of Rock-enrole have become the ideals of youths and there is no left for traditional, social and ethical values.

Recent Trends and Response

In an important development the Maoist Communist Centre of India (MCCI) and the Communist Party of India (Marxist - Leninist) People's

War, also known as People's War Group or PWG merged to form a new entity, the Communist Party of India - Maoist (CPI - Maoist) on September 21, 2004. Officially, the merger was announced on October 14, 2004, by the PWG on the eve of peace talks between the PWG and the State Government. It has given new teeth to the Maoists' movement in India and compelled the Central and State government to address the issue more urgently. It has also cast a dark shadow in all States already facing the Left extremism for decades. From there onwards both these groups of Naxalism agreed to work in unison - a pathbreaking step indeed. Now, as it became stronger the CPI (Maoist) altered its stance regarding revolution in India and were now ready to bring in mass-agitation, supplementing the already existing armed struggle. As a result the total number of people killed by the Naxalite violence rose by 30 per cent between 2003 and 2005 while the number of policeman killed jumped to 53 per cent between 2004 and 2005. Naxalite strength has grown over 50 per cent since 2001.[47] Till 2001, 60 per cent of the weaponary was country made. Today they have AK series, grenade launchers, mortars, carbine etc.

The 'objective of the new movement' was 'seizure of power' through an agrarian revolution. The strategy was the elimination of the feudal order in the countryside to free the poor from clutches of the oppressive landlords and replace the old order with an alternative one that would implement land reforms. The annual report of the Ministry of Home Affairs 2005-06 has also admitted that Naxalism is not merely a law and order problem but has deep socio-economic dimensions.[48] The Naxals, in India, has accordingly modelled themselves on the Indian Army lines from training manuals to undercover training. The fighting forces of Naxals are divided into three categories. The primary force is of extremely well trained personnel who spearhead any attack with superior weapons. The secondary force forms the bulk of a large group with less sophisticated weapons. Finally, the people's militia comprises farmers, labourers and others.

Gradually, Maoist violence gained momentum since the early 1990s and in succeeding years the Maoist-extremists launched such major attacks as killing Madhya Pradesh Transport Minister Likhiram Kavre in 1999, blasting the house of Telugu Desam Party leader G. Sudhakar Reddy in Andhra Pradesh in 2000, and attacking TDP leader N. Chandrababu Naidu in 2001.[49] Apart from this Naxal violence has claimed the lives of over 10,000 civilian and security personnel in the last five years with significant rise in the number of killings in Left-wing extremism hit States. Out of a total of 10,268 casualties' between 2005 and 2010, 2372 deaths have been reported in 2009 as against 1,769 in 2008 and 1,737 in 2007 according to an RTI reply by the Home Ministry. A total of 1,999 civilians and security men had lost their lives in 2006 and 1,952 others in 2005.[50] As of 2009, Naxalites were active across approximately 220 districts in twenty states of India accounting for about 40 per cent of India's geographical area. Naxal-related violence occurs in those areas where the administration has low reach. The people in those areas are living at the mercy of insurgents. The effects of the Maoist insurgency have already taken its toll on business. Rebels sided with farmers during violent protests by farmers, which forced the scrapping of the Tata Motor's Nano car plant and a chemical hub complex in West Bengal. In Odisha, bauxite production at the state-run National Aluminum Co. Ltd. has fallen following attack by Maoists in one of their mines in April 2009.[51] In a major deadliest attack the Maoist rebels killed 74 members of CRPF and destroyed an Armoured Personnel Carrier (APC) on 6th April 2010.

The first State response to Naxals in India was made by the United Front Government of West Bengal in 1967 to handle the first phase of the Naxalite movement, which *The People's Daily* characterised as 'spring thunder'. Hare Krishna Konar, the then Revenue Minister of UF government was of the view that so long there was dissatisfaction among the peasantry, militants could operate freely. He proposed the policy to wean away the angry peasantry from militancy by a massive programme of vesting of ceiling-surplus land of the big Zamindars and landowners. This programme resulted in good results and when the peasantry found that the large areas of land would be distributed amongst them, their loyalty shifted from the Naxalite militants to the normal political process. By its effects the Naxalite movement disappeared in the state in early 1970s.

The recent ferocity and the extent of attacks have reached such proportions as to invite the serious concern and involvement of the Central as well as the State governments. It compelled the Government of India to decide on 22 June 2009 to include 'CPI (Maoist)' in the Scheduled of organisation banned under the Unlawful Activities (Prevention) Act, keeping in mind the growing unlawful activities by the group. The party is regarded by some as a left wing extremist entity and a terrorist outfit and several of their members have been arrested by the Indian government under the Prevention of Terrorism Act (POTA). The group is officially banned by the State Governments of Orissa, Chhattisgarh and Andhra Pradesh, among others. In addition funds are given to the States under the Police Modernisation Scheme to modernise their police forces in terms of modern weaponary, latest communication equipment, mobility and other infrastructure. The Naxal affected States have also been asked to identify vulnerable police stations and outposts in the Naxal areas and take up their fortification under the Scheme.[52] Several new developmental schemes have been launched during the 11th Plan period in the naxalaffected states.

The Government of India has realised the fact that unlike other extremist movement, Naxal activities find it easy to garner mass support as they ideologically seek to render justice to socially backward classes. Blantant use of force and banning the outfit in past has evidently proved to be ineffective in tackling the spread of Naxal menace. If Naxals are to be dissociated from the rural support base, the government must come up with plans to bolster socio-economic activity in Naxal-infested areas which, in turn can act as a means to upgrade standard of living of the poor population. The Indian administration can not escape its due share in the failure of tackling the Naxalite violence. On the other for the Maoists' creating terror and untaking violence is easy but to have a place in the heart and soul of the citizenry is difficult one to achieve. What Maoists are doing is just anarchism against democracy.

6.3 Use and Misuse of Religion in Indian Politics

Without doubt secularism has been one of the essential elements in the basic structure of our constitution which lays down that: (i) the state has no religion; (ii) all citizens however have the fundamental right to follow and propagate their own religion; and (iii) it is the duty of the state to protect life, liberty and property of all citizens, provide security to them and enable them to exercise their fundamental rights. The state will not discriminate between the citizens on the grounds of religion and language. But while our constitution has been based on secularism or *dharma nirapekshita*, our society is steeped in religion. Observance of religious festivals and rituals is part of our day-to-day life. Religious feelings govern our mode of thinking. Thus, there is a clear contradiction between the basic tenets of the Constitution and the character of our society. These get reflected in our politics and public administration, which often work in a manner contrary to what is envisaged in the Constitution.

The caste and communal character of our politics inevitably enters in the conduct of public administration. While the constitution envisages secularism in the sense of *dharma nirapekshita*, our politicians have conveniently interpreted it as *sarva dharma samabhava*. This has given free licence to our politicians holding high positions to freely participate in all religious functions with the official paraphernalia in attendance. Going a step further all political parties use religion to gather votes. This starts from the selection of the candidates taking into account the communal character of the constituency. Vote-banks are systematically built on the basis of caste and religion and the very leaders who take advantage of these vote-banks do so in the name of secularism. This has been the hypocrisy of our secular democracy.

Although it is true that for centuries in India the people of different religious ideas and cultural values have lived together. During this period attitudes of tolerance for each other's religious faith did developed and a process of symbiosis and cultural pluralism resulted. But this was primarily due to two factors. First, sultans and rajas realised the need for accommodation, and along with military and aristocratic forces evolved ways of living together and common style of life. The Rajput-Mughal symbiosis is one example of this, second, at the mass level there were innumerable Sufis and saints who fought, against Mullah Islam and priestly Brahmanism pioneering equalitarian and universalistic values and practices, which established ties among communities rather than dividing them along caste and sectarian lines as part of a critique of existing religious political powers.[53] In the Post-Independence scenario the social dynamics was very complex. The process of secularisation/ industrialisation was going on at a slow pace. Even at this stage, though constitution was secular, the state apparatus: the bureaucracy, the judiciary, the army and the police were infiltrated by communal elements. The Congress government, though predominantly secular, had many leaders in important positions who were influenced by a Hindu communal ideology. This resulted in a social development that was mixed; on the one hand secularism thrived and on the other though communalism remained dormant, was never dead. The political use of Hindu religion begins under the impulse of colonial modernity in which proposals were advanced for a 'semiticised unitary Hinduism.'[54] Originally it was first proposed by nationalists who thought that Hinduism suffered in comparison with Christianity because of its lack of effective ecclesiastical organisation. The idea of Hinduism itself is quasi-political in origin, in the sense that people did not wish to be Hindus in this abstract sense until they felt political need to do so. It is therefore easy to exploit it for overtly political purposes.[55] The reality in India is much more complex than western societies, which have been totally secularised.

Use of religion for political purposes or for gaining victory in elections was almost unknown for political parties at the time of independence. It is curious to note that communal politics gained strength after about forty years of national government. If it was entirely due to the forces of traditionalism it should have appeared at the time when forces of modernity had gained enormously in Indian society and economy. Since the sixties Indian politics has been a massive alteration in style, language, modes of behaviour, reflecting far more the actual cultural understanding of rural Indian society rather than the Westernist cultivation of the elite which inherited power in the Nehru years. It was more compounded by the forgetfulness and negligence of Nehruvian state who not merely failed to create conditions for a common sense in Indian politics, through which liberal secular political ideas could be communicated dialogically to them, rather, its neglect of cultural institutions like primary education which contributed to a further division in society. As a result the benefits of development were so unequally and unjustly distributed that it prepared ground for two types of political dissent - an economic critique of class and an indigenist critique of modernist cultural privilege. The second kind of resentment, naturally, has predominantly found cultural expression through regionalist and communal politics, through the politics of Hindu and Hinduism.

There are two consequences of this mixing up of religion, politics and public administration. First, it has given prominence in public life to religious leaders like 'Sants' and 'Mahants', 'Imams' and 'Priests'. They have started playing an active role in government's decision-making. The interference of religious leaders in administrative matters can prove dangerous to our secular democracy. Secondly, practices and festivals have started making serious inroads into the safety and convenience of our public life.[56] As a result, a sea change of tremendous significance occurred both in Hindu religious community and in its relations to others. In the changed circumstances the Hindu community was now called into action, not as one of the various Indian communities, but as the Indian community. It was not only the religious revivalist, but the modernising reformists as well who identified the Hindu community with Indianism and patriotism. Steps were taken deliberately to create a Sanskrit-based,

Hindu language, Hindi, as against the earlier composite language. Further there are two variants of this expression of Indianness. One is the overt religious concept of Hindutva; and the other is the 'secular' expression of Indianness as based on ancient Indian culture. The first is a religious, the second is cultural concept; but both together relate Indanness to the tradition of what is now identified as Hindu civilisation.[57] On the lines drawn above the political parties of India may be grouped as religion-leaned and secularism-leaned.

India, despite partition on the basis of religion, resolved to be secular state and promulgated its constitution in 1950 accepting equal rights for all citizens irrespective of their caste, creed or race. It was undoubtedly a great step forward. But it was not easy to translate the constitutional ideals into practice in a society as complex as India. Indian state was characterised as 'Soft state' by Gunner Myrdal in his *Asian Drama*. The Indian state remained not only soft towards communalism but it also encouraged it, if it paid political dividends. 1970 onwards Central and different State Governments have started the practice of giving 'Iftar' parties to our Muslim brethren during 'Ramzan'. Now political leaders vie with each other to throw such lavish parties at national and state capitals and the practice continued even in the regime of a BJP Prime Minister. Wide publicity is given in the media as to who attended these parties and what was served. It is forgotten that such politicisation of 'Iftar' is a sacrilege to sacred religious practice much to the disgust of truly religious people. Even the representation of the people act provides that appeals made on the grounds of religion to gather votes would be deemed to be a corrupt practice and would disqualify a candidate but this happen as a rule in all our elections.

Louis Dumont, one of the most influential writer on Indian religion and society viewed sadhus as the agent of the development in Indian religion and speculation, 'the creator of values' responsible for 'founding of sects and their maintenance', and for the major ideas and social innovations.[58] In the changed circumstance, this consensus on the role of religious figures began to change during the time of Mrs Indira Gandhi who relied on populist measures and appeal to specific categories of voters. She drew Hindu religious figures into the lime light through her patronage of religious institution and played the 'Hindu Card' against the minorities.[59] The case of Sikh religious leader Bhindarwala is burning example of her creation. She was systematically encroaching on the traditional vote-bank of Jana Sangh. Mrs Gandhi also co-opted Muslim religious figure in her attempt to hold on to the Muslim vote, pursuing her strategy of what was then called Fatwa Politics. It was seen on certain occasions that persons holding purely religious office play a decisive role to the job of political recruitment. Religious saints and sages are in great demand on the eve of and during election for influencing the voters in favour of or against a particular candidate or party. Political leaders run from one religious leader to another to seek their blessings for their success in elections. The net result is not the secularisation of the socio-economic and political processes but the communalisation of these processes.[60] Thus, the ideology and practice of secularism in actual fact, however, is confronted with multi-faceted and multi-dimensional challenges.

However, Indian secularism began to face a rough weather with the revival and strengthening of religion-leaned political parties in the country. The pro-Hindu strategies of the ruling Congress reminded the BJP, RSS and VHP its actual role for which they had been struggling in previous decades. Earlier in seventies several proposals were made for a judicious deradicalisation of the BJP's slogans from groups inside the party itself. The decade also witnessed communal propaganda seemed to bring in few dividends and the destiny of the Jana Sangh irreversibly on the decline. At the juncture it was felt inside the Party that it should subtly shift its appeal to the middle class. Instead of the traditional appeal to Hindu Chauvinism, it should try to project itself as a substitute for the Congress, asking for support not because of its ideological differences with the Congress, but its similarity - offering a cleaner, more efficient, less corrupt government. After the dramatic success of the rath yatras, its own agenda was rewritten in a retrograde direction, but it is remarkable how clearly the party has not rejected its other, more secular constituency. From the early eighties, Hindu communal organisations increased the scale, range aggressiveness and violence of their operations under the general direction of the militant Hindu ring-wing party Rashtriya Swayam Sevak Sangh (RSS) and its mass fronts: the Vishwa Hindu Parishad (VHP), which coordinates religious bodies, and the Bharatiya Janata Party (BJP), its electoral wing.[61] Again in mid-1980s (1984) elections were held to Lok Sabha in 1984 after Mrs Gandhi's assassi-nation the BJP under the presidentship of Atal Bihari Vajpayee got only two seats. Now Vajpayee resigned and L.K. Advani, considered a hawk in the party, took over and gave BJP a new hope and a decision was taken by the leadership of BJP to promote Hindu militancy to snatch away the Hindu vote-bank from the Congress.

Now, there was a mad race among the national political parties to use religion for strengthening and expanding their political base. This had led to the growth of fundamentalism in India. The growth of strong communalism has made government more and more susceptible to communal pressures exerted by them, thereby finally accommodating and conceding the demands of these organisations. The decision of the Rajiv Gandhi Government to undo the impact of the judgement of Supreme Court in Shah Bano case and the withdrawal of Presidential ordinance (1990) acquiring the disputed land at Ayodhya on the pressure of Babri Masjid Action Committee can be quoted in the context. In the famous Shah Bano case the power elite among Muslims used Indian Secularism for their own power game and resolutely opposed any change or progressive measures in the name of right to practice their own religion and whenever it politically suited them they aroused Muslim sentiment. The Muslim leaders mounted pressure on the then Prime Minister Rajiv Gandhi to change the law in favour of Muslims. The ruling party could hardly resist such pressure and buckled under and changed the law and passed the Muslim Women's (Protection of Rights on Divorce) Bill 1986. This had very adverse effect on an average Hindu mind. It convinced them that Muslim leaders are a fanatic lot and secondly, that the Congress indulges in appeasement of Muslim and treats them as its vote-bank. In addition, it adversely affected our secular polity in two ways: (i) The politicisation of religious entity, and (ii) The legitimisation of communal organisation as the bonafide representatives of the interest of different religious groups.[62] It is true for most of the Indian political parties.

As the political role of Congress in early eighties was nothing but exploitation of religious sentiments to win over certain sections of Indian society, the BJP which is not only a rightist but also a Hindu communal party chose to use the religious controversial issues to capture power at the Centre and some states mainly in Hindi heart land. In its view, the way the secular state has functioned in India has paved way for the growth of fanaticism and fundamentalism, emergence of the anti-national forces posing threat to our unity and integrity and a strong opposition to progressive social legislation. The Bharatiya Janata Party maintains that our present secularism is pseudo secularism as it amounts to "appeasement of the minorities, particularly Muslims. According to their understanding, Muslims constitute the biggest vote-banks as they generally vote as a community while the Hindu consciousness at political level gets fragmented along caste, linguistic and regional lines. In turn, BJP and its groups has come out with a concept of positive secularism of true secularism meaning that the minority should not enjoy any special protection and all such provisions in the Constitution should be done away with. It usually puts it as "justice for all appeasement of none."[63] The RSS and organisations of Parivar have been constantly criticising the Congress rulers for their appeasement of the minority, especially the Muslim. They are saying that though Hindus are in majority they are being discriminated. They want the creation of "Hindu Rashtra." They argue that their definition of Hindu is very wide. Whoever, irrespective of the religion to which he belongs, considers India as his *janmbhumi, karmbhumi* and *pitrubhoomi* is a Hindu.

In a nutshell, the political parties of today, especially the national, are exploiting religious /communal sentiments for electoral gains. Cynical building up of Sant Bhindranwala to marginalise the Akalis or Akalidal, for instance, proved catastrophic not only for the Congress Party but also for the entire country.[64] It is a sorry state of affairs that the polity too has fallen prey to the lobbying of communal organisations and groups as illustrated by the enactment of the Muslim Women's (Protection of Rights on Divorce) Act 1986, banning of *Satanic Verses*, and opening of the locks on the Babri Masjid. Similarly, the wooing of Shahi Imam by the Janata Dal-led National Front resulted into fall of its government at the centre as the after effect of secularism.[65] If mullahs and sadhus, and mahants come to wield political clout, as it happens today, communal forces are bound to get string themed. It is amusing to note that we never hear them speaking against old traditions such as 'pardah' or the 'caste-system,' polygamy or extravagant feasting etc., but they talk of religious identity. In the context if the BJP is blamed to have been practicing majority communalism, the Congress and non-Congress parties should equally be held responsible for pampering minority communalism in our polity for their political gains, forgetting the fact that the indefinite variety of the land can only be preserved and enriched through a policy or substantive decentralisation and that a genuine federal set up is the only solution of our problems.

In fact with social changes of the late 1970s and the early 1980s communalism got a strong boost and it started attacking secularism in a big way. Among political parties, the BJP was quick to take up the mantle of 'the' communal party, riding on the wave of the post-mandal upper class /caste backlash. Supporting the BJP was the Vishwa Hindu Parishad, a relatively new outfit with branches all over the world and drawing on support, both moral and financial, from the Hindu diaspora in the West. This took an aggressive form when the Babri Masjid/Ramjanambhoomi controversy erupted. This period also saw the rise of other militant Hindu organisations such as the Bajrang Dal and the Shivsena. These groups quickly mushroomed and poisoned the social space with communal rhetoric and the agenda of Hindu Rashtra; and launched an ideological, social and political onslaught on secular ethos, syncretic culture and composite nationalism. The attack on the Mosque at Ayodhya led to a rash of violence across the country. The events leading to the demolition of Babri Masjid and their aftermath of communal carnage marked a watershed in the history of free India. The calculated rise of the BJP took place on a fundamentalist Hindu platform to gain dividends in states in principally North India and Maharashtra as well as at national level. India was portrayed as a Hindu India. The BJP and the Sangh Parivar use Ayodhya and other Hindu images continually. The BJP which had got only two seats and seven per cent votes in 1984 got 88 seats 11.4 per cent vote in 1989 in alliance with Janata Dal. And in 1991 election BJP won 120 seats with 20 per cent votes. Something never had happened in the electoral history of the right wing Hindu party. The party in its manifesto for the 1996 elections had proposed that Article 30 of the Constitution giving the right to the minorities to establish their own cultural and educational institutions, be removed. In the same election the number of seats went up to 161 though the vote share remaining stagnant. Finally, it formed government in 1999 with the help of some so-called secular parties on mixed bag of promises.

About the time decades 1980s and 1990s have witnessed violent secessionist movements in Punjab and Kashmir and an upsurge in the use of religious symbols and terminology in politics.[66] There onwards secularism has been challenged by the ascendance of the forces of communalism, fundamentalism and religious revivalism, accompanied by violence. Communal riots continue unabated. Meerut, Bombay, Bhiwandi, Ahmedabad, Surat and Hyderabad and most recently, Gujarat, are just a few cases in point. The ostensible reason for this fury was the burning of a train coach that was carrying Hindu pilgrims returning from Ayodhya. Fifty nine people including women and children died in the fire. But the post-Godhra incidents in 2002 communal riots accompanied by events of arson, loot, and murder in urban as well as rural Gujarat and rural areas of Haryana and Maharashtra have tarnished the image of Indian secularism and the reputation of Hinduism as a tolerant faith. The social climate is thoroughly vitiated and the atmosphere is surcharged with suspicion and hatred reminding of the pre-partition days. This marked the first time when the state has emerged as a major player and actor in violence by mobs, a qualitative change from previous such situations in India. As a climax in May 2002, conference at Bangalore the RSS passed a resolution that the security of the minority community depends on the goodwill of the majority.[67] The resolution was seen as an open threat to the minority, though the spokesman of the RSS tried to explain that it was not meant to be so.

For all this, common but heavyweight cause is that still the political culture of India is unstable and underdeveloped. Political culture depends on the people's attitudes, emotions and beliefs towards the political system of the country, whether it is homogeneous or heterogeneous. Besides, political culture is not static, it is dynamic and therefore, it envisages essentials or needs of the political system within or outside. A pragmatic orientation in this direction is known as the secularisation of political culture. The secularisation of political culture is the process whereby men become increasingly rational, analytical and empirical in their political actions. It is the process of increasing the political awareness of the masses enabling them to have growing information about their political system and their role as political actors in it.[68] The secularisation of political culture has two attributes, first, the pragmatic and empirical orientation, and second, movement from diffuseness to specificity. Times change and change the beliefs and values of the people. Political socialisation through its agencies like family, schools and educational institutes, peer groups, working and informal relations, mass media, government and political parties and leaderships play very major and significant role in the strengthening of secularisation of political culture. In the political systems of the different states of the world, developed or developing, political culture promotes political stability and social change.

The political culture of India, like other developing countries, is in the formative stage and continues to evolve. It is an admixture of historical, geographical, socio-economic structures, the contemporary and ancient social structures, old and new political ideologies and more importantly the practice and tradition of political apathy and non-violence. In Indian political culture, commitment to religious values remained strong. The political and socio-economic changes produced a response along caste lines. The Constitution outlawed caste, but the political institutions continued the same, dividing the country into many castes and sub-castes. As a result, the Indian political system has become the hub of irrational politicians who manipulate the state machinery to advance their personal power and economic gain by disseminating the seeds of social conflict. The secessionist movements, caste assertions, Hindus nationalism and majority - minority schism on cultural identities has been entrenched often inspired by political parties and leaders for electoral gain. The politics of Hindus-Muslims - Dalits vote-bank and more importantly the blame-game become the part and parcel of the Indian political culture.[69] Political system in India is facing plenty of problems such as corruption, extensive centralisation, political criminalisation, declining secularism, rise of national chauvinism based on religion, and growing divide between the included and excluded. In this circumstances, Indian political culture has failed to prevent communal violence, ethnic conflicts and political insurgency. Secularisation does not mean that religious institutions will cease to exist. It only means that they will cease to encompass or regulate all the other institutions of society.

Unlike West where the philosophy of secularism came into existence only as a result of the struggle for powers between the religions and the state, secularism in the Indian context should imply respect for pluralism and a non-coercive and a voluntary recourse to change. Respect for diversity not only embodies the democratic spirit, it is the real guarantee for unity. No democratic society can downgrade diversity and pluralism in the name of unity. In the background, India, shortly after independence adopted a new constitution providing a charter for a secular state and a secular concept of citizenship. Secular ethics can be strengthened only when the acts of vandalism are sternly dealt with and the guilty are made to pay for it. With secularism that insists on the inalienable rights of the citizens and a due process of law, it will be easier to mount public pressure against sectarian killers and those who promote hatred. Secularism begins in the heart of every individual if we have no feeling of "otherness" as we all share a common history that has so far retained the secular character of its polity. It is not only the basic tenet of India's ancient civilisation but also the hallmark of the modern age of globalisation. The new age demands that we should not waste our time in religious discords but rather move ahead with the use of science and technology to make our lives better, richer and fuller.

Secularism and Indian Constitution

India has been declared a secular state by its written constitution but a number of efforts to secure the inclusion of the word 'secular' in the fundamental law of the land did not find favour with the framers of the Constitution.[70] The coming of the partition emphasised the great importance of secularism. Notwithstanding the partition a large Muslim minority, constituting a tenth of the population of India, continued to be citizens of India. Secularism became the mantra of the Indian nation, a nation exhausted by partition and sectarian riots and above all the assassination of Gandhi did not want any more divisive talk. In the circumstances, a secular constitution of independent India, under which all religions could enjoy equal freedom and all citizens equal rights, and which could well together into one nation the different religious communities became inevitable. Our Constitution did not erect any 'wall of separation' between religion and the State. While prohibiting religion-based discrimination between the citizens, it did not prevent the state from participating in the people's religious affairs. It enabled the State to generally "regulate or restrict secular activity associated with religion."[71] First under Jawaharlal Nehru and later under his successors in the Congress Party, the concept of a secular nation state was officially adopted as India's path to political modernity and national integration. Unlike in the West, where secularism came mainly out of the conflict between the Church and the State secularism in India was conceived as a system that sustained religious and cultural pluralism.

The word 'secular' is not written in the Constitution, but it does not mean that the founding fathers of the Constitution had any doubt about the nature of the Indian state being secular. The framers of our constitution properly debated the issue of secularism and individual's religious rights with other members and after due considerations they decided to make India a secular state. While our constitution has been based on secularism or Dharma Nirapekshita, our society is stepped in religion. Religious feelings govern our mode of thinking and we observe religious festivals and rituals as part of our day - to-day life. In comparison to other countries of the world secularism has a very different meaning in India. In the context, wrote Jawaharlal in his autobiography 'no word perhaps in any language is more likely to be interpreted in different ways by different people as the word religion. That being the case, secularism which is a concept evolved in relation to religion can also not have the same connotation for all.'[72] Even during the course of the discussion in the

Constituent Assembly on the fundamental rights relating to religion, the idea of secularism was extensively pressed into service by the members as the most handy tool to substantiate various view points, often diametrically opposed. The members of the Constituent Assembly were in no doubt that the phase 'secular state' and the terms secular and secularism should help us in understanding that the principle is meant the constitutional concept of equality and freedom for all religions, infused every provision of the fundamental rights with this spirit and therefore very wisely avoided institutionalising it in words interminably capable of connoting varying and conflicting meanings.

Several members of Constituent Assembly including K.T. Shah, H.V. Kamath, Tajamul Hussain, Lakshmi Kanta Maitra and Loknath Mishra presented their views/modifications in the fruitful discussion on secularism and religious rights of Indian citizens. In course of the discussion K.T. Shah proposed a new Article 18-A to be inserted under the heading 'rights relating to religion' which would emphasise, 'The State in India being secular shall have no concern with any religion, creed or profession of faith; and shall observe an attitude of absolute neutrality in all matters relating to the religion of any class of its citizens or other persons in the Union. He also added, 'All I wish to say is that with the actual profession of faith or belief, the state should have no concern.[73] India being the secular state with having nothing to do with religion, Tajamul Hussain wanted that caste names, signs and dress be done away with. 'We should not being a secular state, be recognised by our dress'.[74] While H.V. Kamath warned the Assembly not to adopt any religion as it would split the country he made it clear that by this he does not mean to say that a State should be anti-religious or irreligious. According to him, a secular state is neither a Godless state nor irreligious nor an anti-religious state. He even advocated imparting spiritual training in educational institutions.[75] In the debate discussing the right to propagate religion Lakshmi Kanta Maitra laid stress on the fact that there should be no discrimination whatsoever on the ground of religion - means in essence that no particular religion in the State will receive any State patronage but he accepted the fact that even in a secular state there is necessity for religion.[76] However, there was a school of opinion in favour of India being made a Hindu state.

In the Constituent Assembly Loknath Mishra represented Hindu point of view and opposing right to propagate religion said, 'We have declared the State to be a secular State. For obvious and for good reasons we have also declared. Does it not mean that we have nothing to do with any religion? Why do you make it a secular state? The reason may be that religion is not necessary, but as India has many religions, Hinduism, Christianity, Islam and Sikhism, we cannot decide which one to accept. Therefore, let us have no religions. No. That cannot be. If you accept religion you must accept Hinduism as it is practised by an overwhelming majority of the people of India.[77] He continued on saying, 'gradually it seems to me that our secular state is a slippery phrase, a device to by-pass the ancient culture of the land'. He said he failed to understand the 'exact meaning of secularism'. So he wanted that the Constitution should say nothing about right to religion, 'or at least drop the word propagate' from the right.[78] Particularly, the Hindu members in the Assembly totally disagreed with the view that the propagation of religion should be considered a legitimate aspect of religious freedom. But the overwhelming majority of members did not agree with the view. Explaining the word propagate K.M. Munshi remarked, 'Even if the word were not there, he assured under the Freedom of Speech which the Constitution guarantees it will be open to any religious community to persuade other people to join their faith'.

The individual right of freedom of religion as given in the Indian Constitution is of far greater importance, particularly for the religious minorities and for their smooth development. Apart from this, most of the constitutions of the world that provide freedom of religion, such as Switzerland, former USSR, the Peoples Republic of China and Japan do not explicitly guarantee right to propagate religion as a justifiable fundamental right. The word 'propagate' does not find a place in any other constitution where it deals with religious freedom. Despite vehemently opposition to the inclusion of this term by the members as they thought that it might be perilous to guarantee it and might freely be used for the purpose of wholesale conversion. However, it did not find favour of the majority and one member pointed out, 'After all propagation is merely freedom of expression. I would like to point out that the word 'convert' is not there. Those who drafted this constitution have taken care to see that no unlimited right of conversion has been given. People have freedom of conscience, and if any man is converted voluntarily owing to freedom of conscience then well and good. No restriction can be placed against it.[79] Further, it is perhaps in consonance with the provisions of United Nations Declaration of Human Rights, which say, 'Everyone has the right to freedom of thought, conscience and religion:

this right includes freedom to change his religion or belief, and freedom, either alone or in community with others and in public or private, to manifest his religion or belief in teaching, practice, worship and observance'.[80] Thus, without doubt, the scope of the freedom of religion in India is considerably wide and broad.

However, as a result of debates and discussions the term 'secularism' was first defined by the Constituent Assembly on April 3, 1948 , 'Whereas it is essential for the proper functioning of democracy and the growth of national unity and solidarity that communalism should be eliminated from Indian life, this assembly is of the view that no communal organisation, which by its constitution or by the exercise of discretionary power vested in any of officers and organs, admits to, or excludes from, its membership persons on grounds of religion, race and caste or any of them, should be permitted to engage in any activities other than those essential for the bonafide religious, cultural, social and educational needs of the community and that all steps, legislative and administrative, necessary to prevent such activities should be taken'.[81] On the basis of Constituent Assembly's resolution, the provisions of Indian constitution made clear the nature of secularism in India which broadly means four things: (i) the rejection of a theocratic or semi-theocratic state, (ii) the proclamation that religion is of private or group concern, (iii) equality of all citizens irrespective of his caste or creed, and (iv) the right of the state interfere in the religious practices of various communities in the interest of their peaceful co-existence and cultural development.[82] In addition, the freedom of religion guaranteed under Indian constitution is not confined to its citizens but extends to all persons including 'aliens'. This point was underlined by the Supreme Court in Ratilal Panchand vs. State of Bombay as it is very important because substantial number of foreign Christian missionaries in India were engaged at that time in propagating their faith among the adherents of other religions.

January 26, 1950, marked a great event in the long and chequered history as on that day, was brought into force, the present Constitution of India. A constitution is a set of laws and rules setting up the machinery of the government of a State and which defines and determines the relations between the different institutions and areas of government; the executive, the legislative and the judiciary, the central, the regional and the local governments. The Indian constitution is a blend of idealism and realism. In hammering it out, the framers traversed all the processes of "democratic manufactory" and ranged through the whole gamut of democratic factors.

There have been careful thought, close analysis, argument and counter-argument. As a result, the Constitution emerged as a basis for all the people of India to work in cooperation and collabo-ration in a mighty endeavour to build a new, free India. Pandit Nehru contended that a Constitution was not only a legal document but also a social and political document and as such, it must reflect not only the aspirations and wishes of the people, but also serve as an effective instrument for carrying out a socio-economic revolution.[83] The objective of Socialism and Secularism, which they had tried to implement in the past, and would be more and more implemented in the future would have to be more accurately and correctly reflected in it. In particular, the Constituent Assembly was satisfied with other provisions of right and in its bid to infuse complete confidence in the religious minorities, it adopted a separate group of articles dealing solely with the right to freedom of religion.

The Constitution of India provides the freedom of religion in Articles 25 to 30 but in first four Articles (25, 26, 27 and 28) the rights are conceived in most generous terms to the complete satisfaction of religious minorities. They were in fact the result of an agreement with the minorities, almost unanimously arrived at in the Minorities Committee constituted by the Constituent Assembly. Accordingly, part (1) of Article 25 secures to all persons freedom of conscience: and the right to: (i) profess religion; (ii) practice religion; and (iii) propagate religion. The Constitution declares that every person has a fundamental right not only to hold whatever religious belief commend themselves to his judgement, but also to express his belief in such overt acts as are prescribed by his religion and propagate its tenets among others. The scope of this article is very wide and meaningful. Apart from so many other things it declares, 'The state or the Government cannot aid one religion, or give preference to one religion as against another. It means that in India no particular religion will receive state patronage.[84] But Article 25 (2) provides broad sweeping over interference to the state in religious matters. It imposes drastic limitations on the rights guaranteed under Article 25 (1) and reflects the peculiar needs of Indian society. The framers of constitution made Article 25 (2) a part of Article 25 (1) by placing three restrictions to the freedom of religion, namely, public order, morality and health. The Supreme Court of India in the case of Commissioner of Hindu Religious Endowment vs. L.T. Swamiar held, 'Article 25 guarantees to every person, subject to public order, health and morality a freedom not only to entertain such religious belief as may be approved of by his judgement and conscience, but also to exhibit his belief in such outward acts as he thinks proper and to propagate or disseminate his ideas for the edification of others. The expression 'practice of religion' denotes that the constitution not only protects the freedom of religious opinion but also acts done in pursuance of a religion'.[85] In other words the article protects the acts done in pursuance of religious belief as part of religion.

Likewise Article 26 is, in fact, a corollary to Article 25 and guarantees the freedom to manage religious affairs. Under this every religious denomination is given the right: (i) to establish and maintain institutions for religious and charitable purposes; (ii) to manage its affairs in matters of religion; (iii) to own and acquire movable and immovable property, and (iv) to administer such property in accordance with law. In this context, the term 'religious denomination' has not been defined in the Constitution but the Supreme Court of India has accepted the definition as given in Oxford Dictionary, that defines it as 'a collection of individuals classed together under the same name a religious sect of body having a common faith and organisation and designated by a distinctive name'. The Supreme Court in number of cases held that Arya Samaj, Anandmarga, Vaishanave, the followers of Madhawacharya and other religious teachers, though not separate religions yet these are separate religious denomination and enjoys the protection under Article 26 of the Constitution. But the right of a religious denomination to manage its own affairs in matters of religion is subject to any law protected by Article 25 (2) (b) throwing open a Hindu Public temple to all classes and sections of Hindus. The object of this provision is to remove a potent cause of disunion and inequality among the various castes of the Hindu. It is indeed a corollary to the abolition of untouchability.

Undoubtedly Articles 25 and 26 provide every person vast rights pertaining to religious freedom, it however, is not absolute and subject to certain limitations. The text of these articles is concerned with provisions of the constitution and are subject to public order, morality and health. In addition, regarding Article 25 there are two more exception. First, this freedom is subject to the other provisions of Part III of the Constitution and secondly, under clause 2 (3): Nothing in this Article shall affect the operation of any existing law or prevent the state from making any law: (i) regulating or restricting any economic, financial, political or other secular activity which may be associated with religious practice; (ii) providing for social welfare and reform or the throwing open of Hindu religious institutions of a public character to all classes and sections of

Hindus. Judiciary in India has also on various occasions, upheld the view that freedom of religion is not an absolute one. In the case of Masud Alam vs. Commission of Police, it was decided that banning of electrical loudspeakers calling for prayer may be valid. No doubt every religion has a right to have propaganda. But when such propaganda is made through loudspeakers in a crowded and noisy locality to the detriment of public moral, health or order, it is prohibited by Article 25. A loudspeaker may take one to hell instead of Heaven by the very volume of its sound.[86] Similarly Chapter xv, Section 295 to 298 of the Indian Panel Code (IPC) deals with the offences relating to religions that is, injuring or defiling place of worship with intent to insult the religion of any class, disturbing religious assembly trespassing on burial places, etc. Even though these actions might be sanctioned by the offender's own religion, these are offences under the law.

Article 27 of the Indian Constitution provides an additional protection to religious activity by exempting funds appropriated towards the promotion or maintenance of any particular religion from the payment of taxes, while Article 28 lawfully permits to propagate religion by means of religious instructions in educational institutions.[87] Further it also provided that: (i) No religious instruction shall be provided in any educational institution wholly maintained out of State funds; (ii) Nothing in clause 1 shall apply to an educational institution which is administered by the State but has been established under any endowment or trust which requires that religious instruction shall be imparted in such a situation, and (iii) No person attending any educational institution recognised by the State or receiving aid out of State funds shall be required to take part in any religious instruction that may be imparted in such institution or to attend any religious worship that may be conducted in such institutions or in any premises attacked thereto unless such person or, if such person is a minor, his guardian has given his consent thereto.[88] In line, Articles 29 and 30 guarantee cultural and educational rights to: (i) every linguistic, scriptorial or cultural section of the citizens of India; (ii) every citizen of any religion, race, caste or language; (iii) every religious or linguistic minority, and (iv) every religious or linguistic minority educational institution.[89] The object behind Articles 29 and 30 is the recognition and preservation of the different types of people, with diverse languages and different beliefs, which constitute the essence of secularism in India. This aspect is based on the idea that the individual, not the group is the basic unit. The undivided is confronted by the state which imposes duties and responsibilities upon him; in return the state guarantees rights and grants privileges to the individual. The sum of these individual state relationship constitutes the meaning of citizenship. There are numbers of provisions dealing with citizen's relations with state in social spheres. The provisions based on non-discrimination in political functions have also been dealt with under the Constitution.

However, the whole edifice of secularism in India took a large step. By the Forty-second Constitutional Amendment Act 1976 the Preamble was amended for the words 'sovereign democratic Republic' by the words 'Sovereign, Socialist, Secular, Democratic Republic'. For the first time the word 'secularism' was introduced in the Constitution and speaking on the motion for consideration of the Bill in the Lok Sabha on 25 October, 1976, H.R. Gokhale, the Minister of Law, Justice and Company Affairs, justified the inclusion of the words 'Socialism and Secularism' by citing the Congress Resolution passed in 1931 at Karachi in which Pandit Nehru remarked after getting political freedom their further objective was to bring about a socio-economic revolution in the country, 'The objective which we had always in view, namely socialism and secularism, which we had tried to implement, will be more and more implemented and will be more accurately and correctly reflected in a basic part of our Constitution, namely, the Preamble. Sardar Swaran Singh, justifying the addition of the concept in the Preamble observed, '......But secular now is a word which I think has become part of our Indian languages. People of India in their different languages use the word secular because it has assumed a definite meaning and the meaning is that there will be equality before the eye of the law in our Constitution with regard to the people professing different religions.[90] The Lok Sabha, after discussing the Bill for seven days, passed it on November 2, 1976. Two days later, on November 4, 1976, the Rajya Sabha took up the 42nd Amendment as passed by the Lok Sabha, after discussing it for six days, passed it on November 11, 1976.[91] By and large members from both the Houses welcomed the addition of the word 'secularism' in the Preamble. The declaration by the 42nd Amendment, inserting the word 'secular' in the Preamble, amounts to this effect: 'We the people of India, in the Constituent Assembly, on 26th November, 1949, constitute India into a Socialist Secular State as we declare so on 18th December, 1976. It was explained that insertion of the term meant equality, non-discrimination and equal respect for all religions.

The Indian polity having rejected theocracy or state church and adopted equality of all religions as the state policy in the post-Independence constitutional era the term secular had no relevance for the purposes of the interpretation of the Constitution and laws. Actually while, the word, 'secularism' is rather vague and was introduced by 42nd Amendment, Articles 25 to 30 of the constitution relating to the freedom of religion and freedom to manage religious affairs are more specific. The ideals of secular state have clearly been embodied under the Indian constitution and the provisions are being implemented in substantial measure. But the circumstances after independence have posed a challenge before secularism of India for a number of times. India being still a traditional society that contains not one, but many traditions owing their origin in part to the different religions that exist here. While India carries with it many traditions it has managed to retain the secular character of its polity.

However, the overall environment around us do not certify the theme of secularism and when we examine the working of various non-government institutions, the various political parties, especially national parties, which are supposed to have thrown their membership open to all communities, we find that the spirit of secularism is being flouted day after day. We are not completely secular in our approach and attitudes. The universalisation of secular principles should enable secularism not to degenerate into an institutionalised policy of appeasement or domination of religious groups based on the needs of the day. A consensual framework that is based on mutual respect and common principles, not separate beliefs protected by law, needs to develop. The evolution of and adherence to such predetermined but definable principles of state and individual value based behaviour is essential if secularism is to become a universalist social and community ideology and not remain a purely political instrument of societal regulation within the contemporary Indian scenario.

References

1. Alatas, Syed Hussein, *Corruption : Its Nature, Causes and Consequences* (Aldershot : Avebury, 1990), pp. 3-4.
2. Elliot, Kimberly Ann (ed.), Corruption and the Global Economy', *Institute for International Economics*, June 1997 (Washington D.C., 1997) as quoted in Vishnu Bhagwan, 'Corruption and Good Governance', *The Indian Journal of Political Science*, Vol. LXVIII, No. 4, October-December 2007 (Meerut : 2007), p. 728.

3. T.N. Chaturvedi, 'Corruption in India : An Overview' in Subhash C. Kashyap (ed.), *Eradication of Corruption and Restoration of Values* (New Delhi : Sterling Publishers, 2000), p. 41.
4. Dr Dibakar Ch. Das, 'Corruption and Society in India', *Third Concept*, Vol. 20, No. 235, September 2006 (New Delhi : 2006), pp. 26-27.
5. Rajindar Sachar, 'Lokpal Bill 2010 - A Farce on Public', *South Asia Politics*, Vol. 9, No. 10, February 2011 (New Delhi : 2011), p. 7.
6. T.N. Chaturvedi, 'Corruption in India : An Overview', p. 41.
7. Sympson, Antony, E., *The Literature of Police Corruption* (New York : John Jay Press, 1977), p. 20.
8. K. Balachandrudu, 'Understanding Political Corruption, *IJPS* : Vol. LXVII, No. 4, October - December 2006 (Meerut : 2006), p. 811.
9. *Ibid*., p. 809.
10. M. Halaya, *Emergency : A War on Corruption* (New Delhi : S.Chand & Co., 1975), p. 6.
11. Arun Kumar Agrawal, 'Corruption in Historical Perspective : A Case of India' *IJPS*, Vol. LXVIII, No. 2, April - June 2007 (Meerut : 2007), p. 327.
12. M. Halaya, *Emergency : A War on Corruption*, p. 6.
13. Arun Kumar Agrawal, 'Corruption in Historical Perspective : A Case of India', p. 328.
14. *Ibid*.
15. As quoted in *Ibid*., p. 330.
16. H. Harvey, *Cameos of Indian Crime*, as quoted in J.R.B. Jeejebhoy (Bombay: Sant Vartaman Press, 1952), p. 179.
17. Krishna Bhatia, 'The Ordeal of Nationhood', *Imprint*, November 1971 (Bombay : 1971), p. 43.
18. Subhash C. Kashyap, 'Corruption and Criminalisation of Politics', *South Asia Politics*, Vol. 7, No. 9, January 2009 (New Delhi : 2009), p. 21.
19. S.R. Maheshwari, 'Political Corruption : Its Magnitude and Cure', in Subhash C. Kashyap (ed.), *Eradication of Corruption and Restoration of Values*, pp. 85-86.
20. C.B. Muthamma, 'Corruption : Causes and Cures - Need for Systemic Change', in *Ibid*., p. 49.
21. Arun Kumar Agrawal, 'Corruption in Historical Perspective : A Case of India', *IJPS*, p. 332.
22. S.R. Maheshwari, *Administrative Thinkers* (New Delhi : Macmillan, 1998), pp. 27-28.
23. T.N. Chaturvedi, 'Corruption in India : An Overview', pp. 41-42.
24. K. Balachandrudu, 'Understanding Political Corruption', *IJPS*, p. 814.
25. T.N. Chaturvedi, 'Corruption in India : An Overview', p. 43.

26. Myrdal, Gunnar, *Asian Drama*, Vol. 2 (New York : Pantheon, 1968), p. 940.
27. Subhash C. Kashyap, 'Corruption and Criminalisation of Politics', p. 23.
28. S.R. Maheshwari, 'Political Reforms for Good Governance', *The Indian Journal of Public Administration*, Vol. XLIV, No. 3, July - September 1998, pp. 309-10.
29. *Ibid.*
30. R.B. Jain, 'The Art of Political Corruption : An Analysis of Some Major Scams Since Independence', in Subhash C. Kashyap (ed.), *Eradication of Corruption and Restoration of Values*, p. 109.
31. *Ibid.*, p. 96.
32. Arun Kumar Agrawal, 'Corruption in Historical Perspective : A Case of India', p. 333.
33. *The Indian Express* (Bombay), 17 November 1993.
34. *Ibid.*
35. Dwivedy, Surendranath and G.S. Bhargava, *Political Corruption in India* (New Delhi : Popular, 1967), p. 121.
36. Uddipan Mukherjee, 'Maoism and its Future in India,' *South Asia Politics*, Vol. 7, No. 3, July 2008 (New Delhi: 2008), pp. 24-26.
37. T.H. Chowdary, 'Ending the Maoist Menace', in *Ibid.*, Vol. 8, No. 7, November 2009 (New Delhi: 2009), pp. 35-37.
38. Sohail Jawaid, *The Naxalite Movement in India: Origin and Failure of the Maoist Revolutionary Strategy in West Bengal-1967-1971* (New Delhi: Associated Publication, 1979).
39. *People's Daily* (editorial), 5 July 1967.
40. Bipin Chandra, Mridula Mukherjee and Aditya Mukherjee, *India After Independence 1947-2000* (New Delhi: Penguin Books India, 2002), pp. 426-27.
41. Madhumita, 'Naxalism-Development or Discontent-A Study of Jharkhand', *South Asia Politics*, Vol. 9, No. 6, October 2010 (New Delhi: 2010), pp. 27-28.
42. Kartick Das, 'Naxalbari to Today's Maoist: Uprisings and Implications', *IJPS*, Vol. LXXI, No. 2, April-June 2010 (Meerut : 2010), pp. 89-90.
43. *Ibid.*, pp. 429-93.
44. Report of the 1997 international IDEA Democracy Forum, Stockholm, as quoted in Shri Prakash Mani Tripathi and Santosh Kumar Tiwari, 'Socio-Economic Challenges of Globalisation,' *IJPS*, Vol. LXIX, No. 4, October-December 2008 (Meerut : 2008), P. 721.
45. Jean Dreze and Amartya Sen, *India: Economic Development and Social Opportunity* (New Delhi: Oxford University Press, 1995), see also in *Ibid.*

46. Barber R. Benjamine, *Jehad vs. McWorld* (New York: Ballentine Books, 1996), p. 17.
47. Madhumita, 'Naxalism-Development or Discontent-A Study of Jharkhand', pp. 28-29.
48. *Ibid.*
49. *Frontline* (Chennai), 17 July 2009.
50. Biswaranjan Mohanty, 'Tackling the Naxal Insurgency', *South Asia Politics*, Vol. 9, No. 12, April 2011 (New Delhi: 2011), p. 27.
51. Kartick Das, 'Naxalbari to Today's Maoist: Uprisings and Implications', pp. 494-95.
52. Biswaranjan Mohanty, 'Tackling the Naxal Insurgency', pp. 29-32.
53. Md. Mahtab Alam Rizvi, 'Secularism in India: Retrospect and Prospects', p. 908.
54. Rajkumar Singh, *Past, Present and Future of Kashmir*, p. 72.
55. Sudipta Kaviraj, 'Religion, Politics and Modernity', in Upendra Baxi and Bhikhu Parekh (eds.), *Crisis and Change in Contemporary India* (New Delhi: Sage Publications, 1995), pp. 312-15.
56. P.R. Dubhashi, 'Meaning of Secularism', *The Hindu*, 11 June 2002.
57. Dev Nathan, 'India: From Civilisation to Nations', in Kumar Rupesinghe and Khawar Mumtaz (ed.), *Internal Conflicts in South Asia* (Oslo:1996), p. 24.
58. Louis Dumont, 'World Renunciation in Indian Religions', pp. 46-47.
59. Virginia Van Dyke, 'Religious Mobilisation and Sadhus in Politics: The Idealised Versus Real politik', in Paul R. Brass and Achin Vanaik (eds.), *Competing Nationalism in South Asia* (New Delhi: Orient Longman, 2002), p. 144.
60. A.K. Singh, *The Concept and Practice of Secularism in Indian Concept* (1999) p. 24.
61. Rajkumar Singh, *Past, Present and Future of Kashmir*, pp. 74-75.
62. Prashant Amrutkar, 'Indian Secularism: Is It a Way Out to Communalism?' p. 748.
63. Partha Ghosh, *BJP and the Evolution of Hindu Nationalism: From Periphery to Center* (New Delhi: Manohar Publications, 1999), pp. 108-13.
64. P.S. Ghosh, 'Hindu Nationalism: The Politics of Nation Building and Implications for the Legitimacy of the State' in S.K. Mitra and D. Rothermud (eds.), *Legitimacy and Conflicts in South Asia* (New Delhi: Manohar Publications, 1997), pp. 68-76.
65. *Ibid.*
66. Manoranjan Mohanty, 'Secularism: Hegemonic and Democratic', *Economic and Political Weekly*, Vol. XXIV, No. 22, June 3, 1989 (Mumbai: 1989), p. 1219.

67. Naidu Ashok, 'Secularism Re-examined', *IJPS*, Vol. LXVIII, No. 3, July - September 2007 (Meerut: 2007), p. 607.
68. Vinod F. Khobragade, 'The Secularisation of Political Culture', *South Asia Politics*, Vol. 6, No. 6, October 2007 (New Delhi: 2007), p. 38.
69. *Ibid.* pp. 38-39.
70. *Constituent Assembly Debates*, Vol.VII, p. 400.
71. *The Hindustan Times*, 23 August 2003.
72. Jawaharlal Nehru, *An Autobiography* (Bombay: Allied Publishers, 1962), p. 378.
73. *Constituent Assembly Debates*, Vol.VII, pp. 815-16.
74. *Ibid.*, pp. 818-19.
75. *Ibid.*, pp. 831-33.
76. *Ibid.*, p. 834.
77. *Ibid.*, p. 822.
78. *Ibid.*, Vol. I, p. 59.
79. *Ibid.*, Vol.VII, p. 835.
80. R. Rajarajan, 'Secularism in Indian Politics', p. 407.
81. *Constituent Assembly Debates*, Vol. VIII, p. 316.
82. Gani, H.A., *Muslim Political Issues and National Integration* (New Delhi: Sterling, 1978), p. 178.
83. K.C. Markandan, *The Preamble-Key to the Minds of the Makers of the Indian Constitution* (New Delhi: National Publishing House, 1984), p. 63.
84. *Constituent Assembly Debates*, Vol.VII, p. 837.
85. M.V. Pylee, *India's Constitution*, p. 131.
86. *Article 18 of the Indian Constitution*.
87. *Constituent Assembly Debates*, Vol. VII, p. 823.
88. *Ibid.*
89. V.P. Bharatiya, *Religion-State Relationship and Constitutional Rights in India*, p. 360.
90. K.C. Markandan, *The Preamble-Key to the Minds of the Makers of the Indian Constitution*, p. 67.
91. *Ibid.*, pp. 62-63.

Bibliography

Documents

All India Reporter (from 1950 to date) *Constitutional Law Decisions Cabinet Mission Plan* (1946).

Constituent Assembly Debates 1947-1949.

Constitution of India (Draft - 1949).

Constitution of India (Text - 1950).

Government of India's Despatch on Constitutional Reform India Independence Act, 1947.

India Independence Act, 1947.

India Information (Delhi), 1963-65.

India, Muslims in India, Ministry of Information and Broadcasting (New Delhi, 1966).

Indian Round Table Conference : *Proceedings of Federal Structure Committee and Minorities Committee,* 1932.

Lok Sabha Debates (New Delhi).

Memorandum of States Treaties and Paramountcy dated 12 May 1946.

Political Trends, Annual 1976 (New Delhi, 1977).

Report of Linguistic Provinces Commission (Constituent Assembly of India), 1948.

Report of the All Parties Conference, 1928.

Report of the Backward Classes Commission 1955.

Report of the Committee on Emotional Integration, 1962.

Report of the Election Commission of India - First General Elections, 1951-52 and second General Elections, 1957.

Report of the States Reorganisation Commission, 1955.

Report of the Union Constitution Committee.

Report of the Union Powers Committee as Adopted by the Constituent Assembly, August 1947.

Reports (Annual) *of the Commissioner for Scheduled Castes and Tribes* from 1951 onwards.

Resolution of the Constituent Assembly Pertaining to the Head of the State, 20 August 1952.

Resolution UN Security Council, 13 August 1948.

World Press Review (New Delhi, Publication Division, Ministry of Information and Broadcasting, Government of India).

Books

Achin Vanaik, *The Painful Transition : Bourgeois Democracy in India* (London, 1990).

Aiyar, S.P., *Federalism and Social Change* (Asia Publishing House, Bombay, 1961).

Aiyer, S.P. and R. Srinivasan, (eds.), *Studies in Indian Democracy* (Allied, Bombay, 1965).

Akbar, M.J., *India, The Siege Within : Challenges to a Nations Unity* (Penguin, 1985).

Alam Javeed, *Who Wants Democracy Tracts for the Times* (Orient Blackswan, New Delhi, 2012).

Alexandrowiez, C.H., *Constitutional Developments in India* (Oxford University Press, Bombay, 1957).

Ali, Sadiq, *Towards Socialist Thinking in Congress* (New Delhi, 1960).

Allen, Douglas (ed.), *Religion and Political Conflict in South Asia* (Oxford University Press, New Delhi, 1993).

Almond, Gabriel A. and B.G. Powell, *Comparative Politics : A Developmental Approach* (Little Brown, Boston, 1966).

Almond, Gabriel A. and James S. Coleman, (eds). *The Politics of the Developing Areas* (Princeton University Press, Princeton, 1960).

Apter David, *The Politics of Moder*nisation (University of Chicago Press, Chicago, 1965).

Asghar, Ali Engineer (ed.), *Secular Crown on Fire : The Kashmir Problem* (Ajanta, New Delhi, 1991).

Austin, Granville, *The Indian Constitution : Cornerstone of a Nation* (Oxford University Press, New York, 1966).

Bailey, F.G., *Caste and the Economic Frontier*, (Manchester University Press, Manchester, 1957).

Banerjee, D.K., *Sino-Indian Border Dispute* (Intellectual Publisher, New Delhi, 1985).

Banga, Indu and Jaidev (ed.), *Cultural Orientation in Modern India* (Indian Institute of Advance Study, Shimla, 1997).

Bardhan, Pranab, *The Political Economy of Development in India* (Oxford University Press, Delhi, 1985).

Basu, Amrita, *Two Faces of Protest : Contrasting Modes of Women's Activism in India* (University of California Press, Berkeley, 1992).

Baxter, Craig, *The Jana Sangh - A Biography of an Indian Political Party* (Philadelphia, 1969).

Betielle, Andre, *The Backward Classes in Contemporary India* (Oxford University Press, Delhi, 1992).

Bose, Sugata and Ayesha Jalal (eds.), *Nationalism, Democracy and Development : State and Politics in India* (Oxford University Press, Delhi, 1997).

Byres, Terence (ed.), *The State and Development Planning in India* (Oxford University Press, Delhi 1993).

Carras Marry C., *The Dynamics of Indian Political Faction* (Cambridge University Press, Cambridge, 1972).

Cohen, Stephen P., and Richard L. Park, *India : Emergent Power* (Crane, Russak & Company, New York, 1978).

Cormack, Margaret, *The Hindu women* (Asia Publishing House, Bombay, 1961).

Cressey, George B., *Asia's Lands and Peoples,* McGraw-Hill (New York, 1951).

Curran, J.A. Jr., *Militant Hinduism in Indian Politics, A Study of the RSS* (New York, 1951).

Dash, S.C., *The Constitution of India* (Chaitanya Publishing House.

Derrett, J. Duncan M., *Religion, Law and the State in India* (Free Press, New York, 1968).

Dhavan Rajiv and Jacob Alice (eds.), *Indian Constitution Trends and Issues* (1978).

Dube, S.C., *Indian Village* (Routledge and Kegan Paul, London, 1955).

Dutta, Palme, R., *India Today* (1946).

Easton, David, *The Political System : An Inquiry into the State of Political Science* (Scientific Book Agency, Calcutta, 1971).

Friederich, C.J., *Constitutional Government and Democracy* (1966).

Gangulee, N., *The Making of Federal India* (James Nisbet & Co., 1936).

Ghouse, M., *Secularism, Society and Law in India* (Vikas Publications, New Delhi, 1973).

Ghurye, G.S., *Caste and Class in India* (Bombay, 1955).

Gledhill, Alan, *The Republic of India, the Development of its Law and Constitution* (London, 1951).

Gopal, S., *Jawaharlal Nehru : A Biography* (Oxford University Press, Delhi, 1976).

Hartmann, Horst, *Political Parties in India* (Meenakshi, Meerut, 1971).

Hassnain, S.E., *Indian Muslims : Challenge and Opportunity* (Lalvani Publication House, Bombay, 1968).

Hastings, James, *Encyclopaedia of Religion and Ethics* (1959).

Hutton, J.H., *Caste in India* (Oxford University Press, New York, 1963).

Irwin, Lord, *Some Aspects of the Indian Problem* (1932).

Jacob, Alice (ed.), *Constitutional Development Since Independence* (1975).

Jalal, Ayesha, *Democracy and Authoritarianism in South Asia: A Comparative and Political Perspective* (Cambridge University Press, Cambridge, 1995).

Jennings, Sir Ivor, *Some Characteristics of Indian Constitution* (Madras, 1953).

Kohli, Atul (ed.), *Indian Democracy : An Analysis of Changing State - Society Relations* (Princeton University Press, Princeton, 1988).

Kothari, Rajni, *State Against Democracy : In Search of Humane Governance* (Konark, New Delhi, 1988).

Krishnaswami, A., *The Indian Union and the States : A Study in Autonomy and Integration* (Pergamon Press, London, 1964).

Livingston, W.S., *Federalism and Constitutional Change* (Oxford London, 1971).

Ludden, David (ed.), *Making India Hindu* (Oxford University Press, Delhi, 1996).

Mirchandari, G.G., (ed.), *Reporting India 1977* (Abhinav Publications, New Delhi, 1978).

Misra, B.B., *Government and Bureaucracy in India 1947-1976* (Oxford University Press, Delhi, 1986).

Morris, Jones, W.H., *The Government and Politics of India* (Butchinson & Company, London, 1971).

Narain, Iqbal (ed.) *State Politics in India* (Meerut, 1976).

Narayan, Jayaprakash, *A Plea for the Reconstruction of Indian Polity* (Kashi, 1969).

Natarajan, S., *A Century of Social Reform in India* (Asia Publishing House, Bombay, 1959).

Nayar, Kuldip, *The Judgement* (Delhi, 1977).

Nehru : *The Making of India* (Penguin, London, 1988).

Nehru, Jawaharlal, *The Discovery of India* (John Day, New York, 1946).

Nettle, J.P., *Political Mobilisation - A Sociological Analysis of Methods and Concepts* (New York).

Overstreet, Gene D., and Marshall Windmiller *Communism in India* (University of California Press, Berkeley, 1959).

Palmer, Norman D., *The Indian Political System* (Houghton Mifflin, Boston, 1961).

Park, Richard L., and Irene Thinker, (eds.), *Leadership and Political Institutions in India* (Princeton University Press Princeton, 1959).

Patel, Surendra J., *Indian Economy : Towards the Twenty First Century* (Universities Press, Hyderabad, 1955).

Pattabhiram, M. (ed.), *General Elections in India 1967 - An Exhaustive Study of Main Political Trends* (Bombay, 1967).

Rosen, George, *Democracy and Economic Change in India* (University of Colifornia, Berkeley, 1966).

Rosen, Stephen Peter, *Societies and Military Power : India and its Armies* (Oxford University Press, Delhi, 1996).

Roy, S., *Indian Politics and Constitutional Development* (Meerut, 1976).

Rudolph, Lloyd J., Rudolph Hoeber, Susanne, *The Modernity of Tradition - Political Development in India* (Chicago, 1967).

Sathyamurthy, T.V., (ed.), *Region, Religion, Caste, Gender and Culture in Contemporary India* (Oxford University Press, Delhi, 1996).

Sengupta, Bhabani *India: Problems of Governance* (Centre for Policy Research, Konark, New Delhi, 1996).

Shakir, Moin, *Secularisation of Muslim Behaviour* (Minerva, Calcutta, 1973).

Sharma, B.M., *The Republic of India : Constitution and Government* (Asia Publishing House, Bombay, 1966).

Shelat, J.M., *Secularism, Principles and Application* (Tripathi, Bombay, 1972).

Singer, Milton, (ed.), *Traditional India : Structure and Change* (University of Texas Press, Austin, 1959).

Singh, Rajkumar, *Less Tasty Indo-Nepal Political Relations, 1947-1997* (Novelty, Patna, 1998).

__________, *India-South Asia Minus Congress Regimes* (Novelty, Patna, 2000).

__________, *India's Foreign Policy- The First Study in Continuity and Change* (Samiksha Prakashan, New Delhi, 2001).

__________, *Indo-Pak Nuclear Tension 1974-1998* (Samiksha Prakashan, New Delhi, 2001).

__________, *Past, Present and Future of Kashmir* (Gyan Publishing House, New Delhi, 2008).

__________, *India and Pakistan - Social, Political and Military Perspectives* (Regal Publications, New Delhi, 2009).

__________, *Global Dimensions of Indo-Nepal Political Relations Post-Independence* (Gyan Publishing House, New Delhi, 2009).

__________, *Relations of NDA and UPA with Neighbours* (Gyan Publishing House, New Delhi, 2010).

__________, *Contemporary India with Controversial Neighbours* (Gyan Publishing House, New Delhi, 2011).

__________, *Ethnic Politics and LTTE in Sri Lanka* (Kalpaz Publications, New Delhi, 2012).

__________, *Myth and Reality of Terrorism in South Asia* (Kalpaz Publications, New Delhi, 2013).

__________, *Be Update and Face to Face with Indian Republic* (Kalpaz Publications, New Delhi, 2014).

__________, *Nuclear Power and Politics of South Asia-New Disclosures* (Kalpaz Publications, New Delhi, 2014).

__________, *Tireless Border Diplomacy of India with China and Pakistan* (Gyan Publishing House, New Delhi, 2016).

Smith, Donald E. *India as a Secular State* (Princeton University Press, Princeton, 1963).

Smith, Wilfred Cantwell, *Modern Islam in India: A Social Analysis* (Ripon Printing Press, Lahore, 1947).

Srinivas, M.N., *Caste in Modern India and Other Essays* (Bombay, 1962).

Subbarao, G.C.V., *Indian Constitutional Law* (1971).

Suri, Surinder, *1962 Elections - A Political Analysis* (New Delhi, 1962).

Thakur, Janardhan, *All the Prime Minister's Men* (Vikas Publishing House, New Delhi, 1977).

Tharoor, Shashi, *Reasons of State : Political Development and India's Foreign Policy Under Indira Gandhi* (Vikas Publishing House, New Delhi, 1982).

Varadarajan, M.K., *Indian States and the Federation* (1939).

Venkatarama, T.S., *A Treatise on Secular State* (1950).

Venkatarangaiya, M., *Competitive and Cooperative Trends in Federalism* (Gokhale Institute of Politics and Economics, Poona, 1951).

Weiner, Myron, *Party Politics in India : Development of Multiparty System* (Princeton University Press, Princeton, 1957).

Zaidi, A.M., and Zaidi, S.G. (eds.), *The Encyclopaedia of Indian National Congress* (S. Chand and Company, New Delhi, 1981).

Zaidi, A.M., *The Annual Register of Indian Political Parties*, Vols. I and II (New Delhi).

Articles in Books, Periodicals and Newspapers

Abraham, A.S., 'Decade of Turbulence - System Under Growing Stress', *The Times of India*, 21 December 1979.

Agrawal, Arun Kumar, 'Corruption in Historical Perspective - A Case Study of India', *The Indian Journal of Political Science*, Vol. LXIII, No. 2, April-June 2007 (Meerut, 2007).

Aiyar, S.P., 'The Structure of Power in Indian Political System', in Subhash C. Kashyap (ed.), *Union State Relations in India* (The Institute of Constitutional and Parliamentary Studies, New Delhi, 1983).

Amrutkar, Prashant, 'Indian Secularism : Is It a Way Out to Communalism?', *IJPS* Vol. LXXI, No. 3, July-September 2010 (Meerut, 2010).

Ann, Elliot Kimberly, '*Corruption and Global Economy*' (Institute of International Economics June 1997 (Washington, D.C. 1997).

Balachandrudu, K., 'Understanding Political Corruption', '*IJPS* Vol. LXVII, No. 4, October-December 2006.

Balasubramanian, Dr R., 'Indian Polity in Transition', Presidential Address, *53 Annual Conference of Indian Political Science Association*, 27-29 December 2006 (Jaipur, 2006).

Banu, Zenab, 'Religion in Indian Politics: Need to be Value Oriented Not Power-Oriented', *IJPS* Vol. LXX, No. 3, July-September 2009.

Behera, Harish Chandra, 'Political System and Governance in South Asia', *SAP*, Vol. 8, No. 11, March 2010 (New Delhi, 2010).

Beteille, Andre, 'Politics Without Policy', *The Hindu*, 28 June, 2012.

Bhagwan, Vishnu, 'Corruption and Good Governance', *IJPS*, Vol. LXVIII, No. 4, October-December 2009.

Bhatia, Krishna, 'The Ordeal of Nationhood', *Imprint*, November 2007 (Bombay, 2007).

Bhatnagar, Mridula, 'Gender Politics : In the Context of Social Structure and Development', *IJPS*, Vol. LXX, No. 4, October-December 2009.

Bjorkman, J.W., 'Changing State/Society Relations : Broad Brush Approaches and Analytical Models', *Administrative Change*, Vol. XXVIII, No. 2, and Vol. XXIX, No. 1, January-December 2001 (Jaipur, 2001).

Chandra, Bipin, 'Truth is God', *The Hindustan Times*, 5 April 2002.

Chaturvedi, Geeta, 'Democracy in Global India', *IJPS* Vol. LXIX, No. 4, October-December 2008.

Chaturvedi, T.N., 'Corruption in India : An Overview', in Subhash C. Kashyap (ed.), *Eradication of Corruption and Restoration of Values* (Sterling Publishers, New Delhi, 2003).

Chatterjee, Somnath, 'Parliamentary Democracy and Some Challenges', *The Hindu*, 15 November 2007.

Chowdary, T.H., 'Ending the Maoist Menace', *SAP*, Vol. 8, No. 7, November 2009.

Chowla, N.L., 'Indian Democracy in Perspective', *The Times of India*, 22 December 1980.

Das, Ch. Dr Dibakar, 'Corruption and Society in India', *Third Concept*, Vol. 20, No. 235 September 2006 (New Delhi, 2006).

Das, Gupta S., 'Regaining the Faith', *India Today*, 8 April 2002 (New Delhi, 2002).

Das, Kartick, 'Naxalbari to Today's Maoist : Uprising and Implications', *IJPS*, Vol. LXXI, No. 2, April - June 2010.

Das, Shreeram Chandra, 'Political Relevance in Constitutionalism', in Satya Prakash Das (ed.), *Constitutional and Political Dynamics of India* (Sarup & Sons, New Delhi, 2004).

Deb, Papia, P.K. Sengupta, 'Coalition Politics and the Changing Perspectives of India's Federal Governance,' *IJPS*, Vol. LXX, No. 2, April-June 2009.

Dyke, Varginia Van, 'Religious Mobilisation and Sadhus in Politics : The Idealised Versus Realpolitik', in Paul R. Brass and Achin Vanaik (eds.), *Competing Nationalism in South Asia* (Orient Longman, New Delhi, 2002).

Engineer, Dr Asghar Ali, 'Who is for a Common Civil Code ?', *The Hindustan Times*, 3 August 2003.

Evans, Tony, 'Introduction : Power Hegemony and the Universalisation of Human Rights', in Tony Evans (ed.), *Human Rights Fifty Years on- A Reappraisal* (Manchester University Press, UK, 1998).

Faleiro, Eduardo, 'Reflections on the Republic Day', *SAP*, Vol. II, No. 10, February 2013.

Ghose, Moumita, 'Democracy in India-Background and Emerging Challenges', *SAP*, Vol. 9, No. 8, December 2010.

Ghosh, P.S., 'Hindu Nationalism : The Politics of Nation Building and Implications for the Legitimacy of the State,' in S.K. Mitra and D. Rothermud (eds.), *Legitimacy and Conflicts in South Asia* (Manohar Publications, New Delhi, 1997).

Ghoshal, Sarbani Guha, 'Human Rights : Concept and Contestation', *IJPS*, Vol. LXXI, No. 4, October-December 2010.

Gill, S.S., 'Team Secularism', *The Hindustan Times*, 3 March 2003.

Greene, Joseph N., 'Goal of Democracy', in Sardar Patel Institute of Administration (ed.), *Administration and Politics in Modern Democracies* (Allahabad, 1976).

Groethuysen, B., 'Secularism', in Edwin R.A. Seligman (ed.), *Social Sciences* (Macmillan Company, New Delhi, 1959).

Gupta, Dipankar, 'Communalism and Fundamentalism - Some Notes on the Nature of Ethnic Politics in India', *Economic and Political Weekly*, Vol. XXXVI, No. 11 and 12 March 1991 (Mumbai, 1991).

__________, 'Flagging India's Missing Freedom', *The Hindu,* 29 September 2009.

Gupta, Shekhar, 'NAM Change', *The Indian Express*, 16 September 2006.

__________, 'One Dynasty Dimming', *The Indian Express*, 23 February 2013.

Hazary, S.C., 'Wither Indian Party System', *Political Scientist* (Ranchi, 1980).

Iyer, V.R. Krishna, 'Needed a Renewed Socialist Concern', *The Hindu,* 4 February 2008.

Jain, Girilal, 'Language of Indian Politics : Borrowed Idiom Giving Way', *The Times of India*, 2 April 1980.

__________, 'Gandhiji and Mr. Nehru - Two Different Moral Universe', *The Times of India,* 16 November 1980.

__________, 'Effects of Politicisation - Need to Strengthen Institutions', *The Times of India*, 31 December 1980.

Jain, R.B., 'The Art of Political Corruption : An Analysis of Some Major Scams Since Independence', in Subhash C. Kashyap (ed.), *Eradication of Corruption and Restoration of Values*.

Jha, Prem Shankar, 'Overcome by a Sense of Betrayal', *The Hindu*, 15 January 2013.

Kapoor, Suneera and Shrawan Singh, 'Gandhi and Nehru on Religion', *IJPS*, Vol. LXVI, No. 3, July-September 2005.

Kashyap, C. Subhash, 'President-Prime Minister Relationship. Dr Rajendra Prasad's Presidential Years', *SAP* Vol. 8, No. 5, September 2008.

__________, 'Democratic Governance - Space for the Underprivileged', in *Ibid.*, Vol. 7, No. 8, December 2008.

__________, 'Corruption and Criminalisation of Politics', in *Ibid.*, Vol. 7, No. 9, January 2009.

__________, 'Innovative Federal Structures and Conflict Resolution in India', in *Ibid.*, Vol. 11, No. 3, July 2012.

Kaviraj, Sudipta, 'Religion, Politics and Modernity', in Upendra Baxi and Bhikhu Parekh (eds.), *Crisis and Change in Contemporary India* (Sage Publications, New Delhi, 1995).

__________, 'The Modern State in India', in Zoya Hasan (ed.), *Introduction : The Political Career of the State in Independent India* (2000).

Khare, Harish, 'At 60, the Political Culture Needs Renewal', *The Hindu*, 16 August 2007.

__________, 'Time for House - Cleaning in the Congress', *The Hindu*, 4 April 2012.

Khobragade, Vinod F., 'The Secularisation of Political Culture', *SAP*, Vol. 6, No. 6, October 2007.

Kumar, Suresh, 'Human Rights Protection in India - An Institutional Framework', *SAP*, Vol. 7, No. 3, August 2008.

Lasswell, H.D., 'The Policy Sciences', in *Encyclopaedia of the Social Sciences*, Vol. 2 (Macmillan, New York, 1968).

Madhumita, 'Naxalism - Development or Discontent - A Study of Jharkhand', *SAP*, Vol. 9, No. 6, October 2010.

Maheshwari, S.R., 'Political Reforms for Good Governance', *IJPS*, Vol. XLIV, No. 3, July-September 1998.

__________, 'Political Corruption Its Magnitude and Cure', in Subhash C. Kashyap (ed.), *Eradication of Corruption and Restoration of Values*.

Malhotra, Inder, 'The Changing Face of Parliament,' *The Times of India*, 17 August 1980.

Mathur, A.B. , 'The Indian Polity : A Mild Indictment', *Administrative Change*, Vol. XXIX, No. 2, and Vol. XXX, No. 1, January-December 2002 (Jaipur, 2002).

Mavromaras, Marco, 'The Definition of Secularism', *Social Commentary*, Vol. 3, Issue, 5, February 2007.

Mody, Piloo, 'We Have No Parties - Only Leaders', *The Times of India*, 17 August 1980.

Mohammad, Khai Ali Mia, Yasin and Yasmin, 'Gender Equality - Rhetoric or a Panacea ? : A Review of the Present Concerns', *IJPS*, Vol. LXVII, No. 4, October-December 2007.

Mohanty, Biswaranjan, 'Tackling the Naxal Insurgency', *SAP*, Vol. 9, No. 12, April 2011.

Mohanty, Manoranjan, 'Secularism : Hegemonic and Democratic', *Economic and Political Weekly*, Vol. XXIV, No. 22, 3 June 1989 (Mumbai, 1989).

Mukherjee, Uddipan, 'Maoism and Its Future in India', *SAP*, Vol. 7, No. 3, July 2008.

Muthamma, C.B., 'Corruption : Causes and Cures - Need for Systemic Change', in Subhash C. Kashyap (ed.), *Eradication of Corruption and Restoration of Values*.

Naidu, Ashok, 'Secularism Reexamined', *IJPS*, Vol. LXVIII, No. 3, July-September 2007.

Naidu, Gurappa Y., 'Globalisation and Its Impact on Indian Society', *IJPS*, Vol. LXVII, No. 1, January-March 2006.

Nayyar, Sanjeev, 'Definition of Secularism - A Global Perspectives', October 2003.

Ojha, A.K. 'Globalisation and Liberalisation - Prospects of New World', *Third Concept*, August 2002.

Palanithurai, G., 'Indian Democracy - A Rethinking', *SAP*, Vol. 6, No. 5, September 2007.

Parsons, Talcott, 'Political Development : Times Sequences and Rates of Change', in Finkle and A. Gable (eds.), *Political Development and Social Change* (New York, 1971.

Prasad, Ganesh and Anand Kumar, 'The Concept, Constraints and Prospect of Secularism in india', *IJPS*, Vol. LXVII, No. 4, October - December 2006.

Pye, Lucian W., 'Party System and National Development in Asia', in Joseph La alombara and Myron Weiner (eds.), *Political Parties and Political Development* (Princeton, 1966).

Rajarajan, R., 'Secularism in Indian Politics : Theory and Practice', *IJPS*, Vol. LXXIII, No. 2, April - June 2007.

Rawls, John, 'The Law of People', in Belgrade Circle (ed.), *The Politics of Human Rights* (London and New York, 2002).

Rizvi, Md. Mahtab Alam, 'Secularism in India - Retrospect and Prospects', *IJPS*, Vol. LXVI, No. 4, October - December 2005.

Sachar, Rajindar, 'Lokpal Bill 2010 - A Farce on Public', *SAP*, Vol. 9, No. 10, February 2010.

Sen, Amartya, 'Elements of a Theory of Human Rights', *Philosophy and Public Affairs*, Vol. 32 (4), October 2004.

Sharma, C.L., 'State of Democracy in India', *IJPS*, Vol. LXVII, No. 1, January-March 2006.

Siddharth, K., 'Revolution Without Ideas', *The Times of India*, 1 August 2012.

Singh, Deepali, Nafees, A., 'Ansari and Shaifali Singh', Good Governance and Implementation in Era of Globalisation', *IJPS*, Vol. LXX, No. 4, October - December 2009.

Singh, Jaipal, 'Divisive Versus Inclusive Democracy', *SAP*, Vol. 7, No. 3, July 2008.

Singh, Dr Rajkumar, 'State of Indian Democracy', *Third Concept*, Vol. 16, No. 189, November 2002 (New Delhi, 2002).

Sinha, S.K., 'Nehru - Gandhis in Indian Politics', '*The Hindustan Times*, 30 June 1991.

Singhvi, Abhishek, 'Secularism Unwrapped', *The Hindustan Times*, 22 September 2004.

Suroor, Hassan, 'Looking Beyond Ballot Box Democracy', *The Hindu*, 22 August 2007.

Tariq Thachil, 'Can Hindutva Win Votes ?', *The Indian Express*, 25 February 2013.

Thakur, K.S., 'Indian Economy After Globalisation', *Third Concept*, June, 1997.

Tripathi, Sri Prakash Mani and Santosh Kumar Tiwari, 'Socio-Economic Challenges of Globalisation', *IJPS*, Vol. LXIX, No. 4, October-December 2008.

Tripathi, Sudhanshu, 'Globalisation and Its Consequences', *SAP*, Vol. 9, Nos. 3 and 4, July-August 2010.

Varadarajan, Siddharth, 'Politics After President Pranab', *The Hindu*, 19 June 2012.

Vishwanathan, V.N., 'Human Rights in a Globalised World : The Indian Experiences', *IJPS*, Vol. LXIX, No. 1, January-March 2008.

Yadav, Yogendra, 'Imagining a New National Politics', *The Hindu*, 12 August 2012.

Newspapers

The Amrit Bazar Patrika (Calcutta).

The Commoner (Kathmandu).

The Dawn (Karachi).

The Financial Times (London).

The Hindu (Madras).

The Hindustan Times (New Delhi).

The Indian Express (Delhi).

The Indian Nation (Patna).

The Nagpur Times (Nagpur).

The National Herald (New Delhi).

The New York Times (New York).

The Patriot (New Delhi).

The Sunday Standard (New Delhi).

The Statesman (Delhi).

The Times of India (New Delhi).

The Times (London).

The Tribune (Chandigarh).

Periodicals

Administrative Change (Jaipur).

American Political Science Review (New York).

Eastern Economist (Bombay).

Economic and Political Weekly (Bombay).

Illustrated Weekly of India (Bombay).

India Today (New Delhi).

Indian Journal of Political Science (Hyderabad and Meerut).

Political Science Quarterly (New York).

SAARC News (Calcutta).

South Asia Politics (New Delhi).

Third Concept (New Delhi).

Time (New York).

World Politics (Princeton).

World Today (London).

Index

C

E

K

L

S